I0902394

IMAGES
of America

ATLANTIC CITY

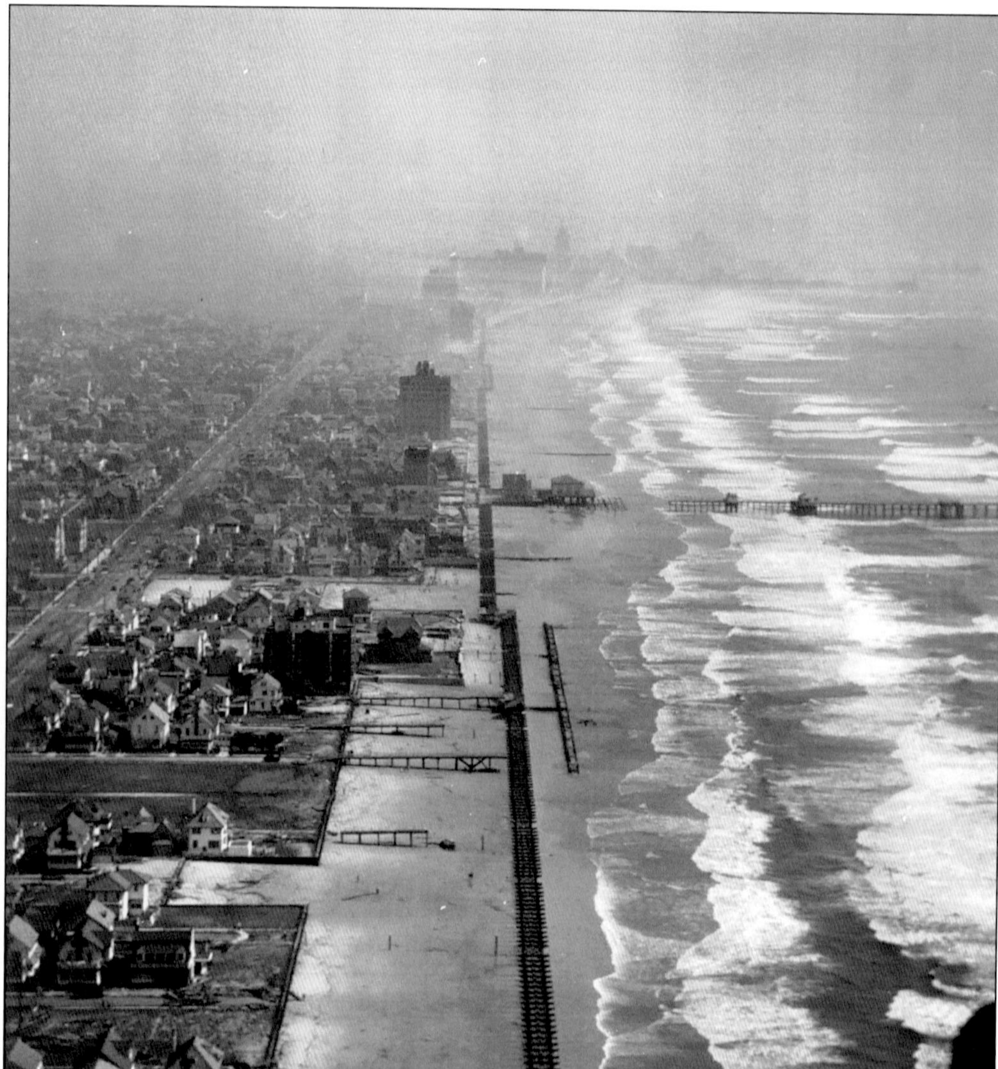

The hurricane of 1944 unleashed its fury on Atlantic City, wrecking portions of the world-famous Boardwalk and Steel Pier. The hurricane also destroyed the H.J. Heinz Pier beyond reconstruction. (ACFPL.)

IMAGES
of America

ATLANTIC CITY

John T. Cunningham and Kenneth D. Cole

ARCADIA
PUBLISHING

ISBN 978-0-7385-0426-1

Published by Arcadia Publishing
Charleston, South Carolina

Printed in the United States of America

Library of Congress Catalog Card Number: 00-102557

For all general information contact Arcadia Publishing at:
Telephone 843-853-2070
Fax 843-853-0044
E-mail sales@arcadiapublishing.com
For customer service and orders:
Toll-Free 1-888-313-2665

Visit us on the Internet at www.arcadiapublishing.com

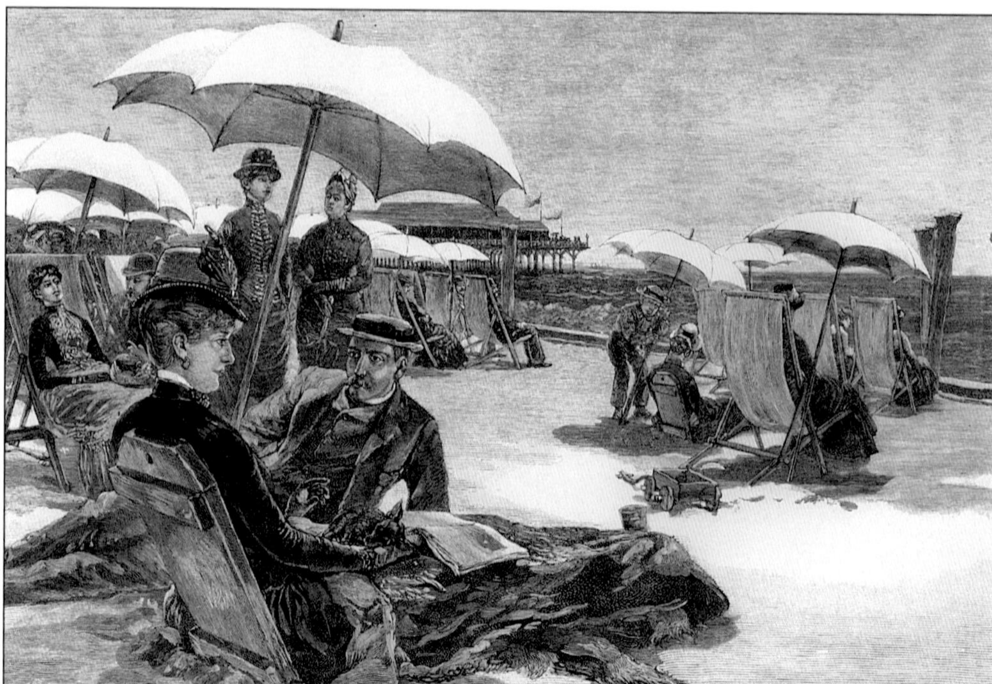

The city's Sand Pier is shown as it appeared in the August 1885 *Harper's Weekly*. Atlantic City may not have introduced amusement piers to the world, but it made the most of them, including this simple one for fashionable lounging.

Cover: A photographer captured this unique view of the 1930s Easter Parade in Atlantic City.

Contents

Acknowledgments

We thank a number of people for their assistance in this undertaking, but none more than the staff of the Atlantic City Free Public Library with Maureen Frank as director. To Julie Senack, the library's reference supervisor, and her desk assistants, Patricia Rothenberg and Madeline Ianni, we owe the deepest debt of gratitude. Always courteous, helpful, patient, and professional despite multiple demands on their time, they assisted us with the library's Alfred Heston Collection, from which most of the book's images come. Named for former city official and amateur historian Alfred Heston, it is an Atlantic City treasure that deserves high rank among New Jersey's archives.

We also acknowledge the assistance of several others. Betty Kennedy in the public relations office at Conectiv, the corporate successor to the Atlantic City Electric Company, graciously shared the company's file. Robert Ruffolo Jr., the owner of Princeton Antiques Bookshop and himself an Atlantic City institution, was generous with his time and his own significant collection. Serving as a resource for this book was Robert E. Kent's *Atlantic City: America's Playground* (Encinitas, California: Heritage Media, 1998), for which Mr. Ruffolo served as historical consultant. At the Miss America Organization, administrator Marie Nicholes and purchasing agent Carol Sprouse were always helpful and provided invaluable insights into America's oldest and best-known pageant. We also appreciate the fine craftsmanship of Andrew Bobeck, who salvaged some battered images with his technical skills.

The Drew University Library offered the quiet space in which to plan this book. Ken thanks his wife, Jane, and his daughter, Grace, for sharing him with this project. John's family, which has been through the process two score times, also deserves our thanks.

Credits appear parenthetically at the end of each block of text. Images from the Heston Collection of the Atlantic City Free Public Library are denoted by the abbreviation "ACFPL." Those from the Miss America Organization collection are noted by "MAO." Those owned by Robert Ruffolo and Princeton Antiques Bookshop are designated "Ruffolo." The images from Conectiv are designated "Conectiv." Images from the personal collection of John T. Cunningham are marked "JTC." All copyrighted images depicting facets of the Miss America pageant are reprinted here with the permission of the Miss America Organization, Atlantic City, New Jersey.

INTRODUCTION
THE MYSTIC ISLAND

From any approach, the low-lying island called Atlantic City is mystical, whether from the north, as migrating birds see it across green sedges; from the west and south, as vacationers have glimpsed it for a century and a half; or from across ocean waves, as recorded by awed boatmen since the beginning of written history.

The island has been called Atlantic City since 1853, when only 21 registered voters shared the pristine beach with squawking sea gulls, horseshoe crabs, and dancing sandpipers. A few visitors rowed across Absecon Bay in summertime to frolic on the dunes. Only one of them, Dr. Jonathan Pitney, visualized how wondrous this land could be.

As he strolled along the deserted beach to breathe clean seaside air or mounted the rolling dunes to gaze over green ocean waves, young Dr. Pitney told friends, "This should become the El Dorado of the Atlantic Coast!"

Pitney thought the riches of his El Dorado to be fresh salt air, warm sands, and cooling breezes. Today's Atlantic City combines will-o'-the-wisp hopes with the belief that the treasures of the casinos will be spread among the hordes of slot machine manipulators and card players. This will not happen, however; no El Dorado ever played fair with everyone.

The first visitors came on July 1, 1854, riding the jolting, dirty cars on the maiden trip of the Camden & Atlantic Railroad. On the island, they headed for the half-completed United States Hotel, returning home before dark. Three days later, the first excursion train made the same round trip; the incoming crowds have never vanished—in summertime, at least.

Those early visitors initially supplied their own amusements, clambering over the skeletons of wrecked ships, eating picnic lunches on the dunes, and wading in the ocean. Pleasures had to be hastily enjoyed since their trains returned to Camden or Philadelphia before twilight.

Boardinghouses rose, followed by small wooden hotels. The first Boardwalk, conceived in 1870 and laid directly on the beach, heralded a new day. Several boardwalks have followed, culminating in the modern permanent fixture. In 1882, the first of Atlantic City's famous amusement piers opened, encouraging others to build piers stretching from the Boardwalk out into the ocean, in effect increasing the Boardwalk's scope.

Huge brick hotels were in place or were being built at the end of the 19th century. Already known as the "Queen of Resorts," the city knew well the three elements that one promoter of the 1950s would call "Ocean, emotion and plenty of promotion." One of the heralded annual events of the late 19th century, the Easter Parade, each year attracted crowds of visitors and small armies of photographers. The appeal continued well into the 20th century.

Atlantic City entrepreneurs believed that the beautiful years would last forever. The rich and the famous strolled the Boardwalk in the 1920s. Miss America made her debut in 1921.The huge Convention Hall opened in 1929. City visitation swelled, and the city reached its prime. Thus, the Great Depression of the 1930s struck with savage intensity.

World War II was a dramatic turning point. German submarines lurking off the coast actually sank about a dozen ships. By 1942, the armed services began taking over Boardwalk hotels to house and feed thousands of military personnel. Eventually, almost 50 hotels were under military control, and the Convention Center was the armed forces' headquarters. About 30,000 new men and women arrived monthly, and by war's end more than one-half million persons had trained or been hospitalized in the city. The Thomas L. England Hospital, which opened in 1943 in the Chalfonte-Haddon Hall, treated a steady stream of thousands of wounded personnel.

Atlantic City had fully returned to its pre-war status by 1950, attracting huge state and national conventions and millions of regular visitors. The Easter Parade flourished. Hotels were filled, although many of the huge, outmoded wooden hotels and boardinghouses were demolished in the 1960s to make room for higher profit-yielding motels. Still, the city grew increasingly shabby as competition from other resorts increased. Miami Beach, only a short flight away, became a major competitor for New York City vacationers.

New Jersey voters approved casino gambling in 1976, believing it to be a cure-all. Famous old hotels fell before wrecking balls and explosives, to be replaced by the glittering palaces housing the gambling facilities.

Today, although it has changed tremendously, Atlantic City may be more mystical than ever. At night, the brilliant lights reflect far out into the ocean, putting the moon to shame. Huge crowds storm the doors of the casinos, as if mere entrance assured good fortune.

The old recipe for success has been changed (however unofficially) to "promotion, emotion, and very occasionally, the ocean."

One

Railroad to Paradise

Atlantic City came into being on Absecon Island as the eastern terminus of the Camden & Atlantic Railroad, chartered in 1852. At the time, seven families lived among the island dunes, which the railroad promoters believed could become a thriving "bathing village" if rapid transportation were provided from the Philadelphia area. The first train reached the island in 1854, creating an overnight demand among Philadelphians for ocean breezes, white sand beaches, grass-covered dunes, and the hulks of wrecked ships stranded on the beach. Within less than 50 years, large hotels had risen, and sophisticated amusements had been built. Hundreds of thousands of tourists each year stormed into the erstwhile village lured by posters such as the one seen here. Atlantic City and the railroads had created what was called the "Queen of the Coast." (ACFPL.)

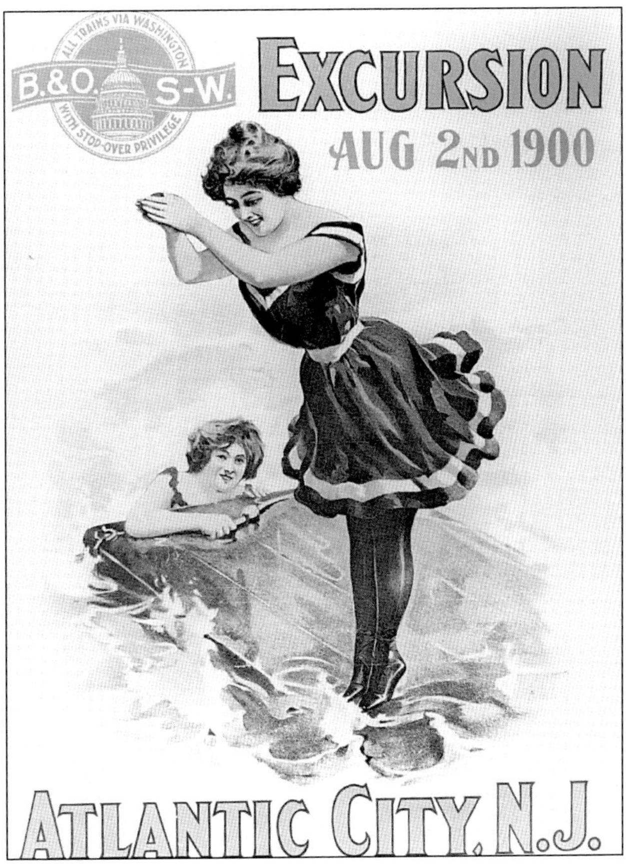

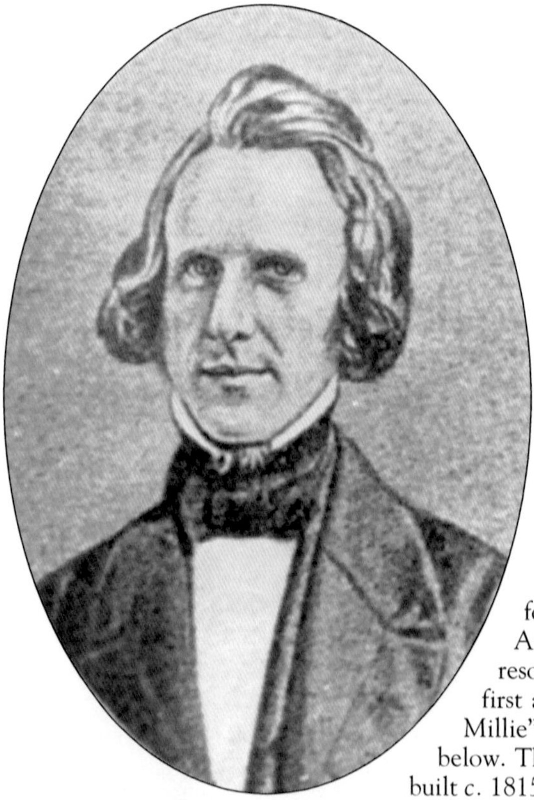

Dr. Jonathan Pitney, left, is properly called the "Father of Atlantic City." He had been touting Absecon Island's healthy climate for many years before convincing Camden & Atlantic Railroad entrepreneurs that a beach resort could draw customers via the railroad. The first accommodations for tourists were in "Aunt Millie" Leeds's substantial two-story frame house, below. This oldest Atlantic City rooming house was built *c.* 1815. (top, JTC; bottom, ACFPL.)

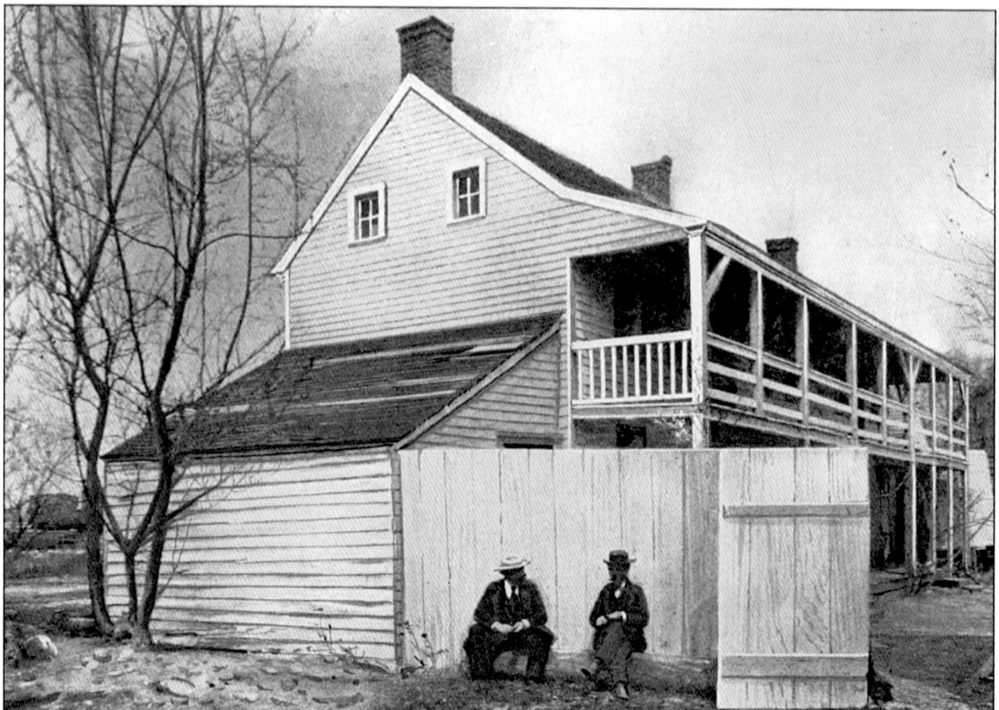

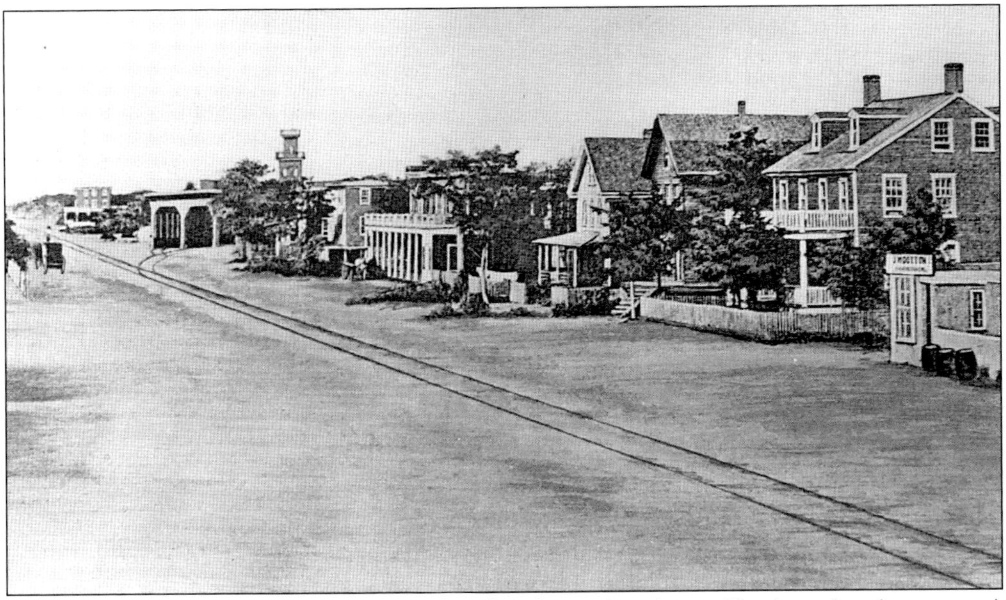

Within three years of the coming of the railroad, Atlantic City (named by the railroad promoters) had begun rapid growth. Rails were laid directly on the sand, which at the time was packed hard enough to support trains. Owners of large houses along the railroad's right-of-way quickly took in vacationers for short or long stays. (JTC.)

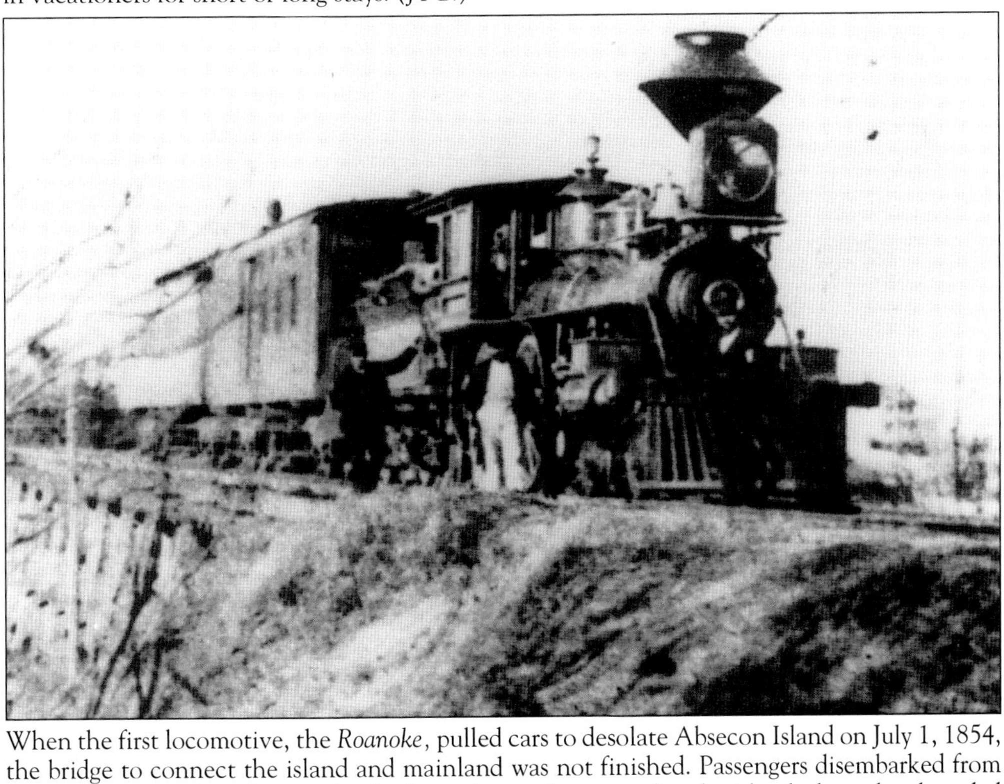

When the first locomotive, the *Roanoke*, pulled cars to desolate Absecon Island on July 1, 1854, the bridge to connect the island and mainland was not finished. Passengers disembarked from trains that stopped on the mainland side, and were then rowed to the island where they boarded cars behind the *Roanoke* to complete the trip. (JTC.)

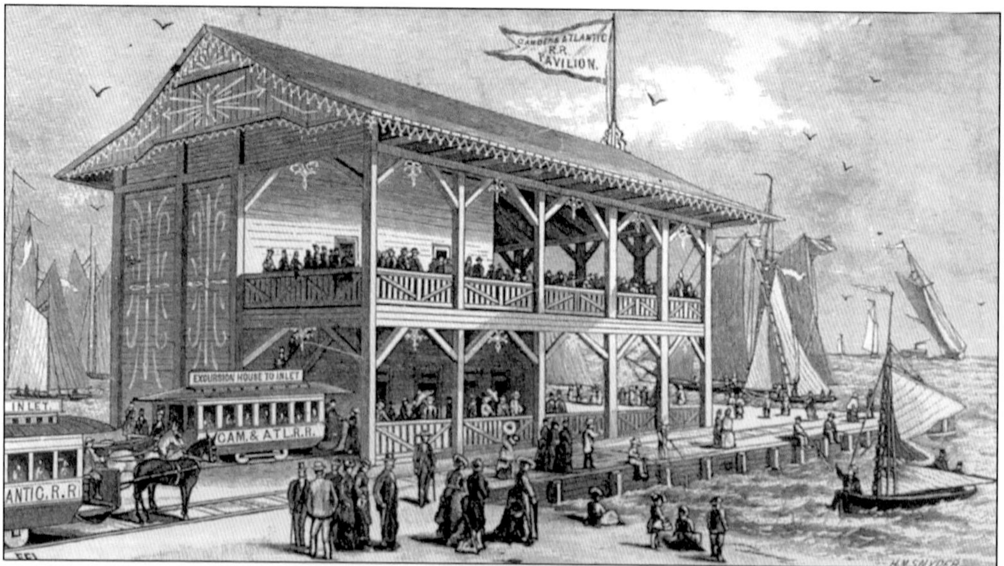

When the long day on the beach neared its end, Camden & Atlantic Railroad passengers wended their way toward the railroad's pavilion at the north end of the island. Little horse-drawn cars carried tourists to most points in the city or picked them up for the return home. Waiting passengers watched yachts on Absecon Bay. (JTC.)

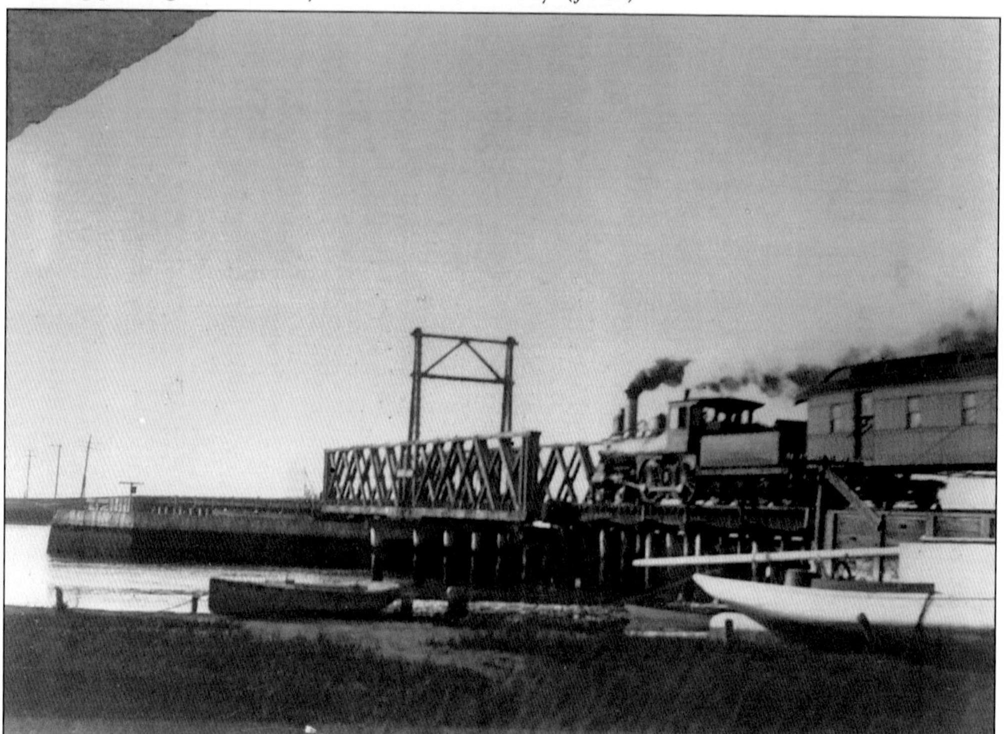

By 1880, many speeding trains headed eastward to Atlantic City during the vacation months, crossing Beach Thoroughfare (the bay) on a sturdy trestle. By then, other railroads—particularly the well-known "narrow gauge" railroad—had been built to compete for the lucrative tourist trade. (JTC.)

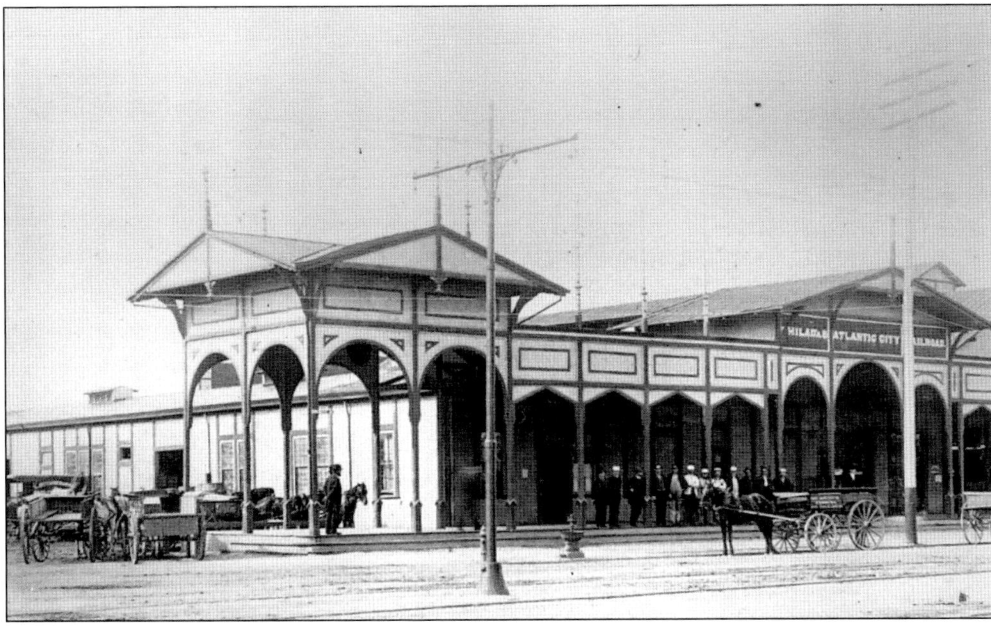

Rivals of the Camden & Atlantic Railroad—the Philadelphia & Atlantic City Railroad—erected the resort's first handsome depot. It incorporated Victorian structures taken down after the 1876 Philadelphia Centennial Exposition closed. Pieces of buildings were brought to the island by train. (JTC collection.)

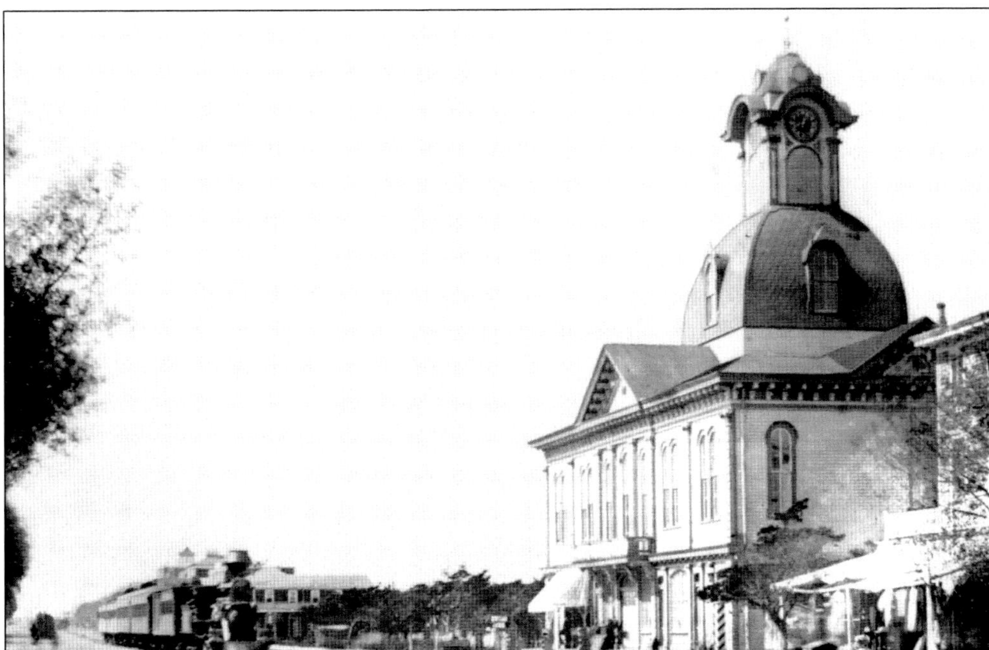

In Atlantic City *c.* 1880, hotels and boardinghouses had proliferated across the island. In this view, a long train passes the splendid new municipal building and courthouse, recently erected, and heads for the varied hotels and boardinghouses along the right-of-way. (ACHS.)

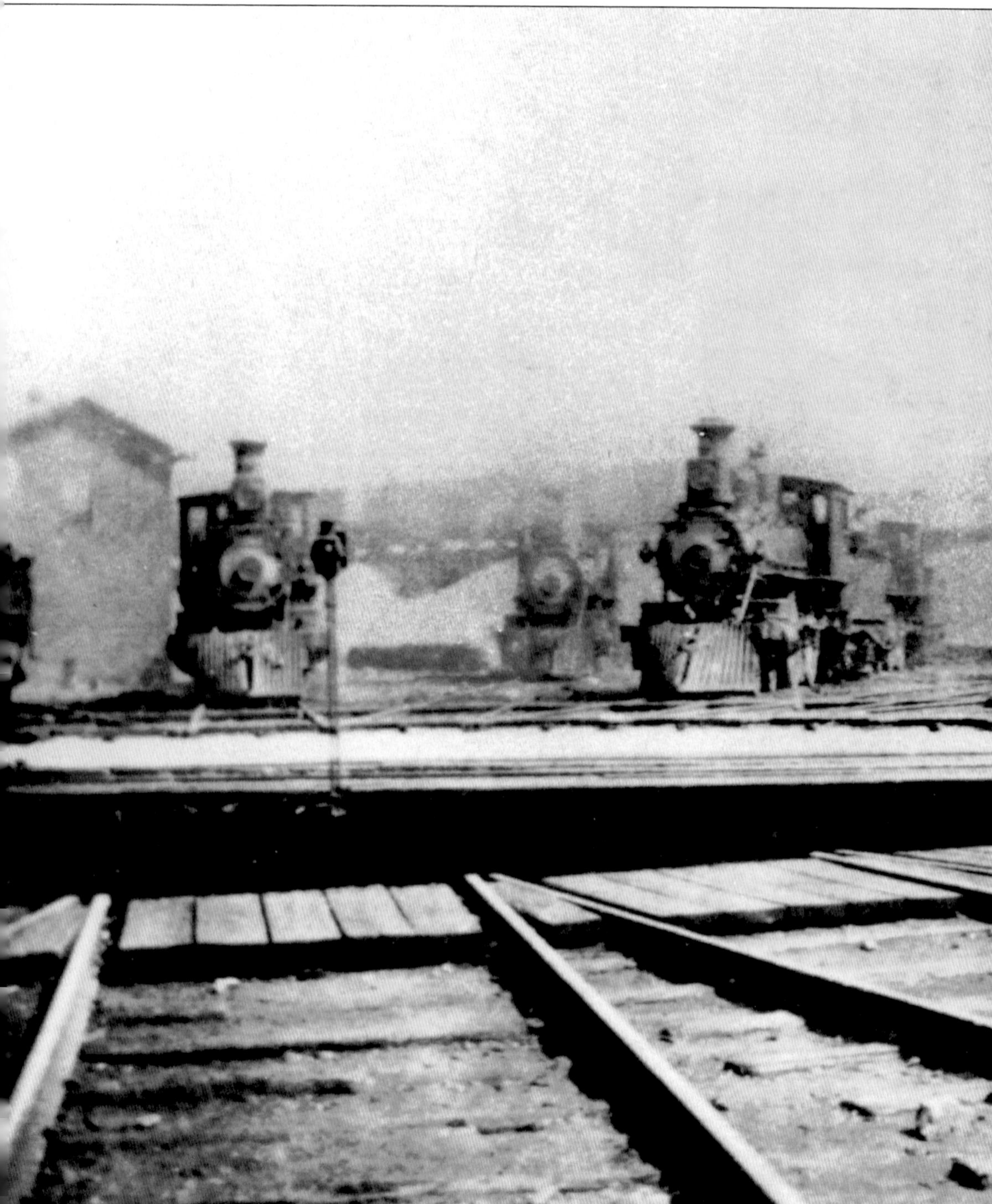

By 1885, Atlantic City's several railroads comprised the most extensive resort railroad network in the country. The lines competed with increased riding comforts and new speed records beyond 70 miles per hour on the straight tracks west of the city. Every Sunday afternoon during

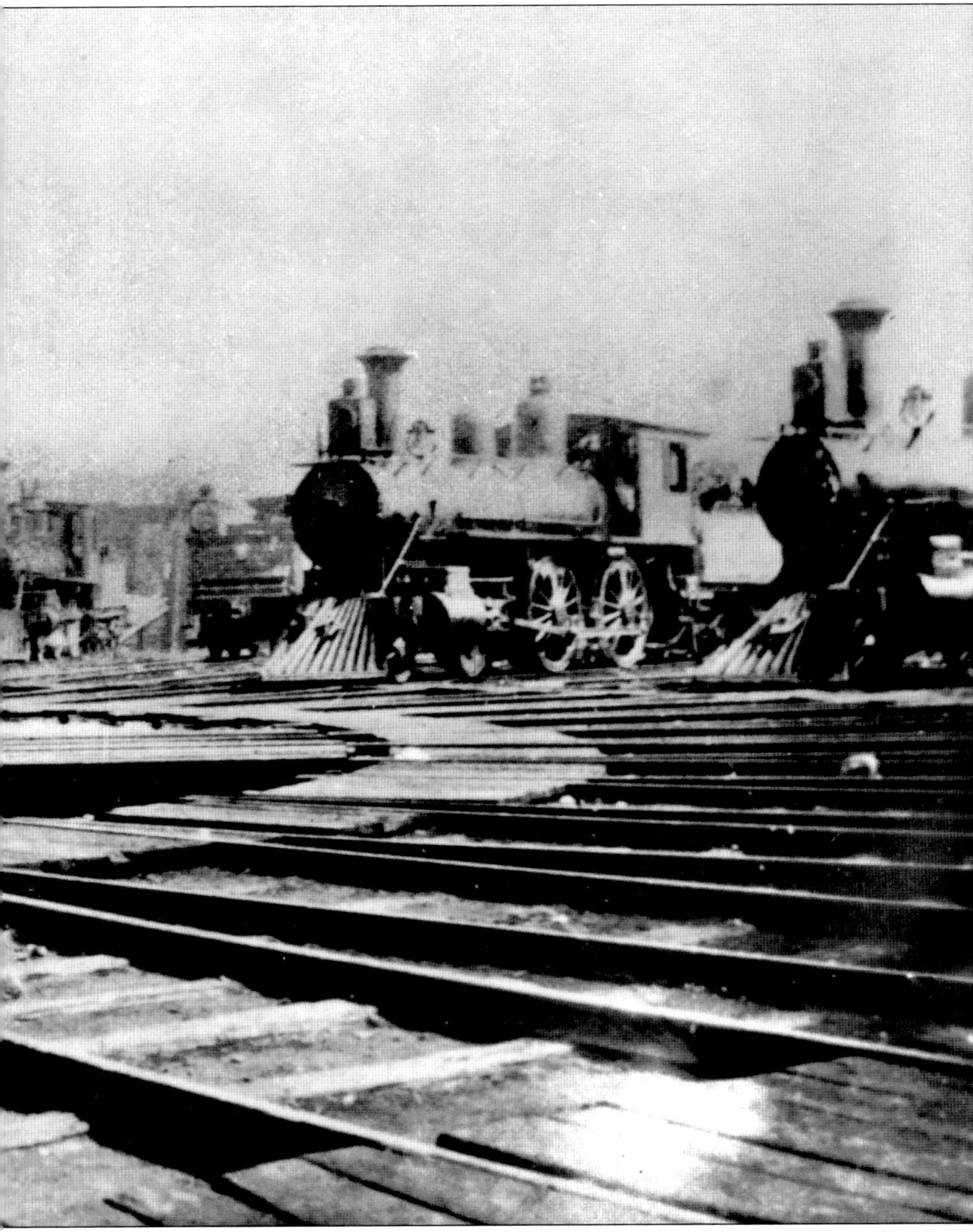

the 1880s and for one-half century beyond, powerful locomotives lined up at day's end to pull happy one-day tourists home. Atlantic City was as much a railroad town as it was an impressive tourist destination. (H. Gerald MacDonald.)

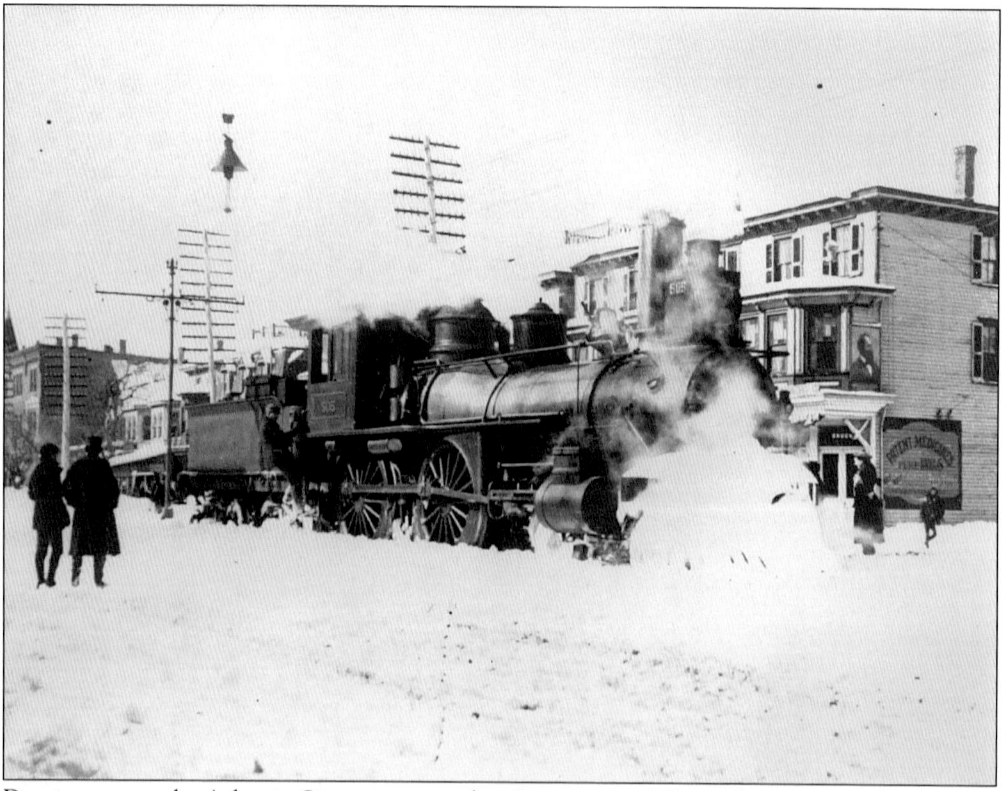

Despite protests by Atlantic City promoters that "snow never falls on the city," this locomotive had trouble moving along an Atlantic City street during a heavy snowstorm before World War I. It was off-season, of course, so no tourists were involved, and the slow pace disturbed no one. (ACFPL.)

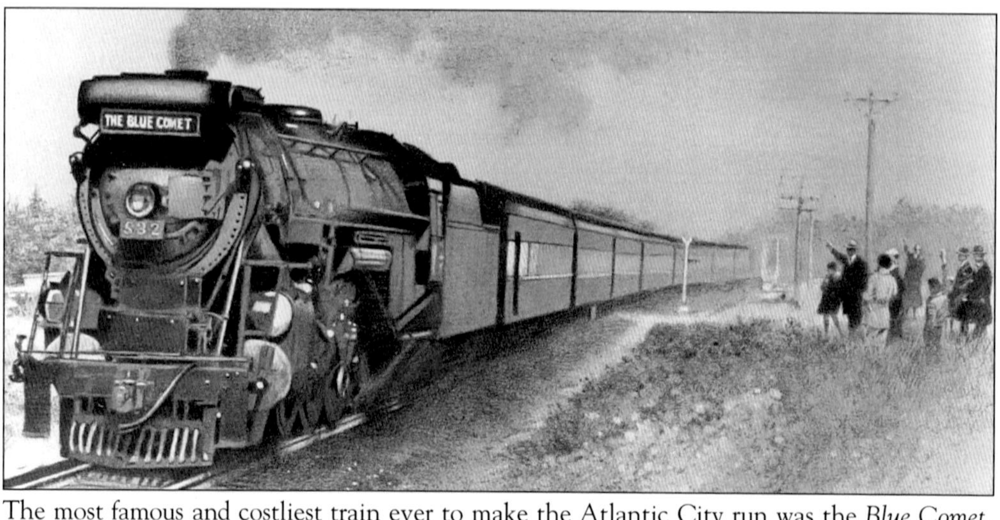

The most famous and costliest train ever to make the Atlantic City run was the *Blue Comet*. Painted in soft blue and cream colors, each car of the train was named after a comet. Introduced in 1928, the tasteful train attracted spectators along the route. It started in Jersey City, raced through the lonely Pine Barrens, then sped to Atlantic City. The luxurious train's last run was in 1941. (ACFPL.)

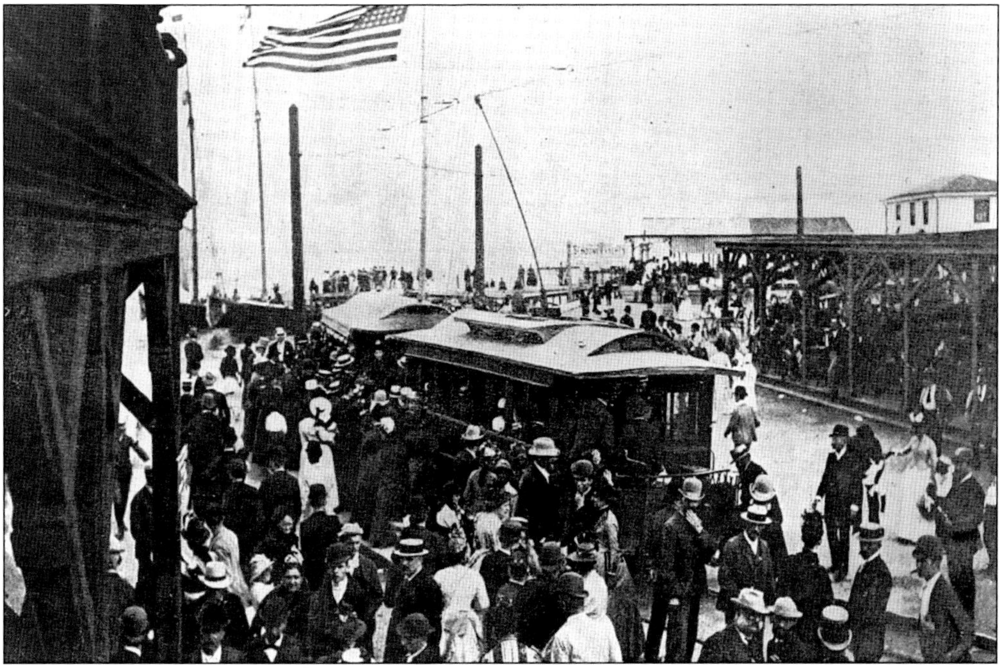

Trolleys became popular after 1900, both within the city and in the long-distance "fast line" that ran from Philadelphia to the resort. One of the city's earliest lines, shown above, ran from the inlet to points within the city. (ACFPL.)

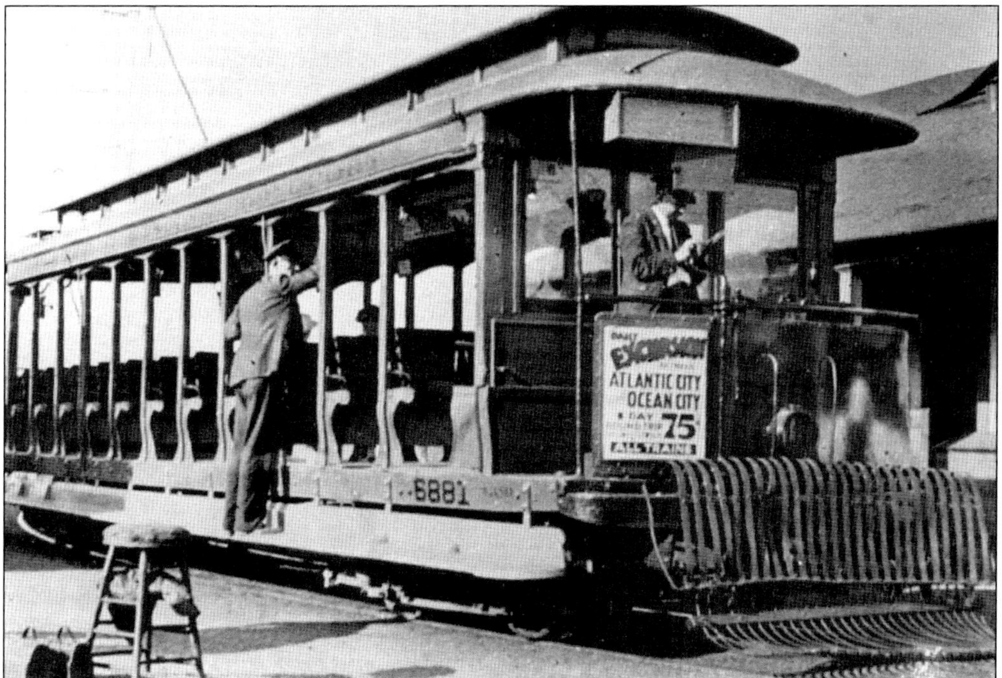

Open summertime trolley cars let cooling ocean breezes flow across warm passengers who boarded this excursion car that ran from Atlantic City to Ocean City (round trip, 75¢). The conductor walked along a narrow outside platform to collect the fares. (ACFPL.)

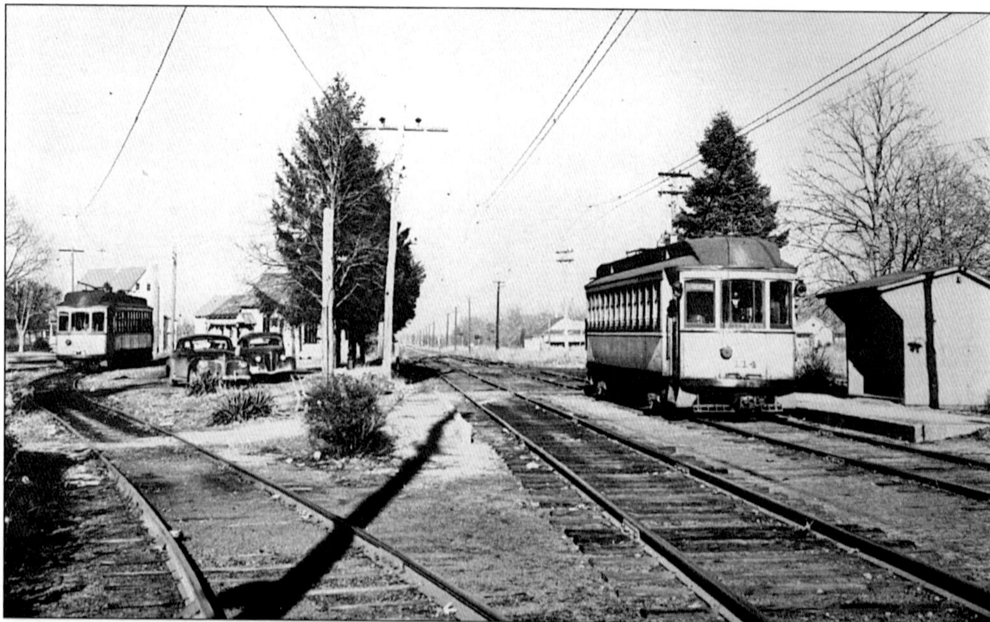

These are two of the trolleys on the Shore Fast Line, which ran on a double-tracked roadbed from Atlantic City near Steel Pier to the boardwalk in Ocean City between 1906 and 1948. The line provided an alternative to trains, although trains were much faster. The car on the left has pulled off at a passenger station. (ACFPL.)

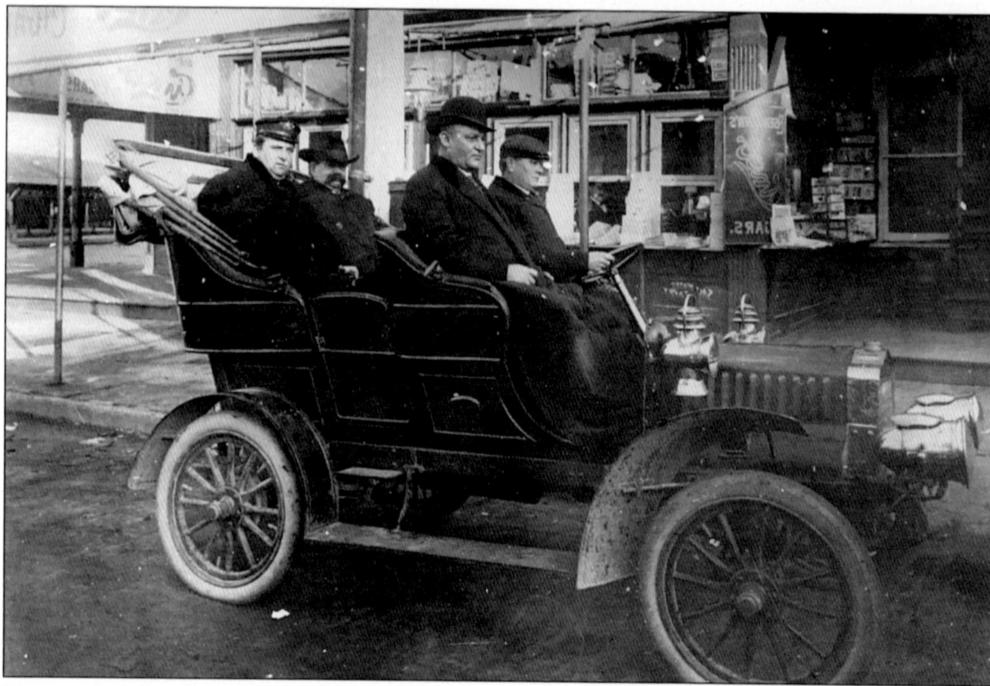

Transportation competition was underway by 1910: automobiles had been added to trolleys. One of Atlantic City's first automobiles, owned by the Atlantic City Electric Company, included among its passengers Commodore Lewis Kuehnle (rear left) and Lewis P. Scott (with derby hat). (Conectiv.)

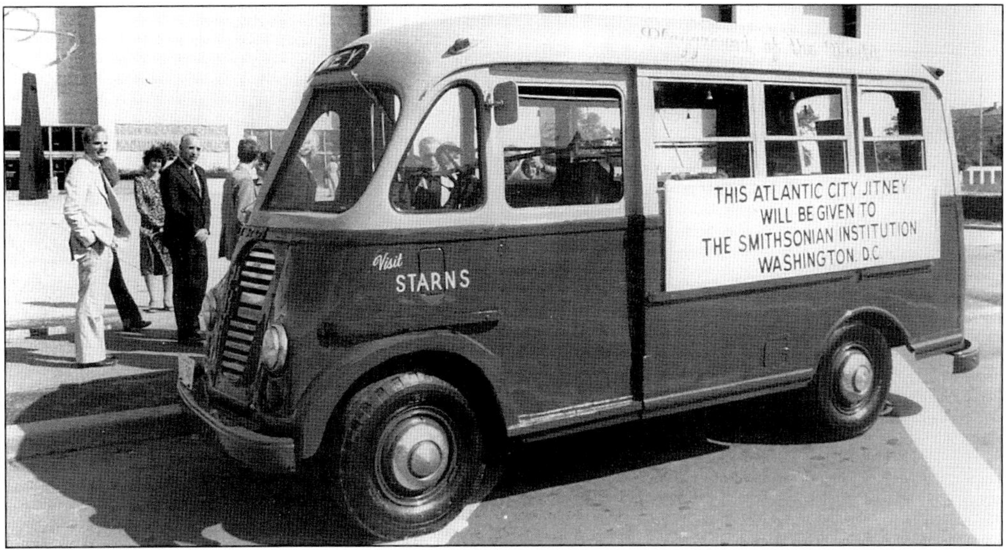

No means of transportation in the city was ever remembered more fondly than the jitneys that streamed up and down Pacific Avenue in all seasons and at all hours. One of the jitneys made it all the way to the Smithsonian. The name jitney was bestowed because the first rides cost only a nickel: the five-cent piece was known as a "jitney." (ACFPL.)

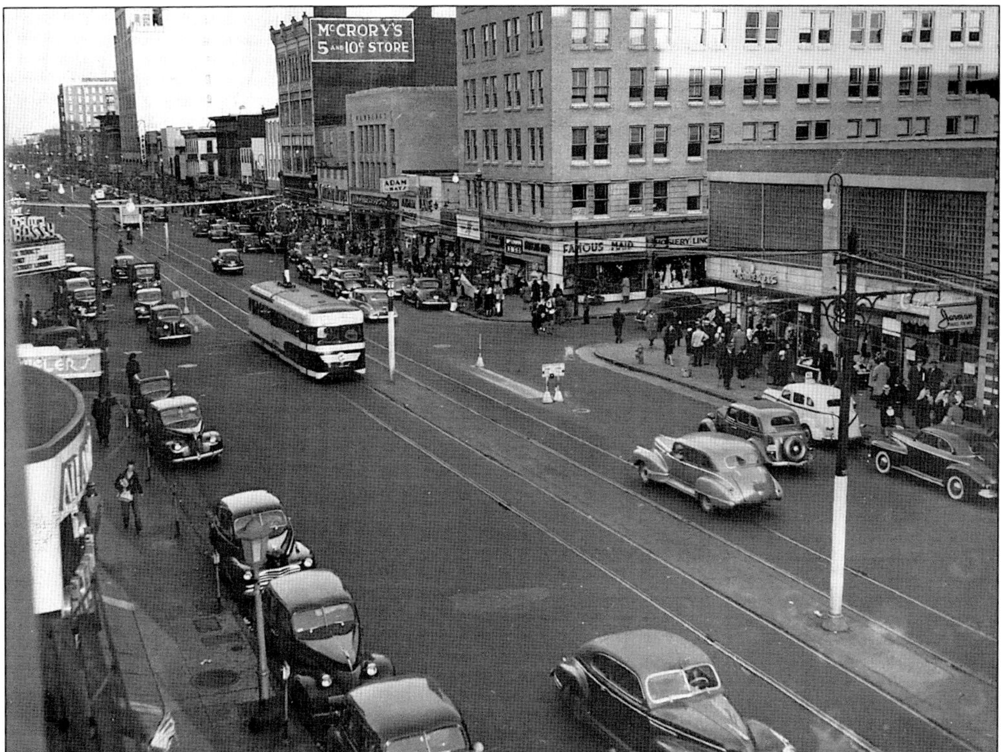

By 1946, wide Atlantic Avenue was a mix of automobiles and streetcars. The double-tracked streetcar line occupied the middle of the street, and even with street parking for automobiles there was ample room to keep all traffic moving smoothly. (ACFPL.)

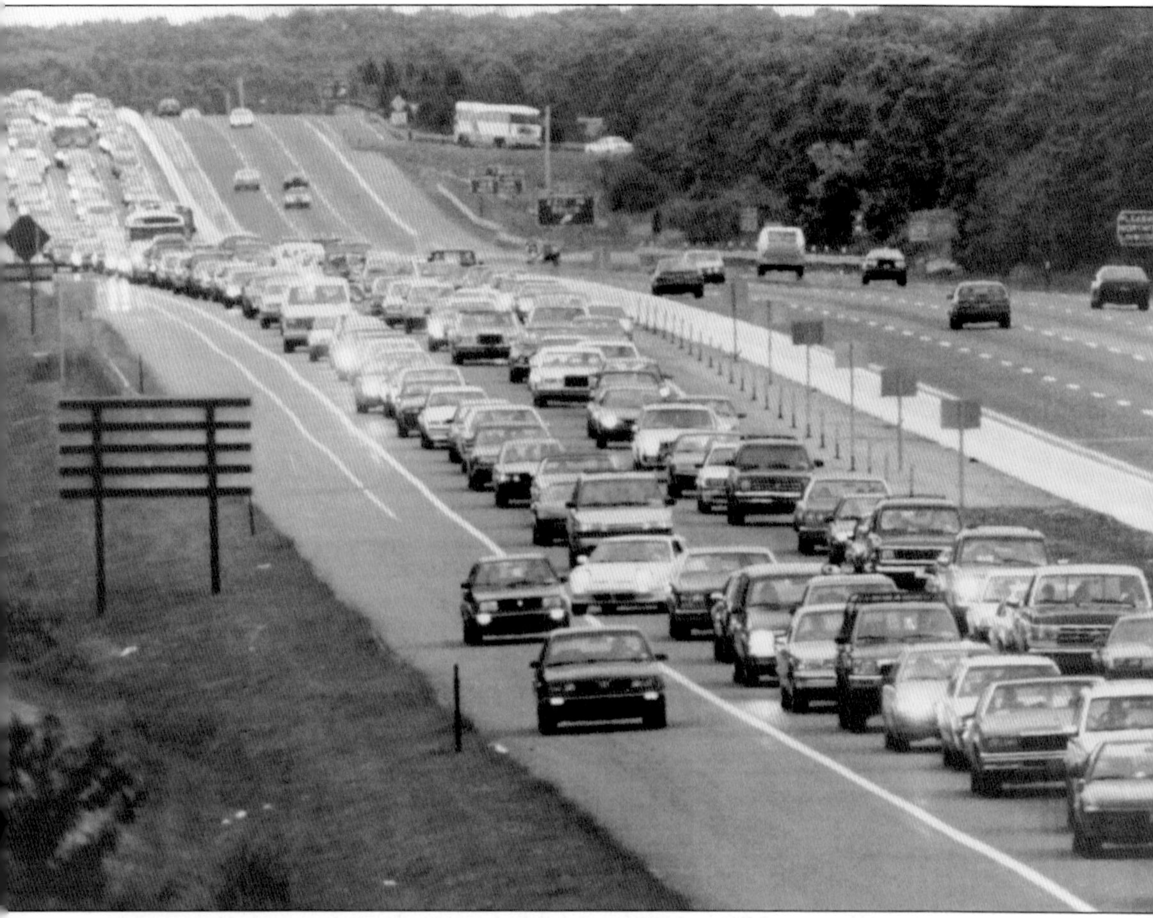

Automobiles dominated transportation after the Atlantic City Expressway was completed from Camden to the city in 1965. Cars usually move swiftly on the expressway, but during holiday or summer weekends, the nearly overwhelming influx of automobiles can test the ability of any road to move people rapidly toward the Boardwalk. (ACFPL.)

Two

ON THE BOARDWALK

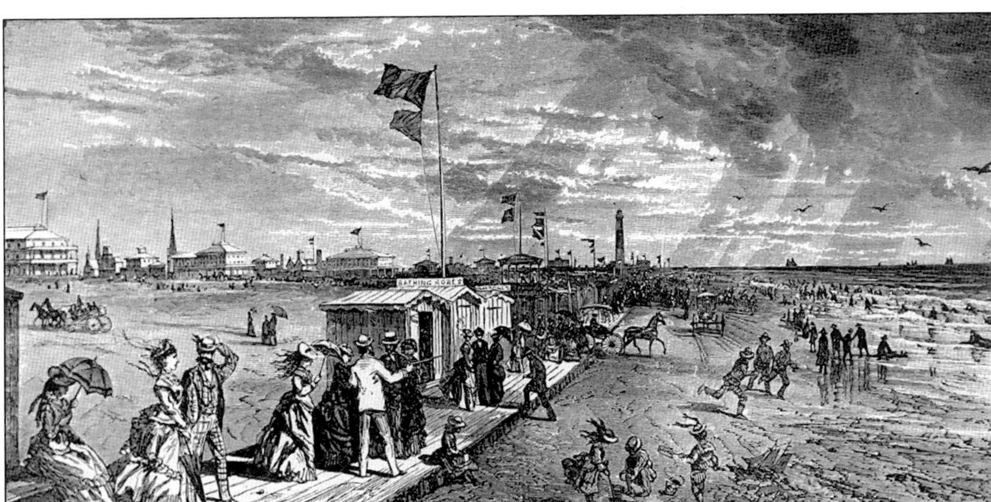

When hotel owners complained in 1870 about the sand that was tracked into their establishments, train conductor Alexander Boardman and hotel keeper Jacob Keim suggested building a wooden walkway atop the beach. By that June, Atlantic City had spent $5,000 on a moveable boardwalk, seen in this 1876 engraving. In the decades ahead, those 12-foot sections of pine planks, only 8 to 10 feet wide, grew into a business and entertainment legend. (ACFPL.)

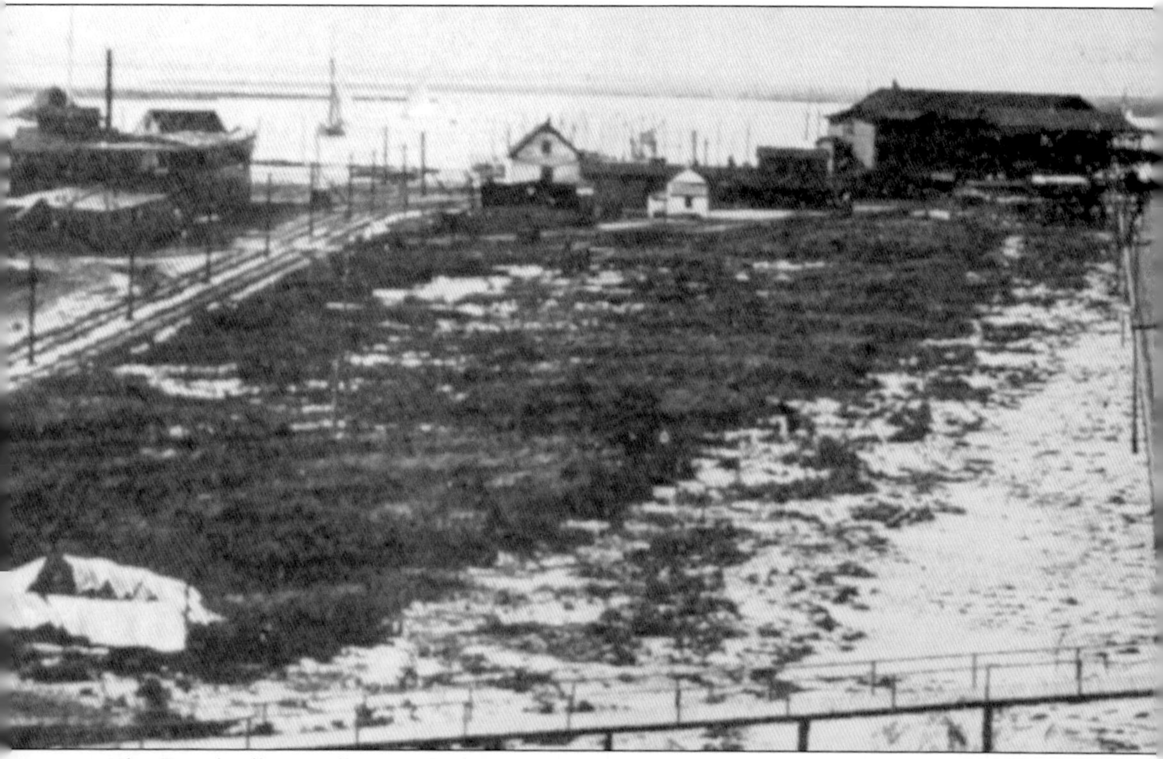

The Boardwalk initially stretched from near Absecon Inlet (above, 1910) and south to the railheads at Georgia Avenue. Although the Inlet section was at first a fashionable district, the

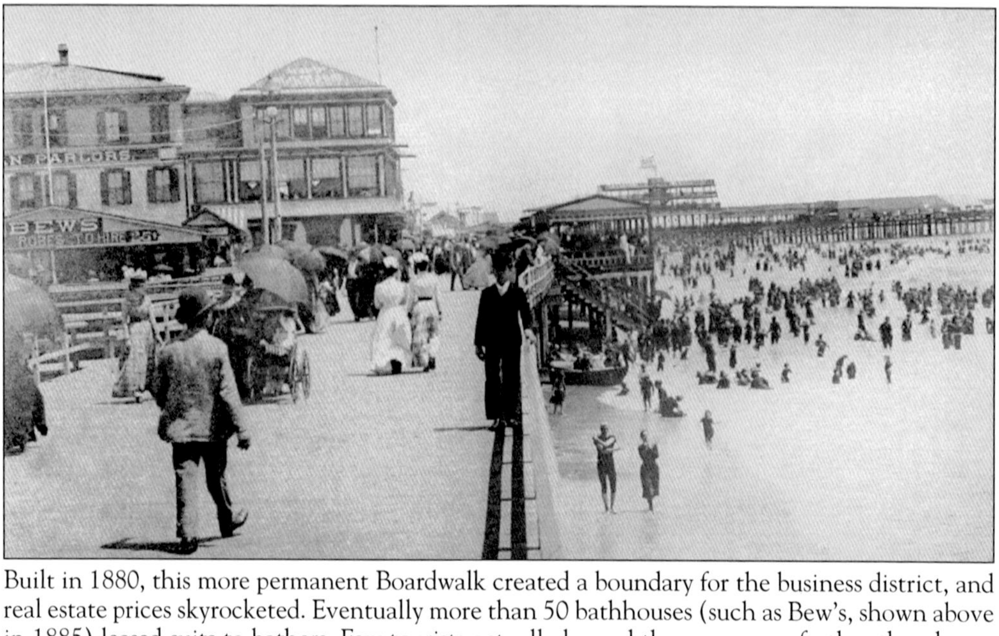

Built in 1880, this more permanent Boardwalk created a boundary for the business district, and real estate prices skyrocketed. Eventually more than 50 bathhouses (such as Bew's, shown above in 1885) leased suits to bathers. Few tourists actually braved the waves any further than knee-deep. Few knew how to swim. Besides, Atlantic City's promoters had championed the benefits of sea air, not seawater. (ACFPL.)

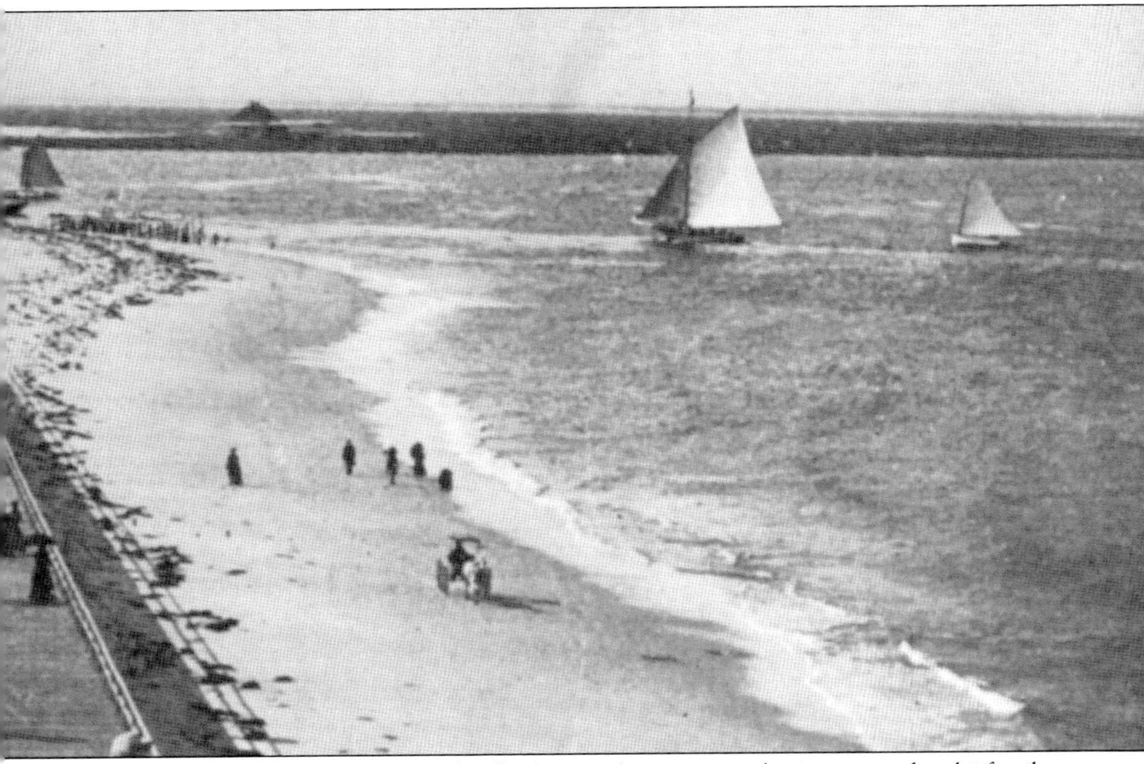

wealthy migrated south along the Boardwalk when working marinas, businesses, and multi-family houses for servants and tradespeople crept too close to their sumptuous cottages. (ACFPL.)

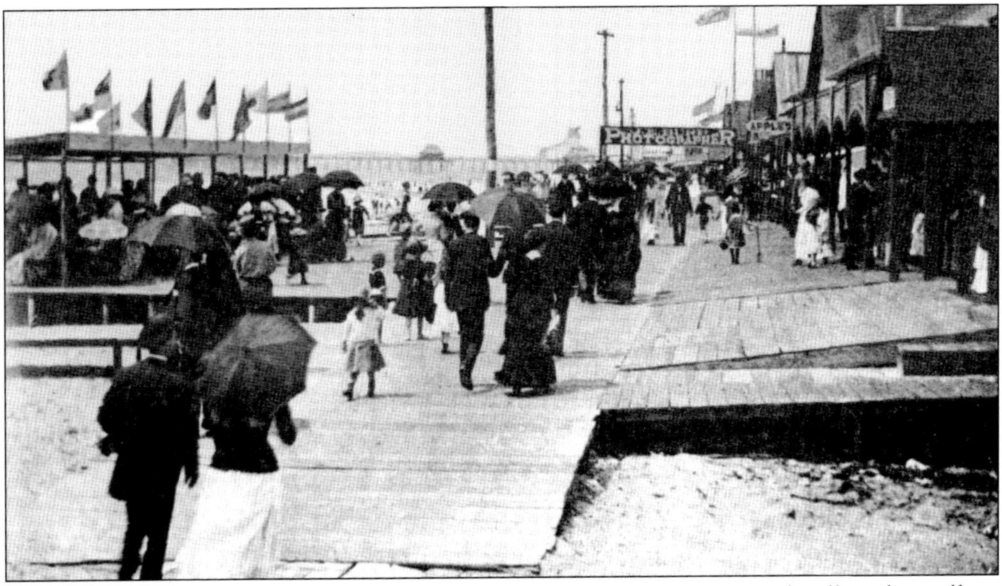

From the beginning, Boardwalk businesses catered to both day-trippers and well-to-do strollers. Besides bathhouses, photographic studios like the one above in 1884 were another staple. Proprietors charged patrons for photographing them and for the custom postcards printed for those clients to mail home to friends and relatives. (ACFPL.)

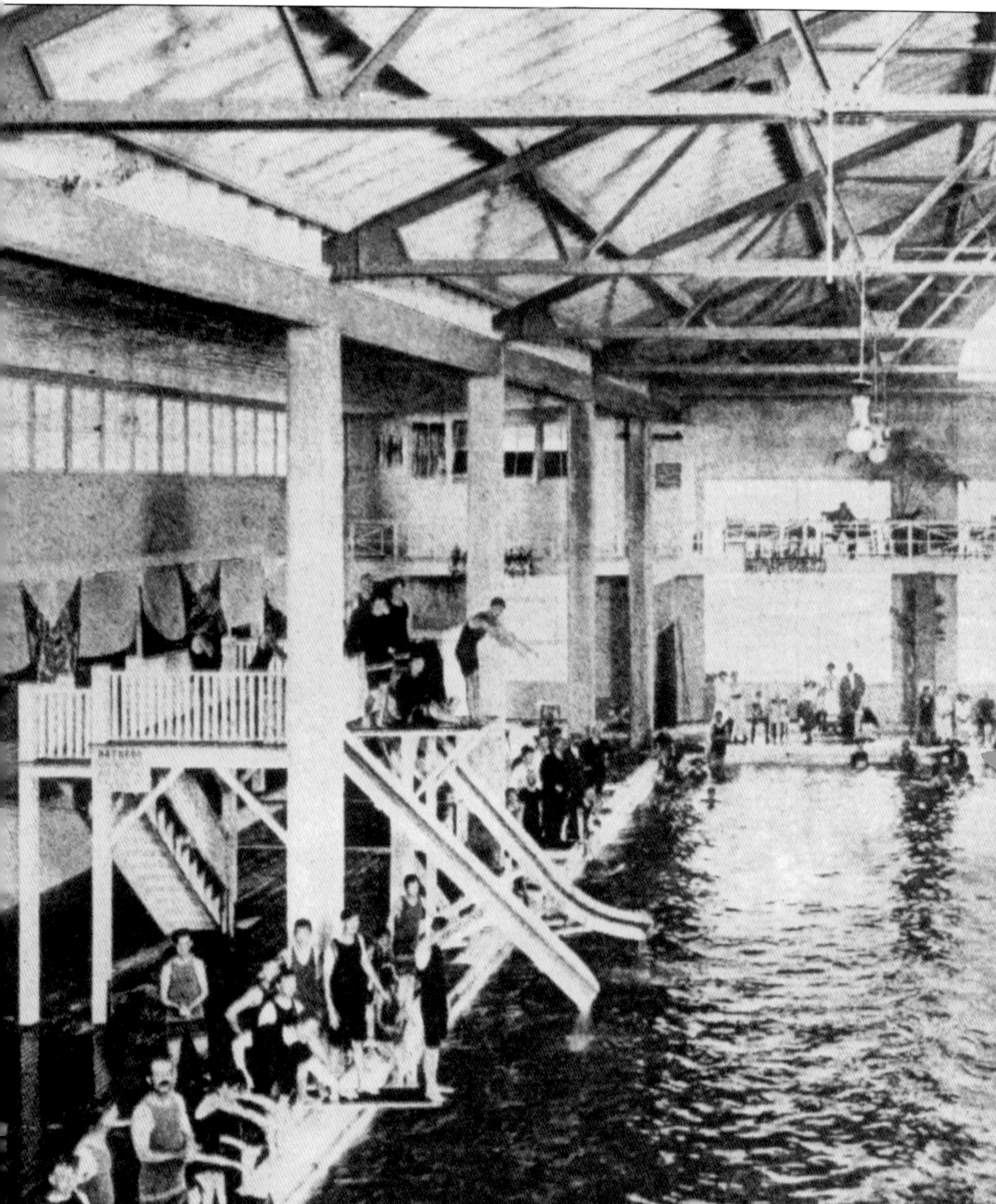

Attractions such as the Hygeia Baths, seen on a 1911 postcard, soon lined the Boardwalk. Located at Rhode Island Avenue, the Hygeia Baths offered bathing either along the ocean, in hot or cold seawater tubs, or in pools. Its advertisements boasted that the baths were open 24 hours a day, every day of the year. Named for the Greek goddess of health, it was *the* place

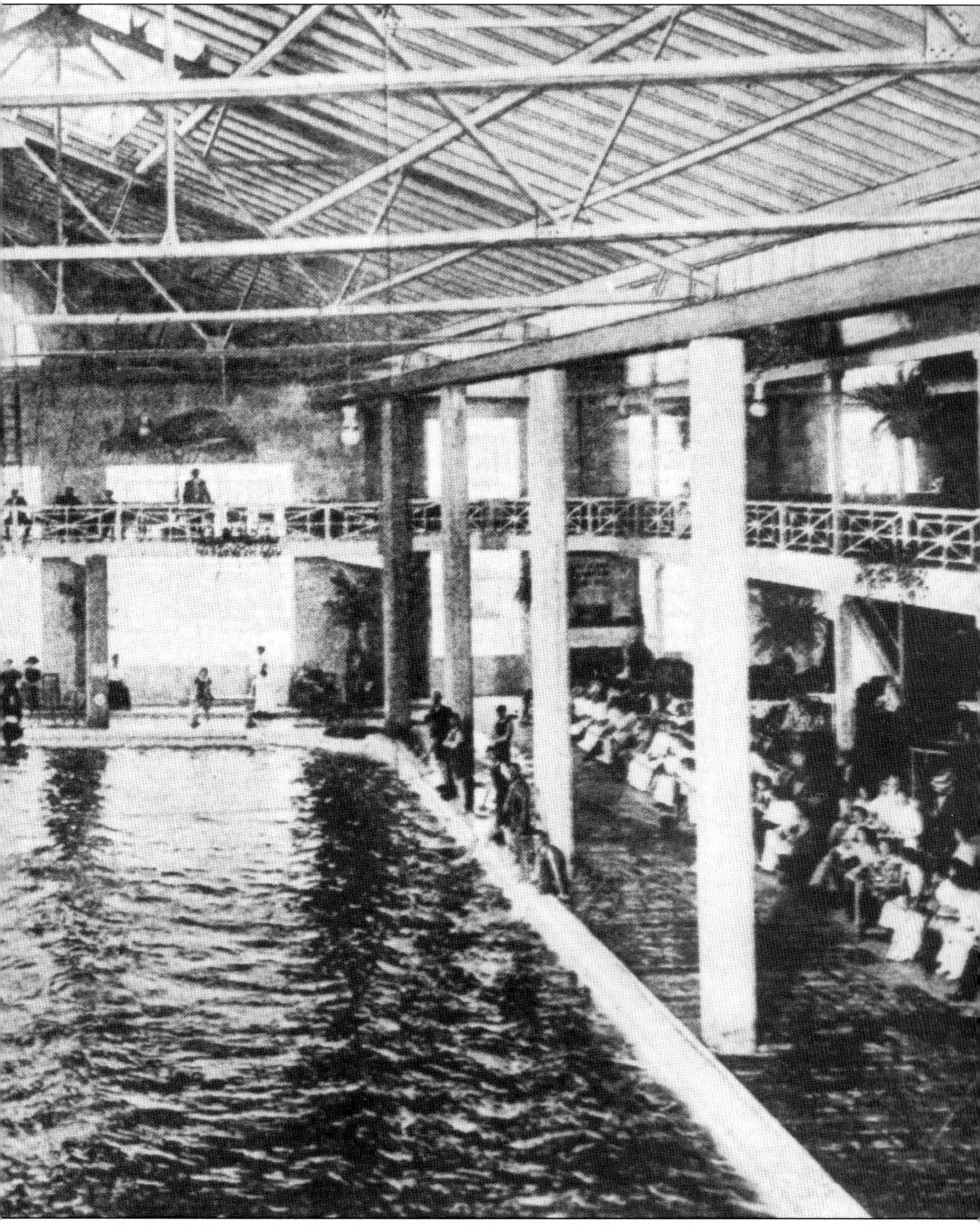

to swim before Atlantic City hotels maintained their own baths or pools. Hygeia sponsored a swimming team whose members won a number of the Round-the-Island races and marched in early Miss America parades. Once the hotels built pools, however, Hygeia Baths faded in popularity and fell into disrepair. (ACFPL.)

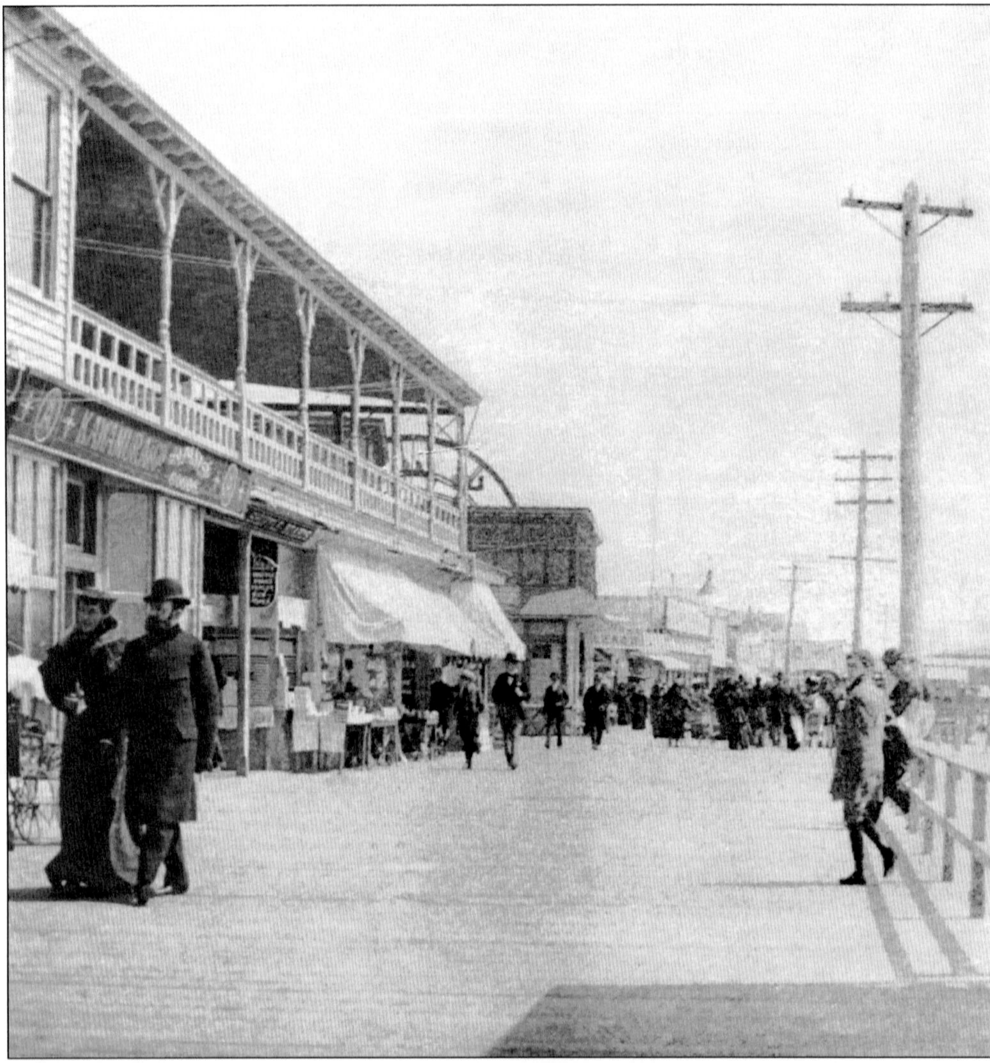

When President Ulysses S. Grant strolled the Boardwalk in 1874, he made it Atlantic City's main stage. Peppered with the exotic—including the Japanese goods advertised here near Kentucky Avenue—the Boardwalk welcomed America's first carousel and the world's first Ferris wheel, seen through the balcony. Local businessman William Somers invented the latter ride, calling it the Observation Roundabout when it debuted in 1872. George W.G. Ferris became famous when he adapted the design for Chicago's 1873 Columbia Exposition. Somers sued Ferris (and won) but never profited from his invention. (ACFPL.)

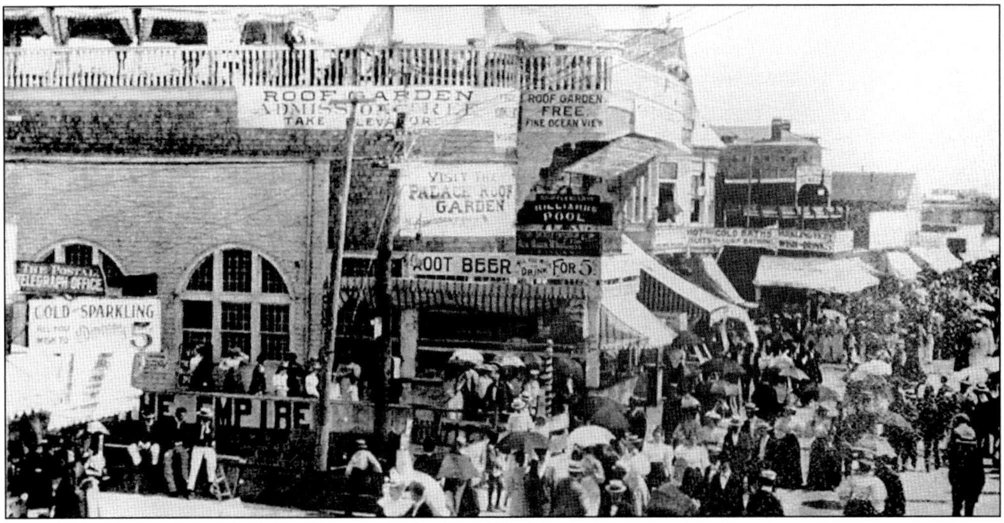

Like all Boardwalk businesses in 1900, the Empire, with its roof garden, advertised heavily. The competition for attention was so intense that outlandish promotion became an Atlantic City hallmark. For example, film star W.C. Fields started in Atlantic City as a juggler; between acts, however, he was paid to pretend to drown near Fortescue's Pier. The mock rescues, as many as 12 per day, attracted crowds to the pier. (ACFPL.)

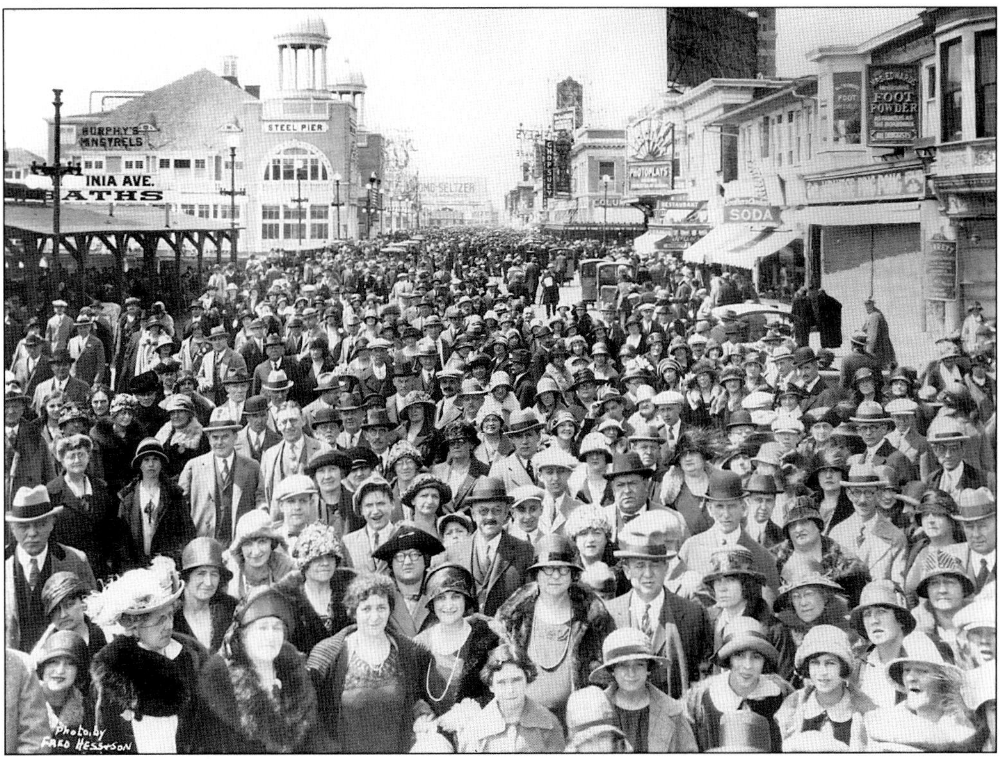

Atlantic City promoted itself, too. The annual Easter Parade, above in 1930, was started in 1876 to stem the loss of visitors to Philadelphia's Centennial Exposition. Although New York City had an older event, Atlantic City offered prizes and attracted crowds of up to 500,000. Rain, shine, or snow, it has been held every year since. (ACFPL.)

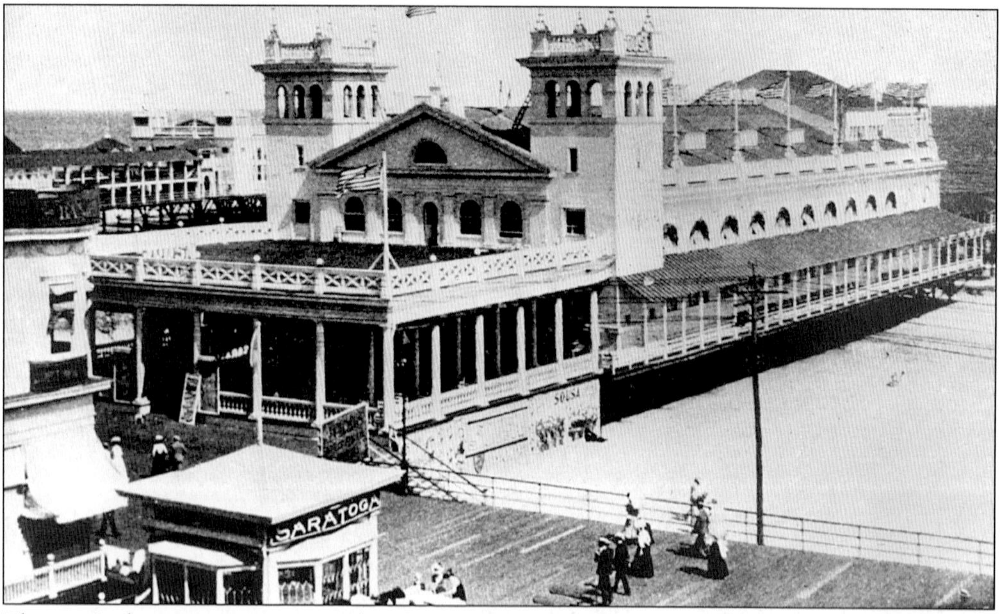

The city's first ocean pier was the West Jersey & Atlantic Railroad's extension into the ocean. There, riders waiting for the train could peer down into the surf. Other dreamers saw the financial potential. Howard's Pier opened in 1882. Applegate's Pier followed in 1884, featuring a freshwater fountain filled each day in summer with 3,000 pounds of ice. Steeplechase Pier, as it appeared in 1897 (top) and in 1920 (bottom) billed itself as the "funniest place on earth" and used every available surface to peddle its consumer products and attractions to Boardwalk crowds. (ACFPL.)

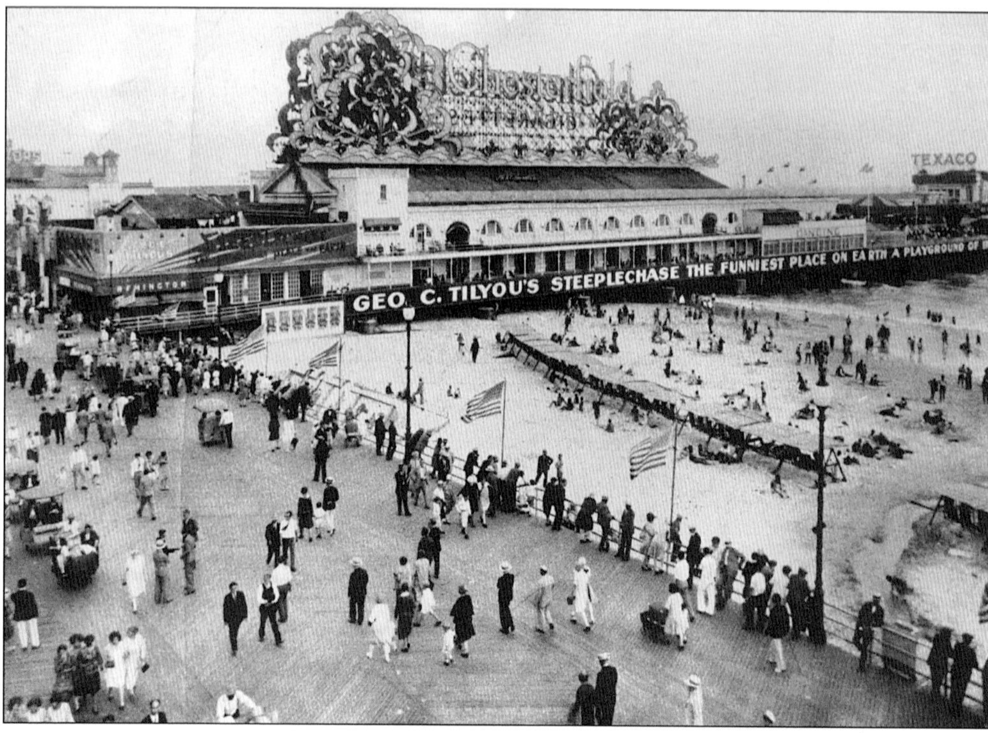

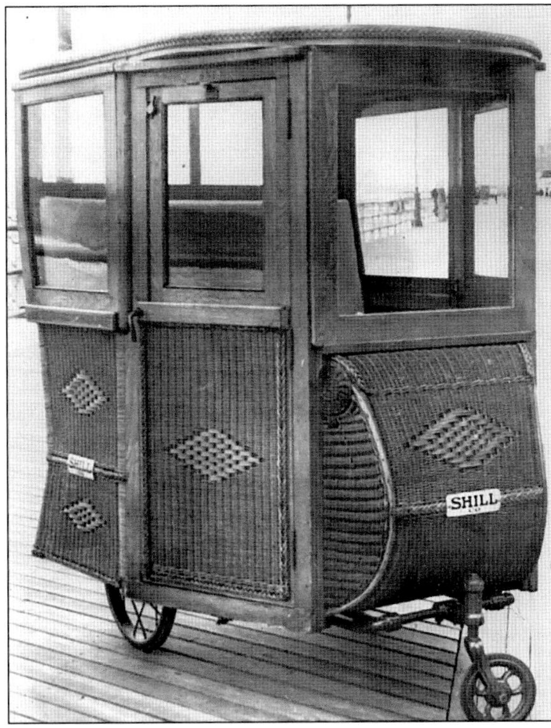

The 1887 introduction of rolling chairs added a touch of luxury to the Boardwalk. Adapted from wheelchairs, the wicker chairs, right, of Philadelphian Harry Shill earned a place in the Smithsonian. Rolling chairs had their own parade, the Floral Parade, before Miss America festivities subsumed it in 1921. The chairs, however, carried contestants down the Boardwalk for decades thereafter. By 1940, some chairs accommodated up to four people, below, with two men pedaling. Motorized chairs appeared briefly before being banned in the 1960s. (ACFPL.)

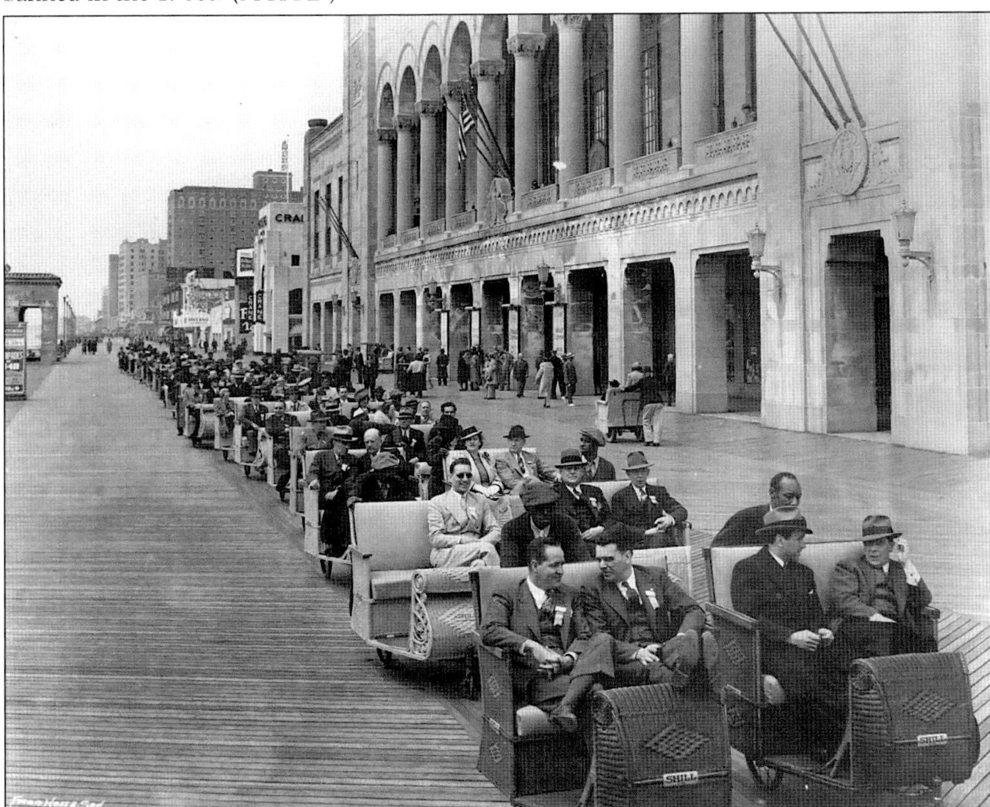

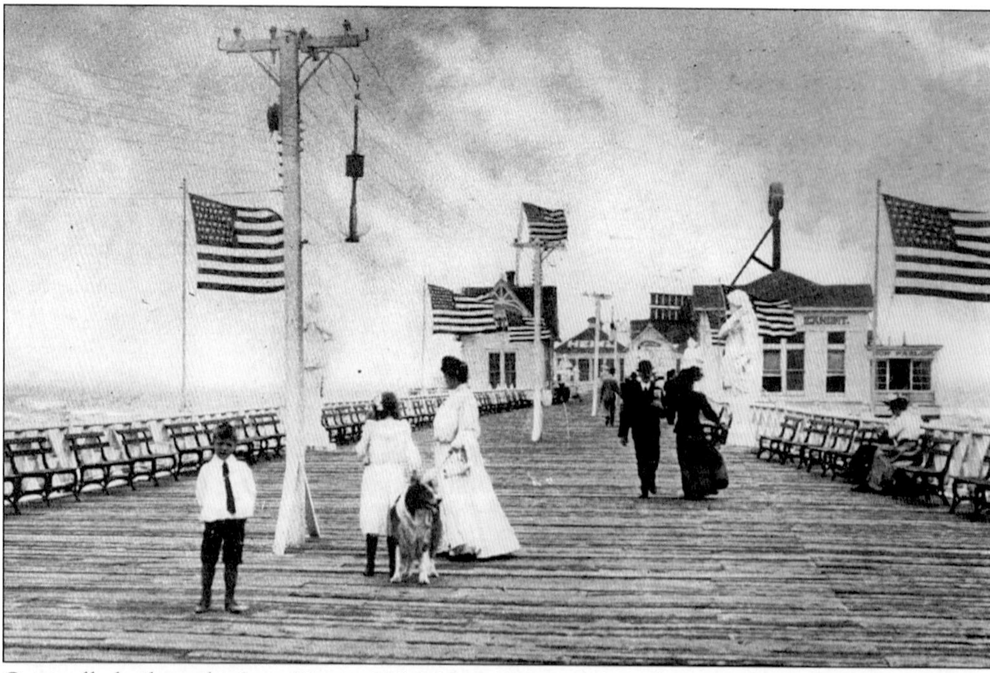

Originally built as the Iron Pier in 1886, Heinz Pier at Massachusetts Avenue, above in 1905, marketed H.J. Heinz brands for more than 40 years. This was done with exhibits, cooking demonstrations, model interiors such as a sun parlor, below in 1910, and souvenir pins shaped like pickles. Although located well north of the main business district, it remained a Boardwalk mainstay until the hurricane of 1944 damaged it beyond repair. (ACFPL.)

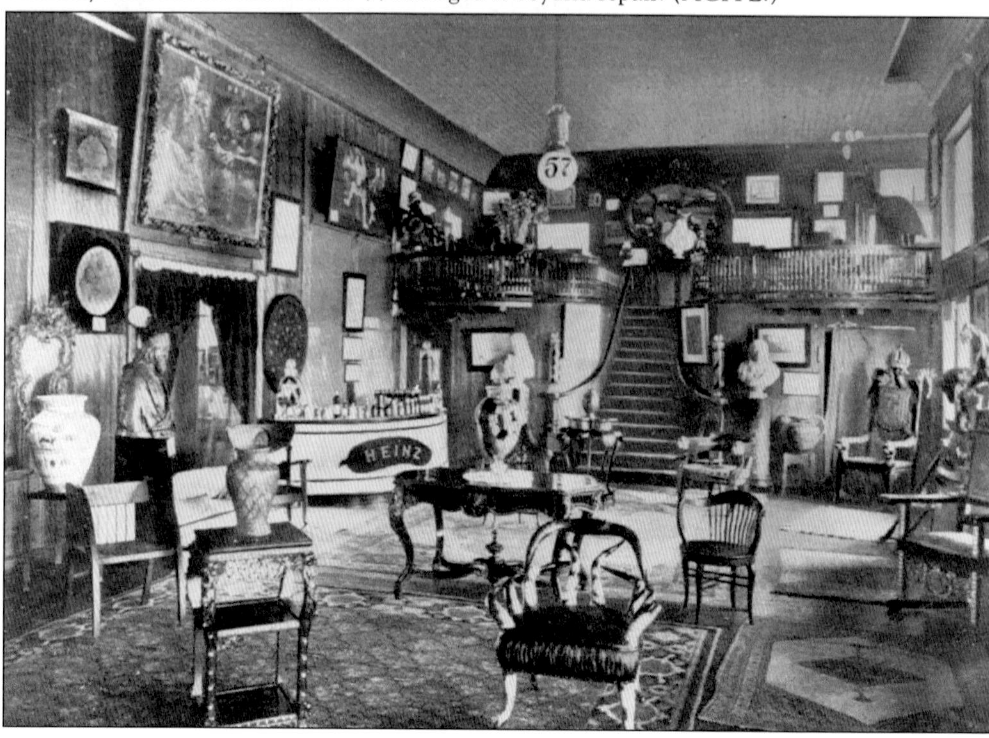

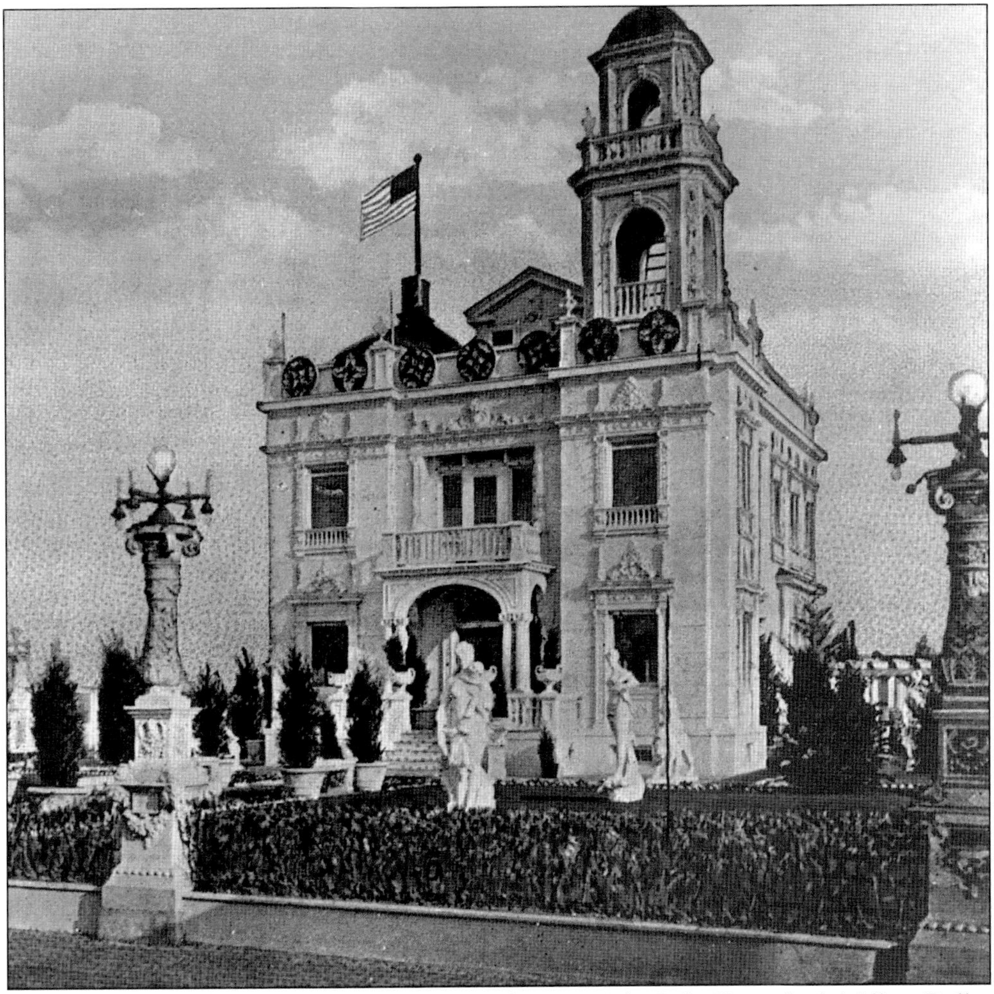

After buying Applegate's Pier and rebuilding its fortunes, John Lake Young built Million Dollar Pier in 1906 at Arkansas Avenue. Its name announced the phenomenal cost of its appointments. Its most famous attraction, the Net Haul, raised creatures twice daily from the deep for all to inspect. The pier also touted "the most famous address in the world," Number One Atlantic Ocean, seen above in 1910. Young claimed to fish from a bedroom window of the Italian Revival mansion, constructed of imported marble and located 1,700 feet out to sea. Among the luminaries he welcomed to the pier was President William H. Taft. (ACFPL.)

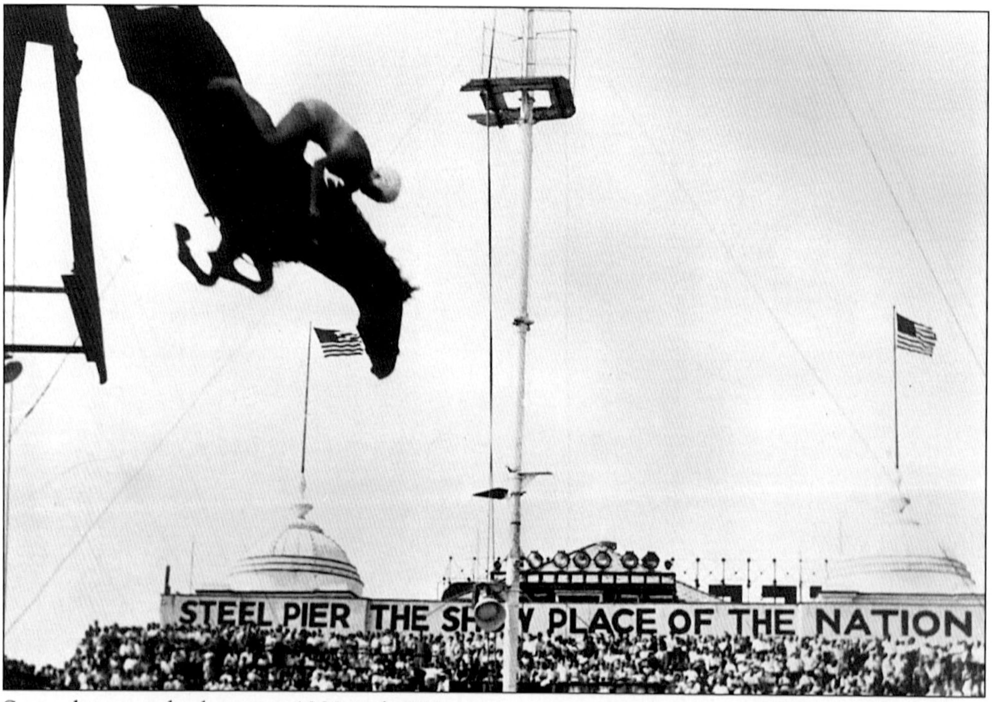

Several times a day between 1929 and 1978, young women in swimsuits coaxed trained horses off a 40-foot tower into 12 feet of water, as seen here in 1933. Although it originated in the Midwest, the diving horse act made the Steel Pier the most famous amusement pier in the world. Neither horses nor riders suffered serious injuries, and few other acts attracted larger crowds. (ACFPL.)

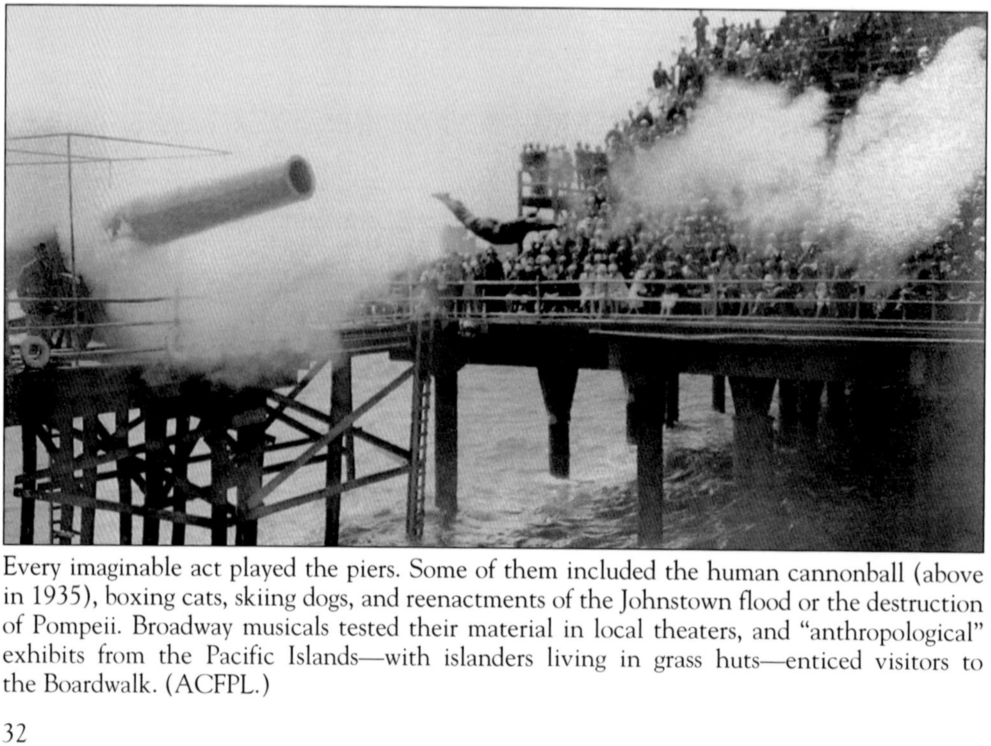

Every imaginable act played the piers. Some of them included the human cannonball (above in 1935), boxing cats, skiing dogs, and reenactments of the Johnstown flood or the destruction of Pompeii. Broadway musicals tested their material in local theaters, and "anthropological" exhibits from the Pacific Islands—with islanders living in grass huts—enticed visitors to the Boardwalk. (ACFPL.)

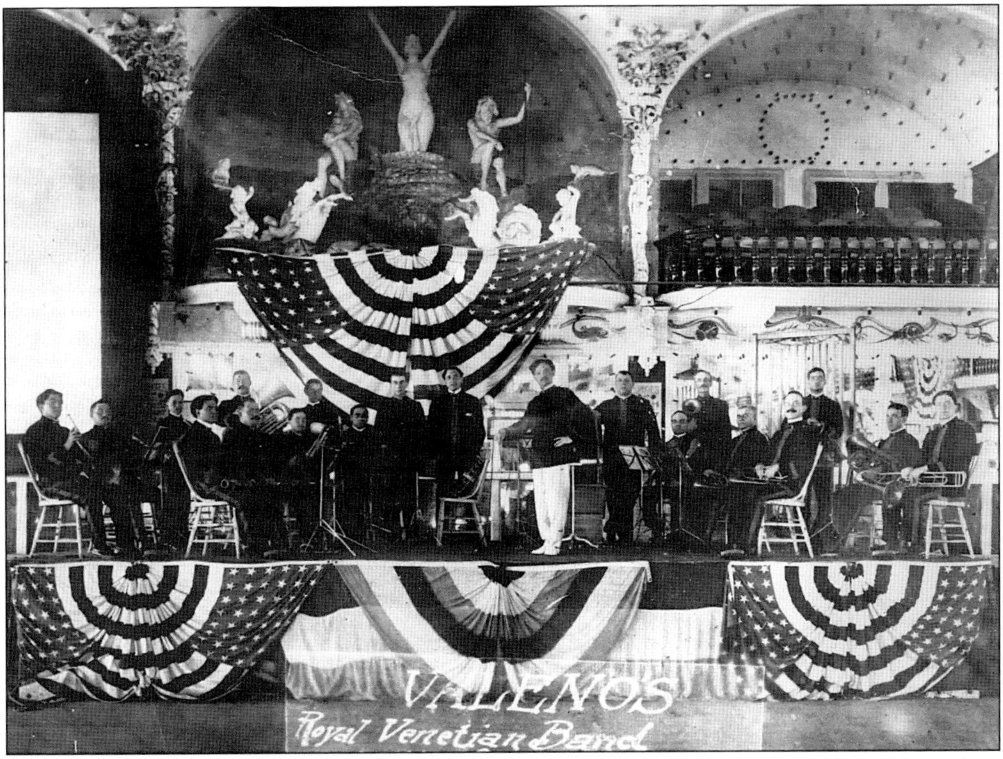

The city danced its nights away along the Boardwalk. In 1914, the Valenos Royal Venetian Band, above, kept the beat in Million Dollar Pier's ornate ballroom. John Philips Sousa was the city's favorite music maker from 1892 to 1927, when each summer he appeared at the Steeplechase or Steel Piers. Before his fame as director of the U.S. Marine Corps Band, however, Sousa toiled anonymously in an Atlantic City hotel. (ACFPL.)

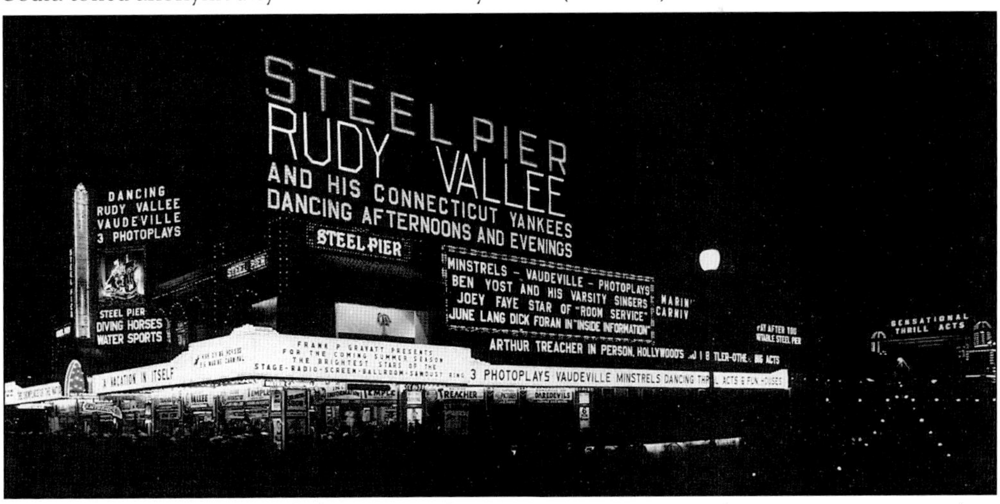

The piers eventually placed the names of every major entertainer (many minor ones too) in lights, including Rudee Vallee's, seen above in 1935. Atlantic City's penchant for promotion painted Boardwalk nights in dizzying colors. Only Broadway and later Las Vegas ever rivaled the city's display of light. The coming of casinos in 1976 revived Atlantic City's reputation for illumination. (ACFPL.)

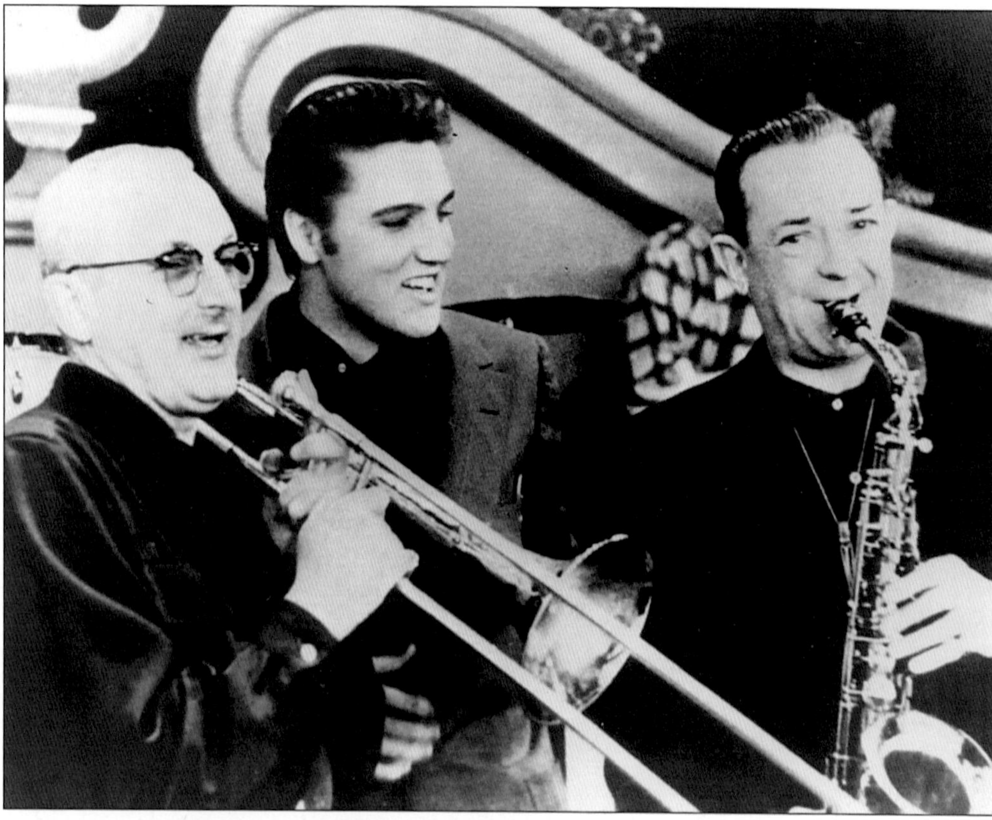

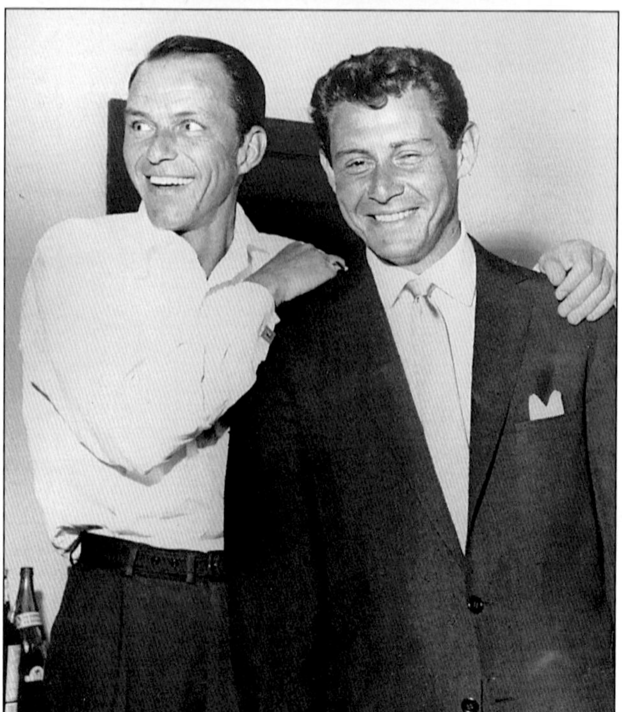

Elvis Presley may have been the only major star never actually to play Atlantic City, thanks to an error in judgment by impresario George Hamid. But that did not stop Presley from dropping in on Tommy and Jimmy Dorsey, above. Such famous clubs as Chez Paree entertained at New York Avenue and the Boardwalk until the 1960s, while Club Harlem was on Kentucky Avenue. (ACFPL.)

New Jersey native Frank Sinatra (seen at left with Eddie Fisher in 1958) made the 500 Club on Mississippi Avenue a legend along with Martin and Lewis, Louis Armstrong, and others. The clubs were one of the few places African-Americans could mingle with whites, but the popularity of the clubs faded as the city declined. (ACFPL.)

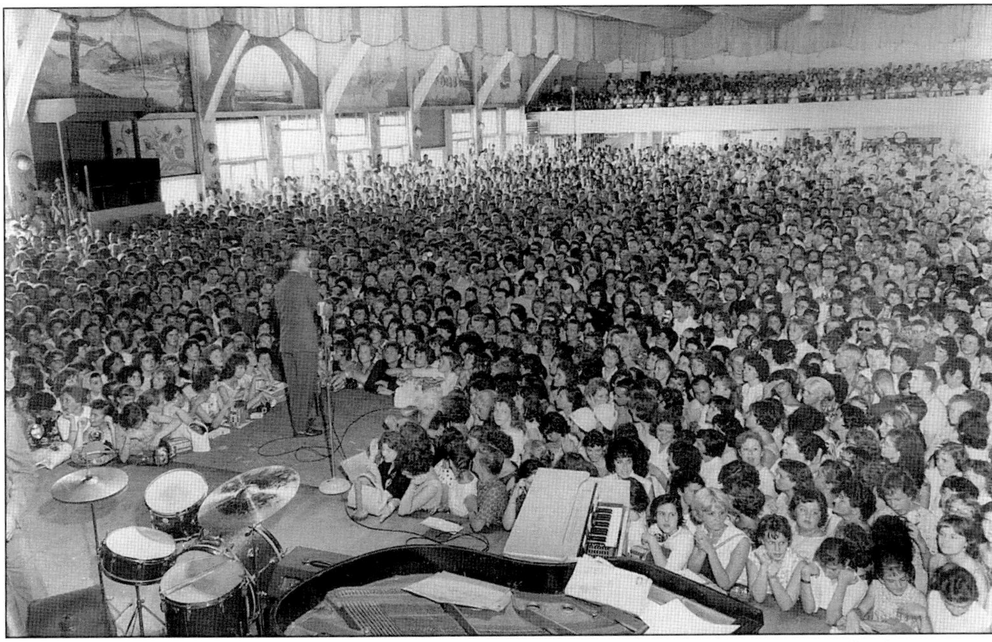

Rock and roll eventually furnished the city's beat, and "Under the Boardwalk" became an Atlantic City anthem. Standing-room-only crowds lured Dick Clark, above in 1960, from his Philadelphia television station to the ballroom of the Steel Pier for summer shows. One night, 44,000 people packed Steel Pier for a concert by Rick Nelson and Dr. John. (ACFPL.)

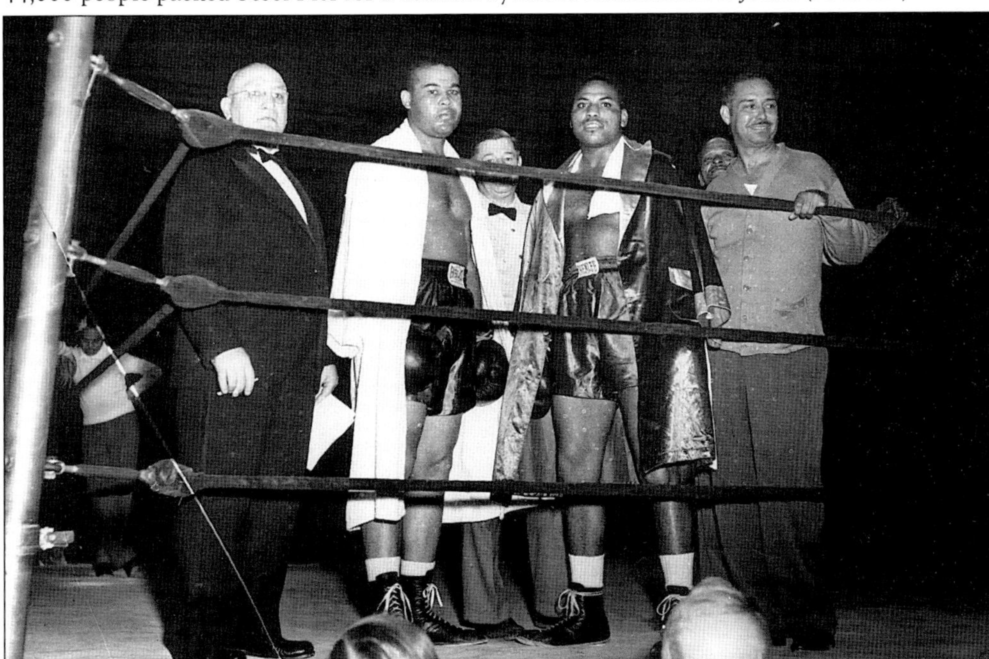

The piers attracted other amusements as well. With a relaxed attitude toward liquor during Prohibition and toward gambling before the casinos, the city also prized its fights and fighters. Even in the twilight of his career after WWII, Joe Louis, shown in trunks on the left, drew thousands to the Boardwalk for training sessions and bouts. (ACFPL.)

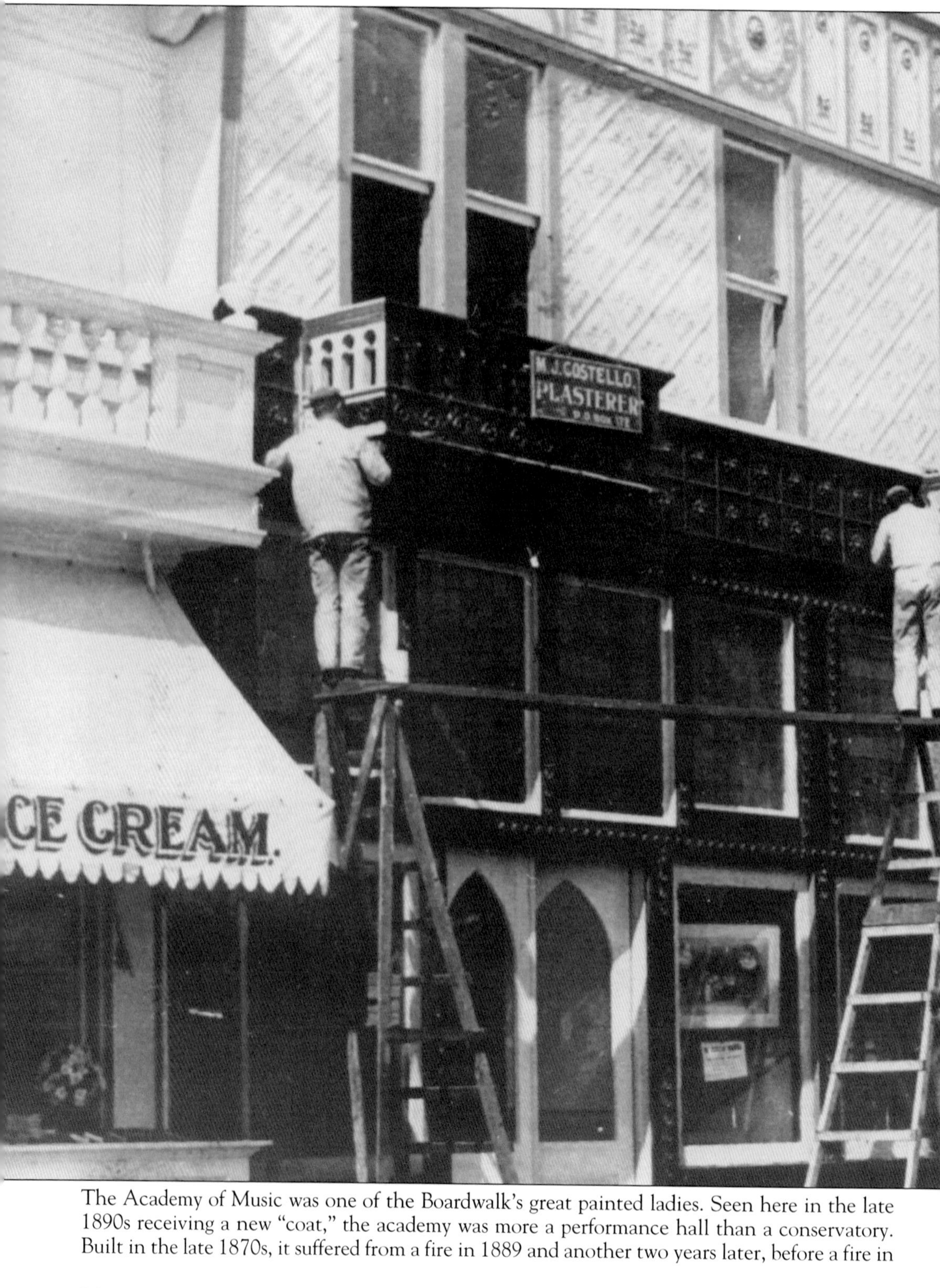

The Academy of Music was one of the Boardwalk's great painted ladies. Seen here in the late 1890s receiving a new "coat," the academy was more a performance hall than a conservatory. Built in the late 1870s, it suffered from a fire in 1889 and another two years later, before a fire in

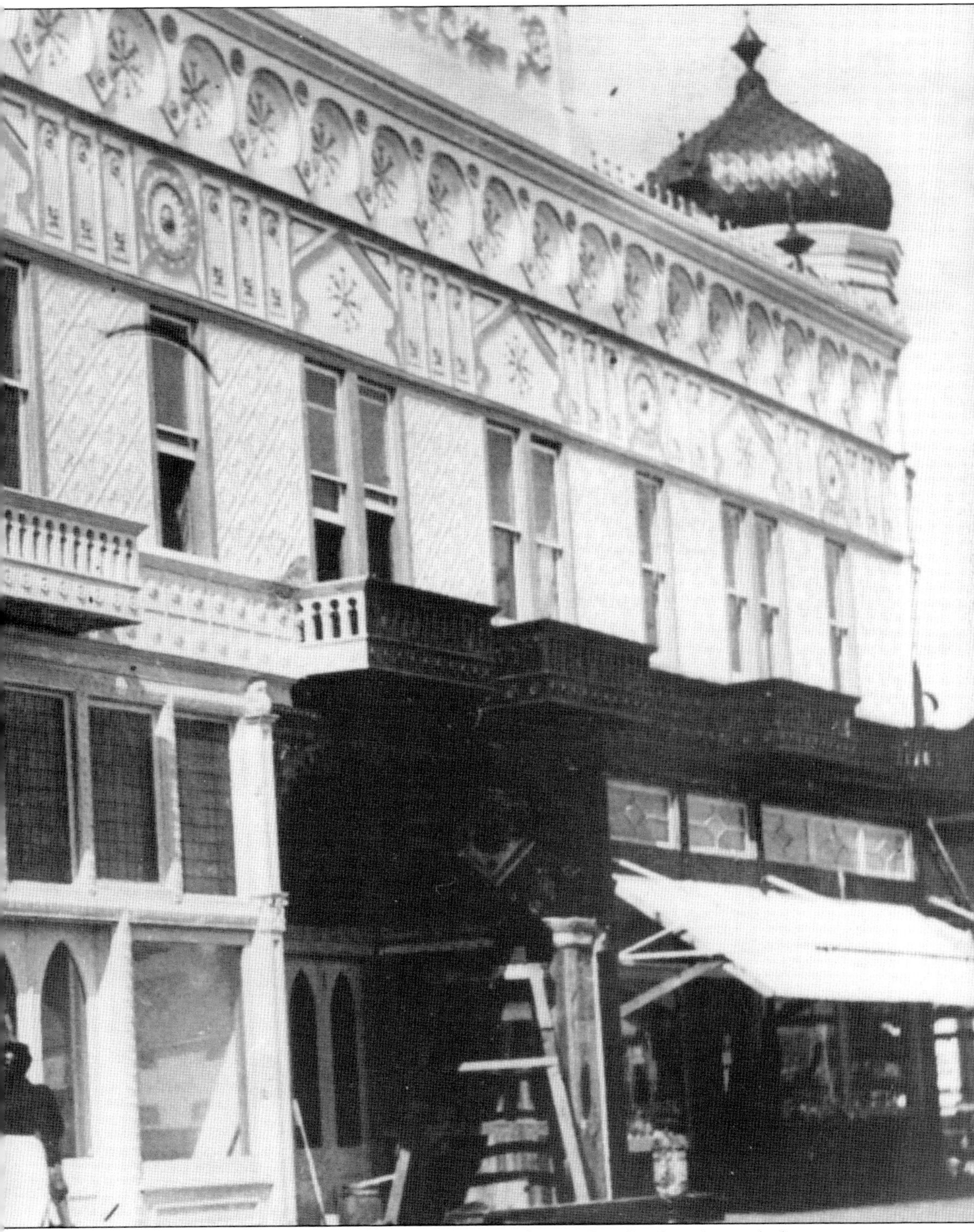

1901 destroyed it altogether. Flames claimed many Atlantic City landmarks, including portions of the Boardwalk itself. (ACFPL.)

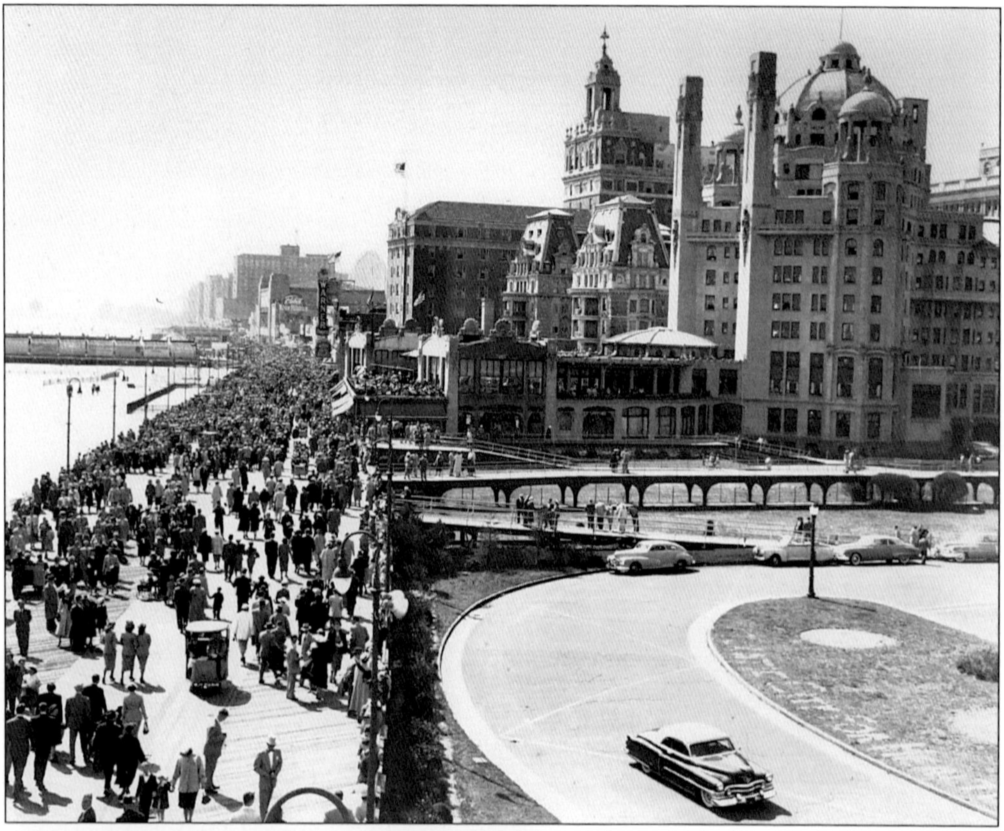

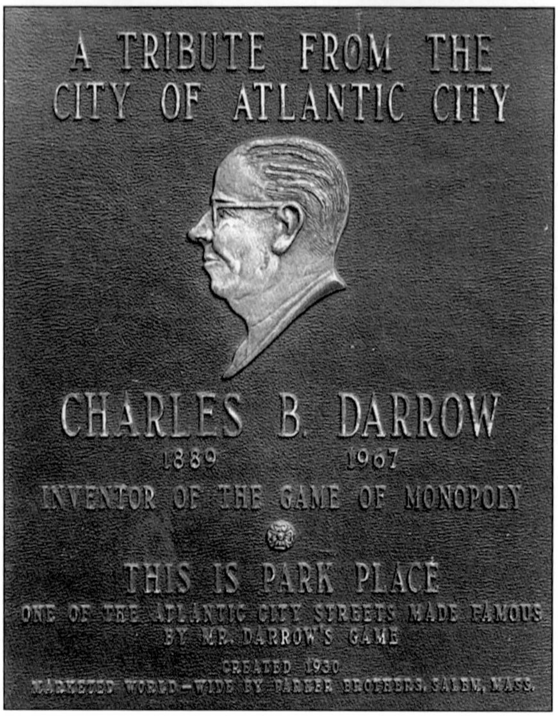

The Boardwalk at Park Place, above in 1955, was famous even before Charles Darrow's Monopoly game made its real estate the game's costliest properties. Bounded on the south by a tiny street named Park Place, Brighton Park, at left, was an 1879 gift to the city by the owner of the Brighton Hotel and a Philadelphia saw maker. The grand Traymore and Marlborough-Blenheim hotels were just a few yards beyond. An unemployed heating contractor when he invented Monopoly in 1930, Charles Darrow created the 20th century's best-selling game and earned a plaque, left, at Boardwalk and Park Place for immortalizing Atlantic City's streets and landmarks. (Conectiv; JTC.)

Three

ALWAYS THE BEACH

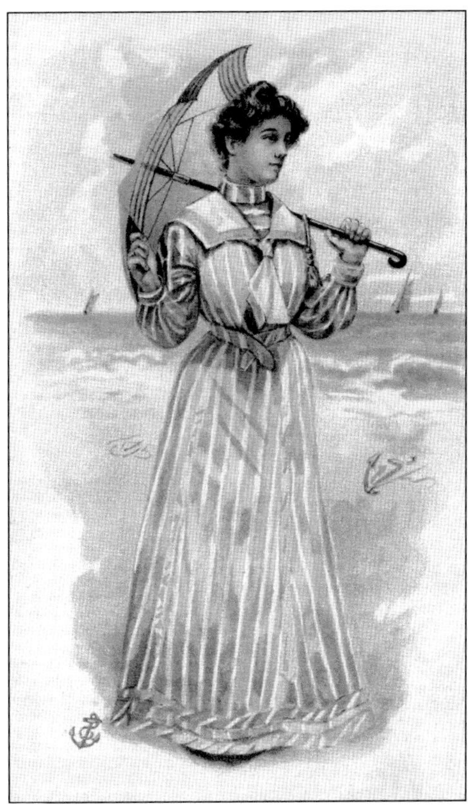

First promoted for its healthy air in an era when cities reeked during the summer, Atlantic City enticed visitors to the ocean's edge, but few into the ocean's waves. The beach, not the water, was the site of the action (or inaction). Languishing in full dress with parasol was all the fashion—and a titillating attraction. (Ruffolo.)

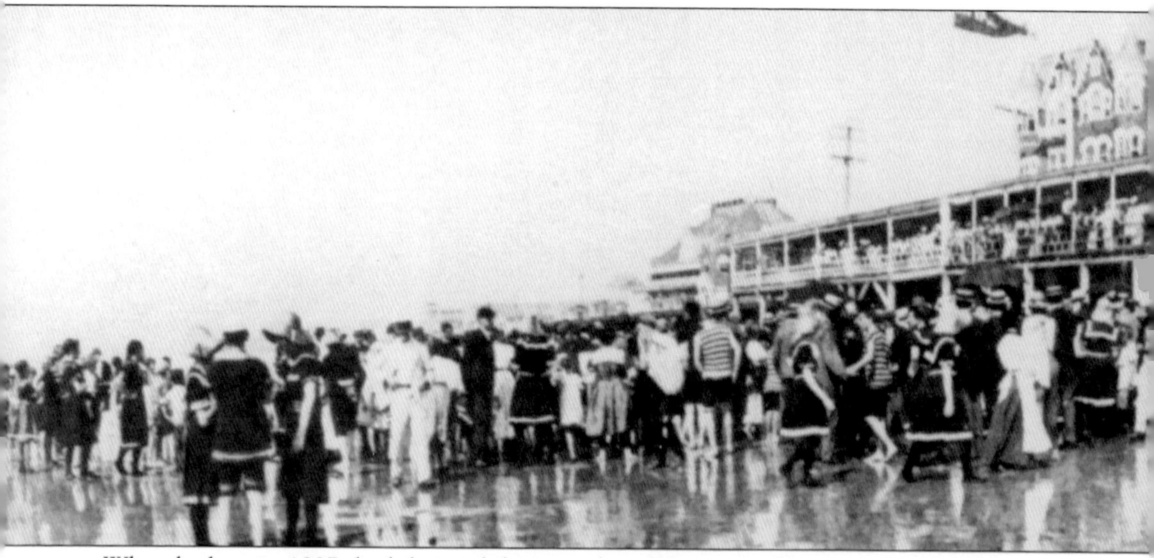

When bathers in 1887 shed their inhibitions, they did so in bathhouses such as Brady's Baths, above. Each day, tourists leased suits from Brady's for wading in the water. For those who abstained, Brady's built a covered observation deck, center, just off the Boardwalk. The woolen

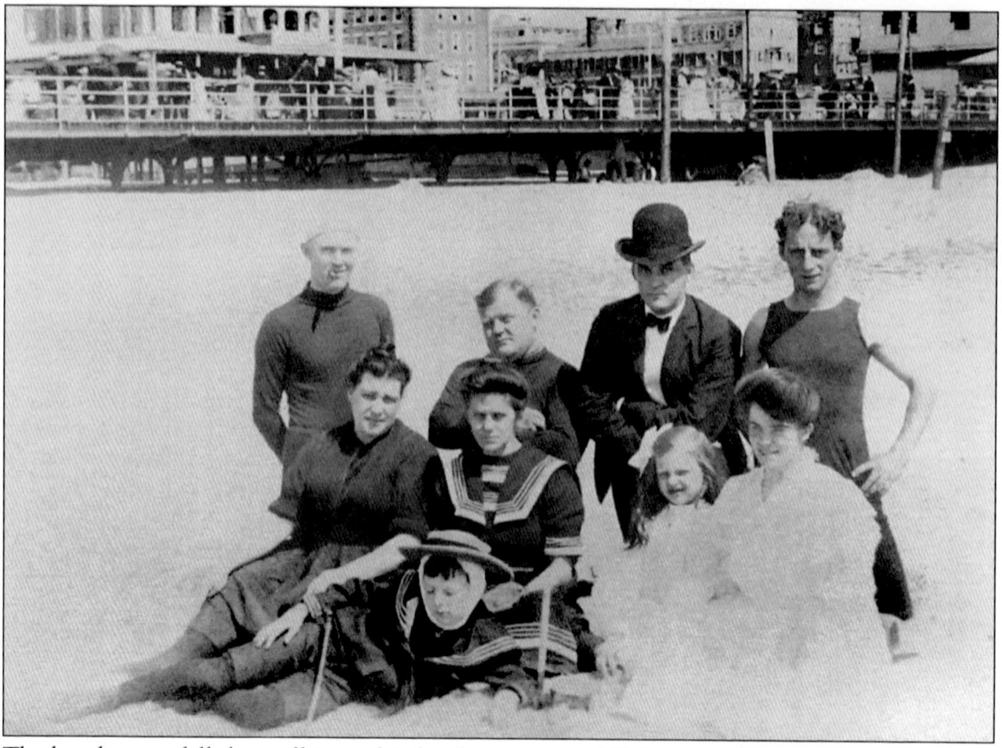

The beach was a full-dress affair, as this family portrait in 1900 attests. Women donned bathing dresses and stockings to sit on the beach, if they changed at all. Men could bare their arms and some of their legs, but the law prevented any greater a display of skin. Non-bathers in the party dressed almost as formally to sit in the sand with their families as to go to work or church. (ACFPL.)

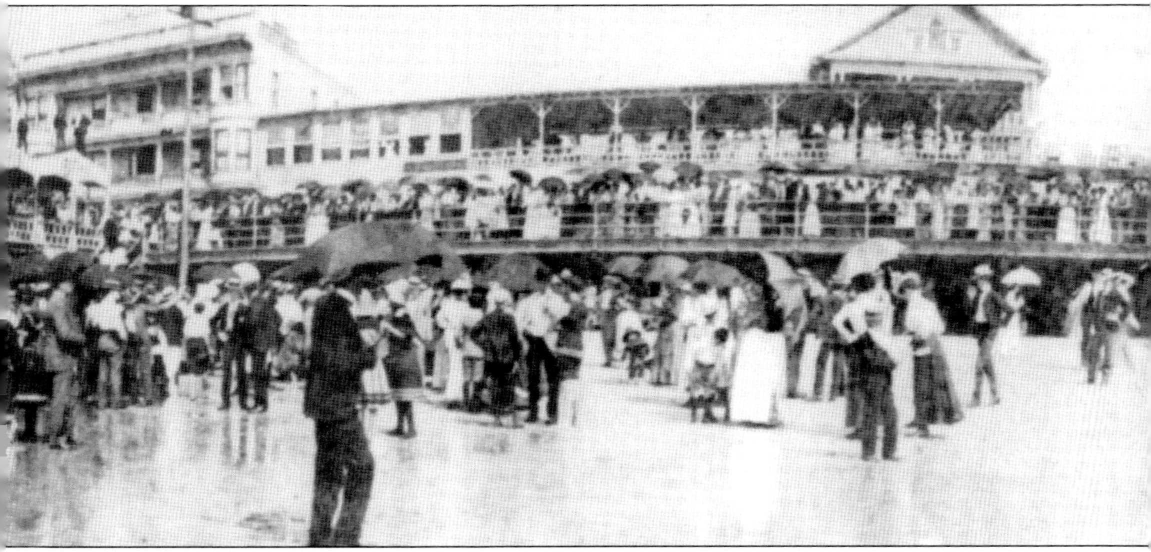

or flannel suits may have endangered bathers had they ventured too far into the water, as the suits became heavy when waterlogged. (ACFPL.)

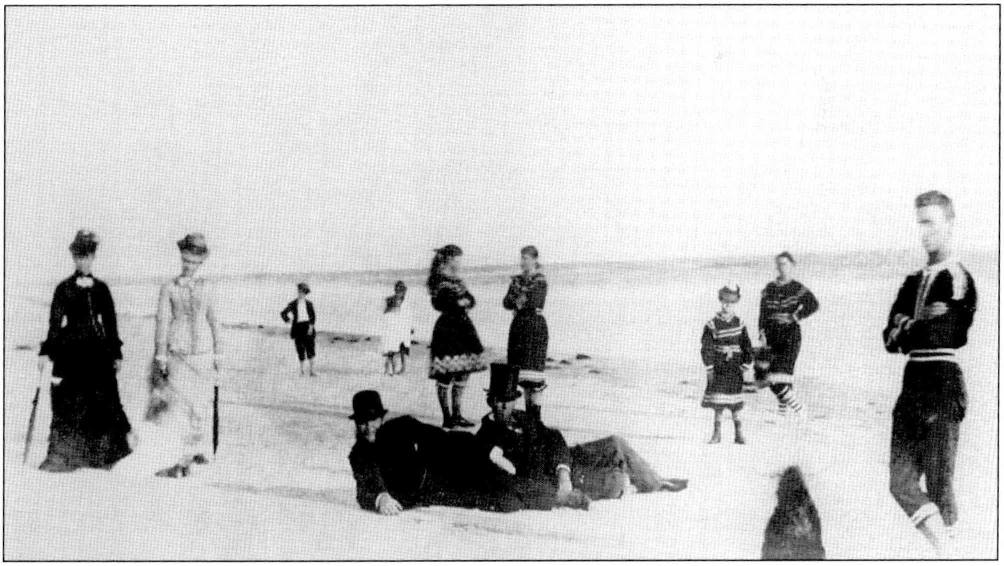

The only accommodation Victorian-era visitors occasionally made to the summer heat was the lighter color and weight of clothing. In 1878, hats remained *de rigeur* for the older generation. Tanning was taboo. Aside from what the exposure of skin entailed, people viewed tanning both as a threat to health and as a sign of low status. Only laborers had tans. (ACFPL.)

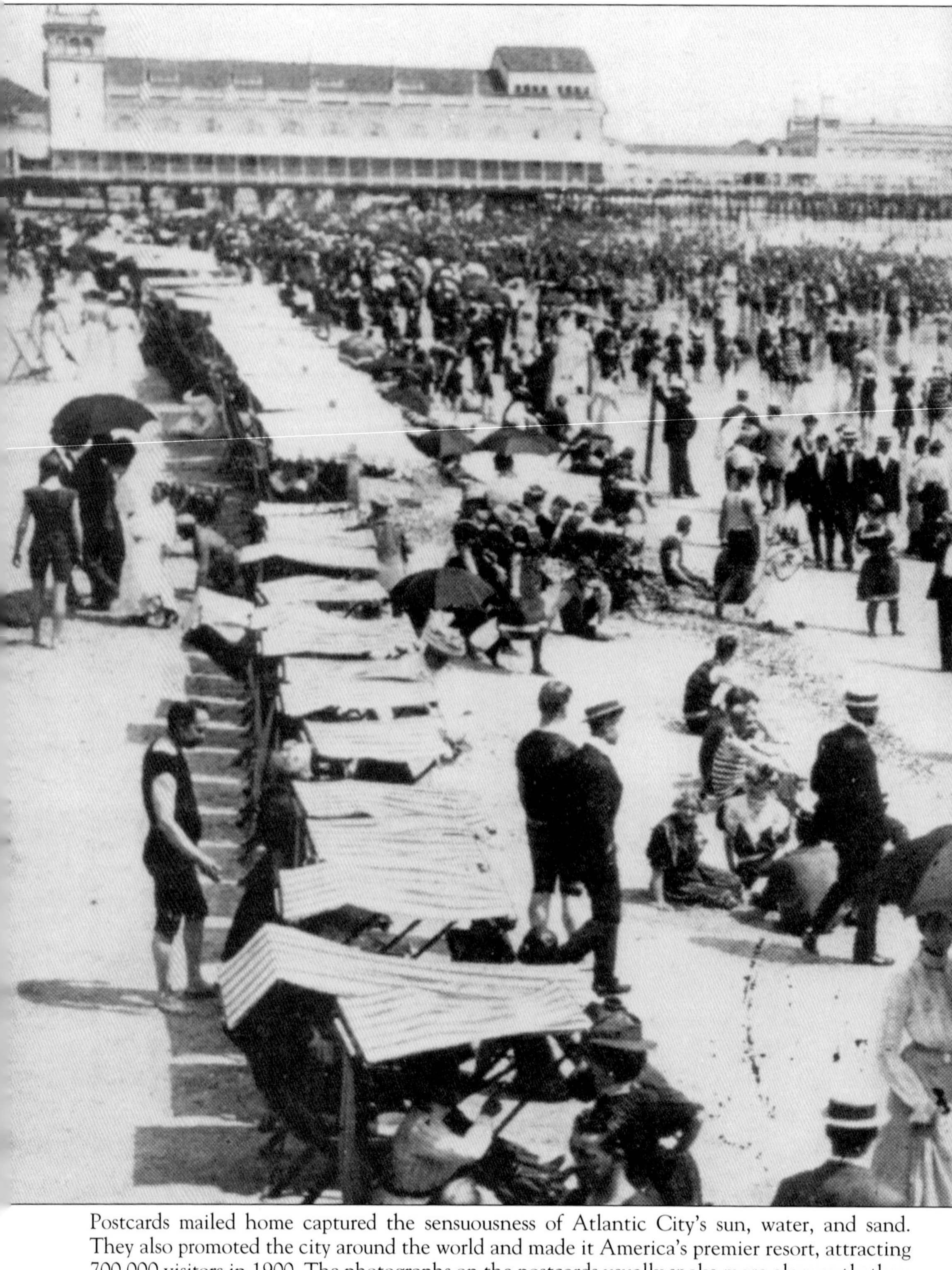

Postcards mailed home captured the sensuousness of Atlantic City's sun, water, and sand. They also promoted the city around the world and made it America's premier resort, attracting 700,000 visitors in 1900. The photographs on the postcards usually spoke more eloquently than

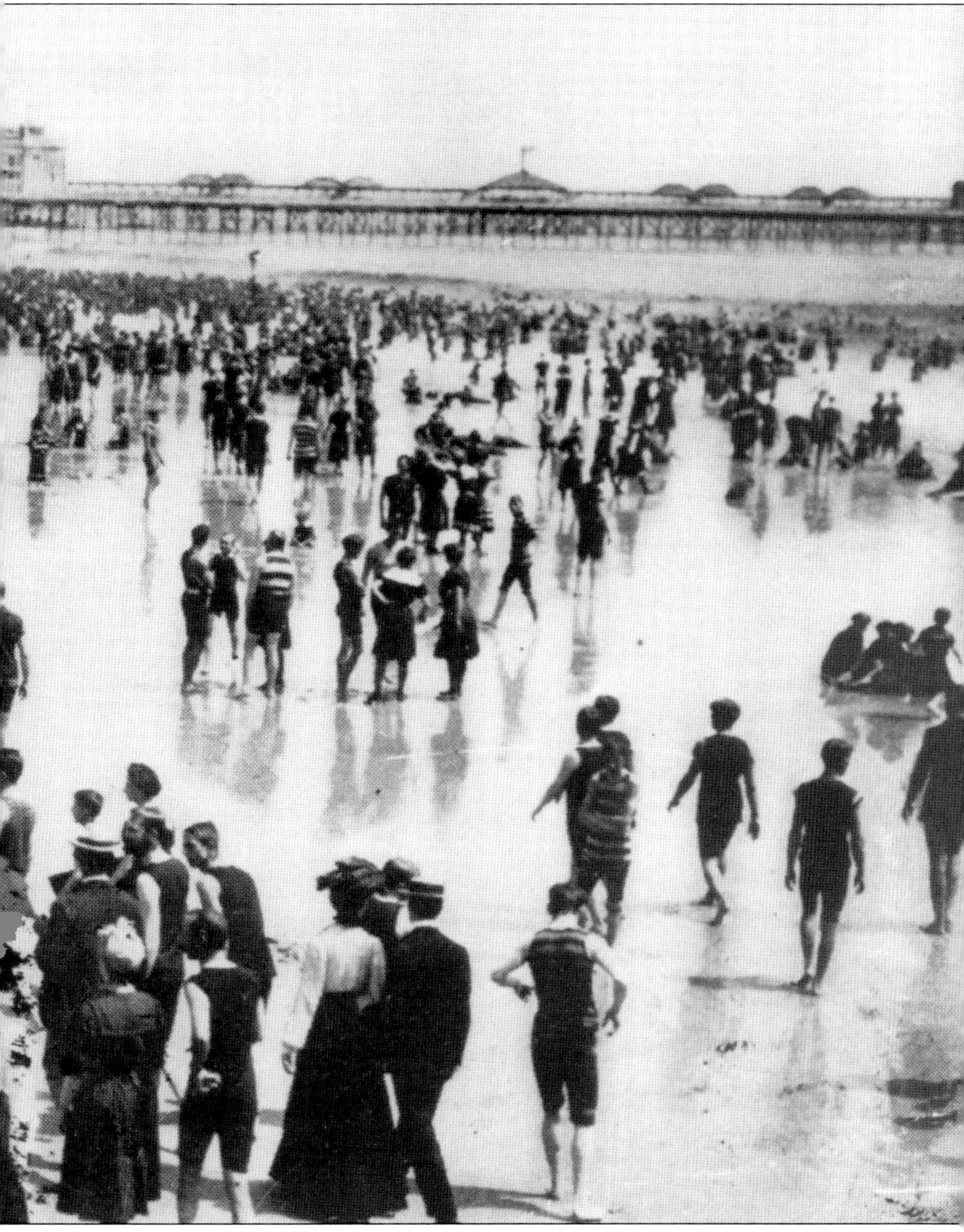

the correspondents who used them. Here, a writer named Izzie wrote, "I had a letter from Giogri saying you were not at market. I hope none of you are sick." (ACFPL.)

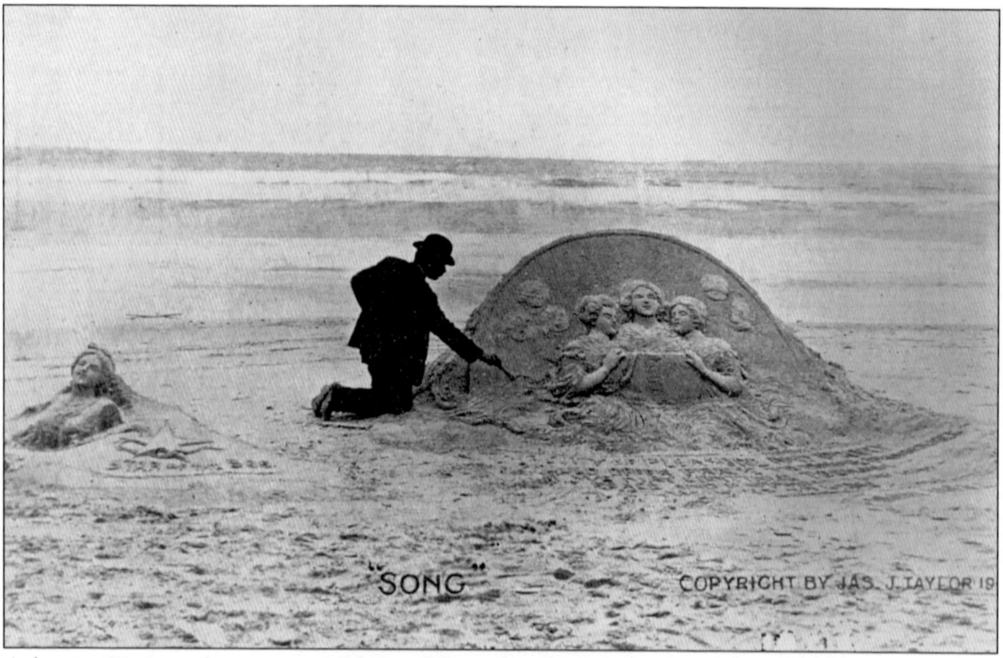

Atlantic City's early promoters claimed their beach gave birth to the art of sand sculpture. True or not, the form flourished after the 1890s. Early artists attracted crowds and then steered onlookers to photographic studios on the Boardwalk. Later ones accepted donations and could make more than $30 per day in the 1920s and 1930s. Masters of the form included James J. Taylor—seen above in 1908, finishing a piece entitled *Song*—and the gentleman posing with his gas-less roadster below in 1907. (ACFPL; Ruffolo.)

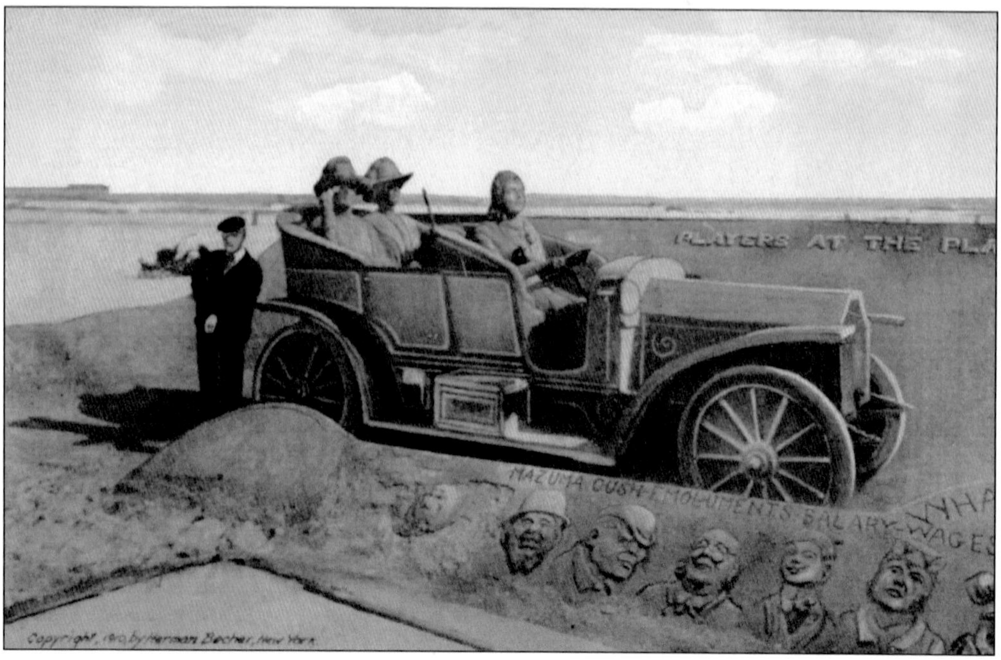

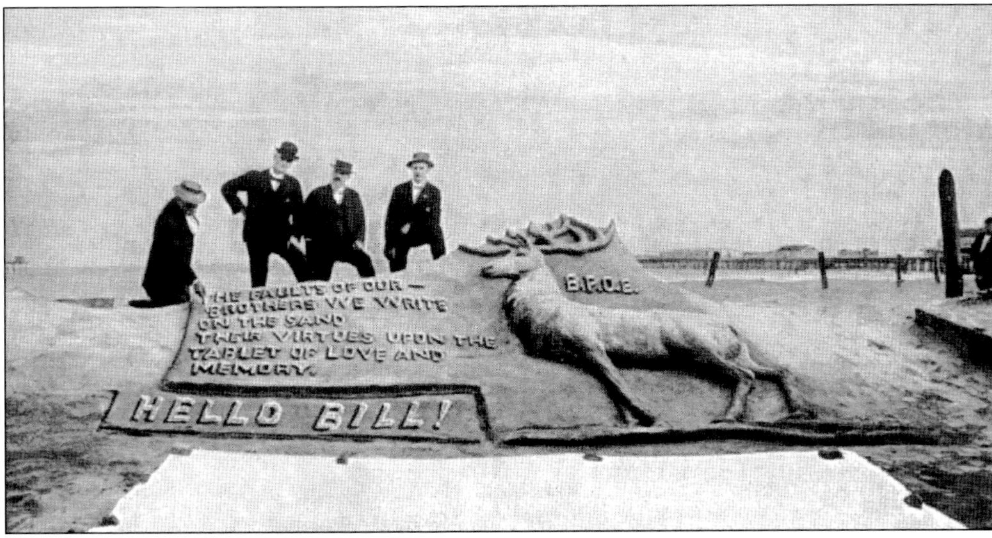

Life-sized sand tableaux may have advertised the artist, a restaurant, an amusement pier, or a fraternal organization, as demonstrated above in 1907. Sand sculpture was banned for years after 1944, however, when a number of sand artists were unmasked as con artists. The attraction to the sculpture is easy to understand, especially for a youngster digging on the Atlantic City beach, below, in 1975. (ACFPL.)

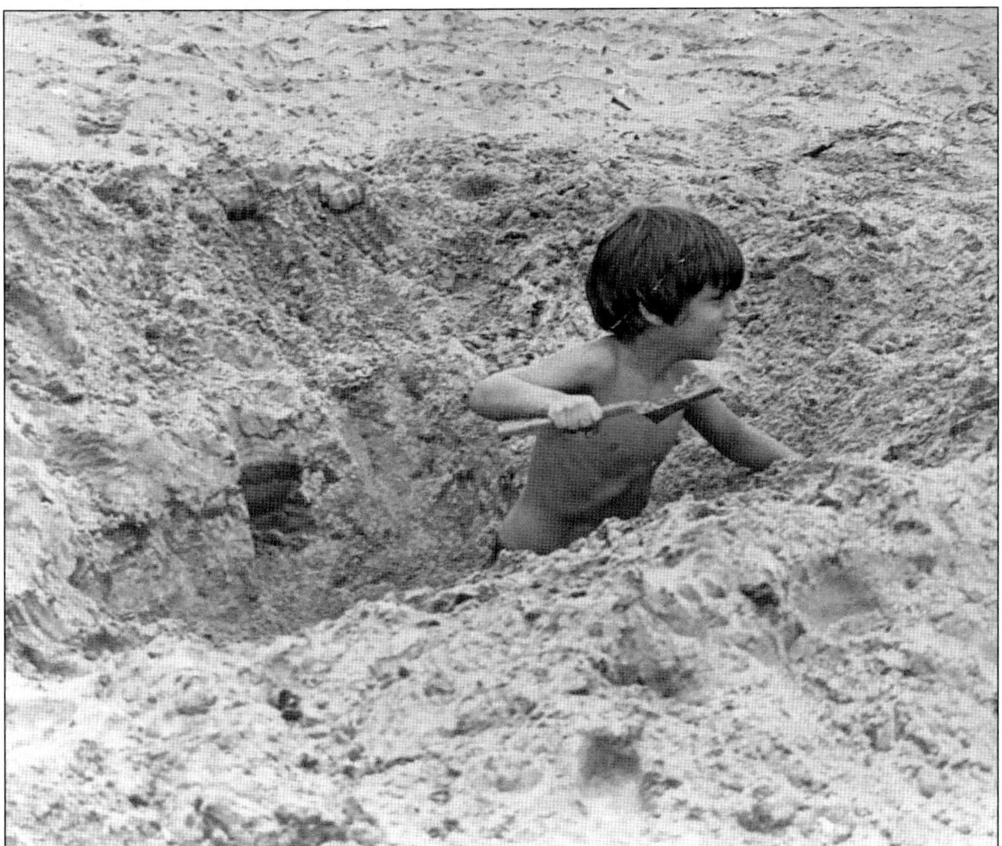

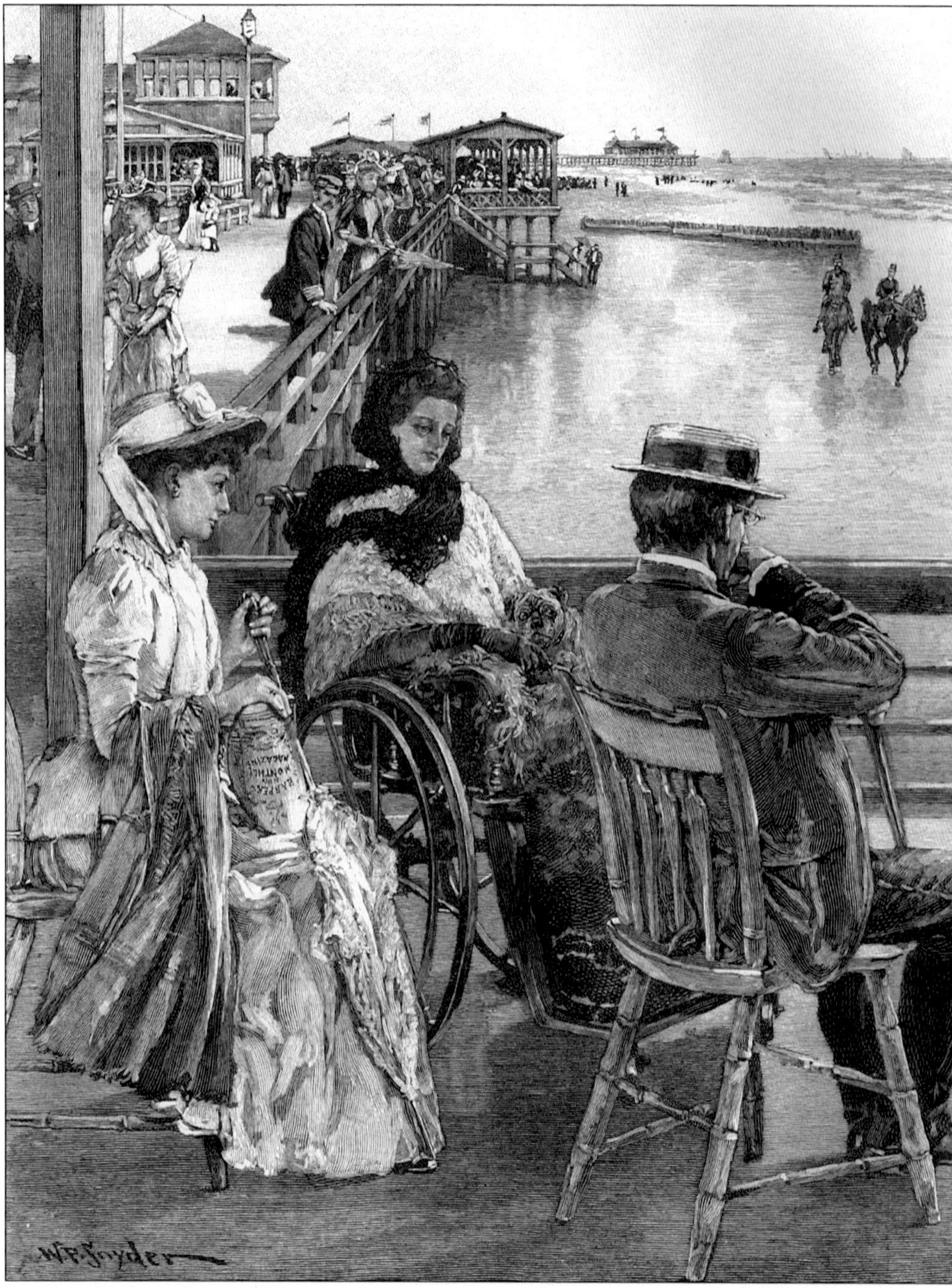

In its early days, the Atlantic City beach admitted all sorts of recreation. Note the horseback riders in the surf in this July 1890 illustration from *Harper's Weekly*. The woman in the wheelchair demonstrates that the city's alleged health benefits attracted visitors for decades after the city's founding. (Ruffolo.)

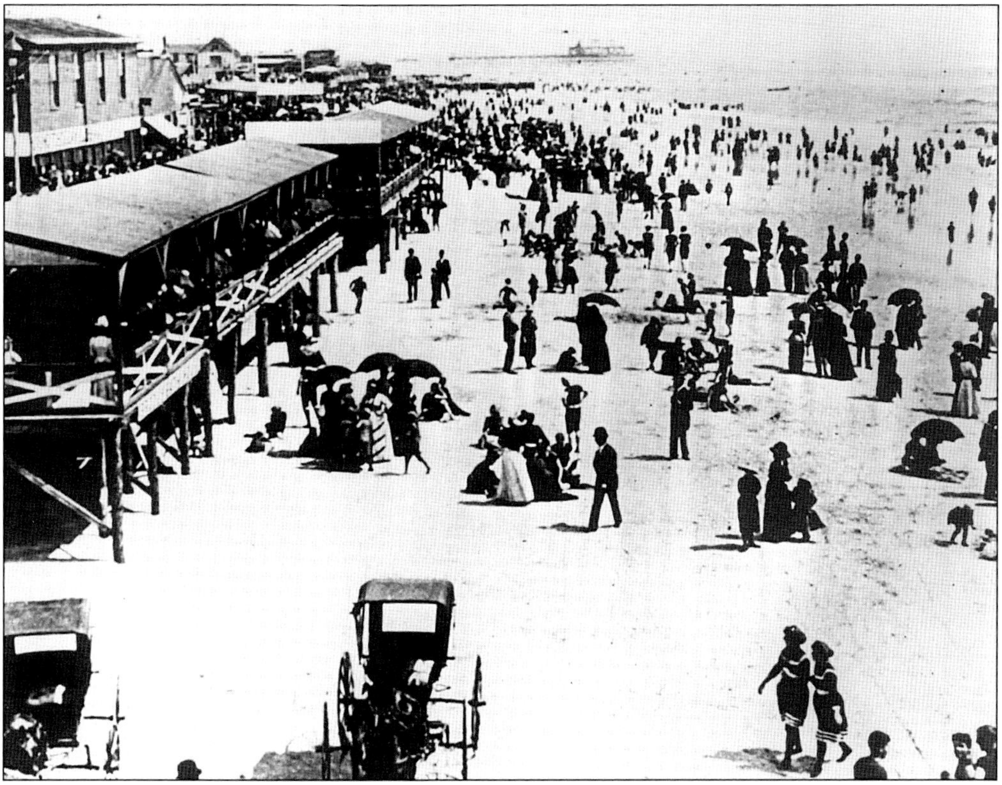

To be safe, people on the beach needed to be watchful. Among the dangers they faced were horse-drawn carriages, seen above in 1890. The carriages disappeared by the early 20th century, but horses and donkeys pulled vendors' carts through the sand for several more decades. Horseback riding, seen below, lasted into the 1960s and beyond. It was eventually restricted to the off-season months. (ACFPL, ACFPL.)

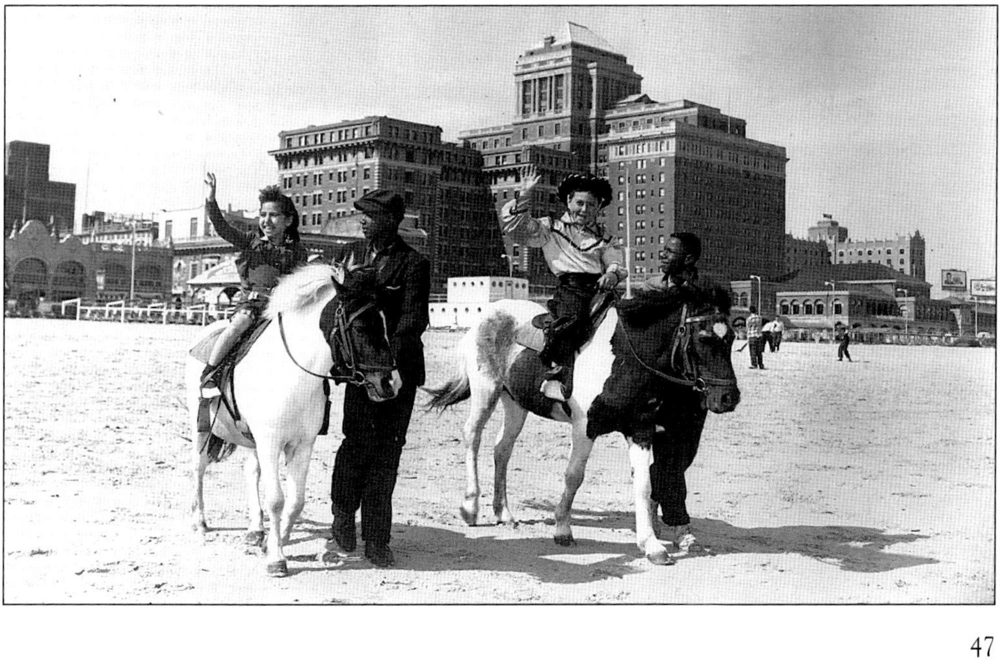

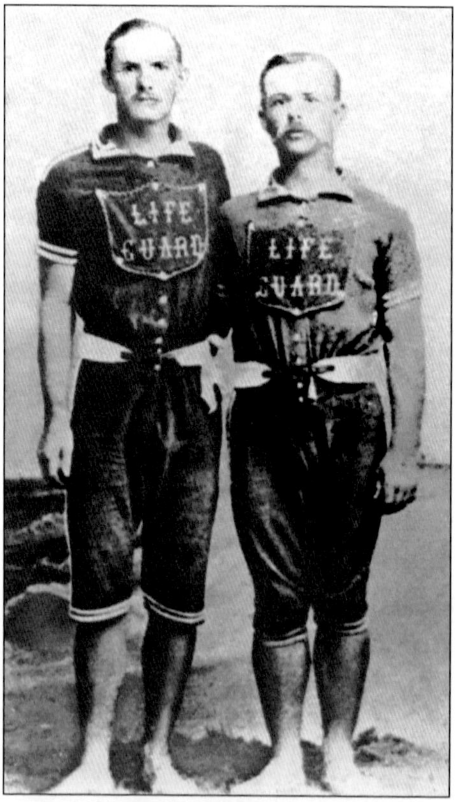

Hired in 1892, the pair at the left—variously identified as Dan Headley and Nick Jefferies or the Jeffrey brothers—patrolled the Atlantic City beach as the city's first paid lifeguards. Before them, small groups of men might occasionally watch stretches of the beach and jump in when swimmers needed rescuing. Afterward, the group would likely pass the hat for a gratuity. The lifeguard chair appeared early on, as seen here in 1916. Then as now, guards sat near the water's edge. (ACFPL, ACFPL.)

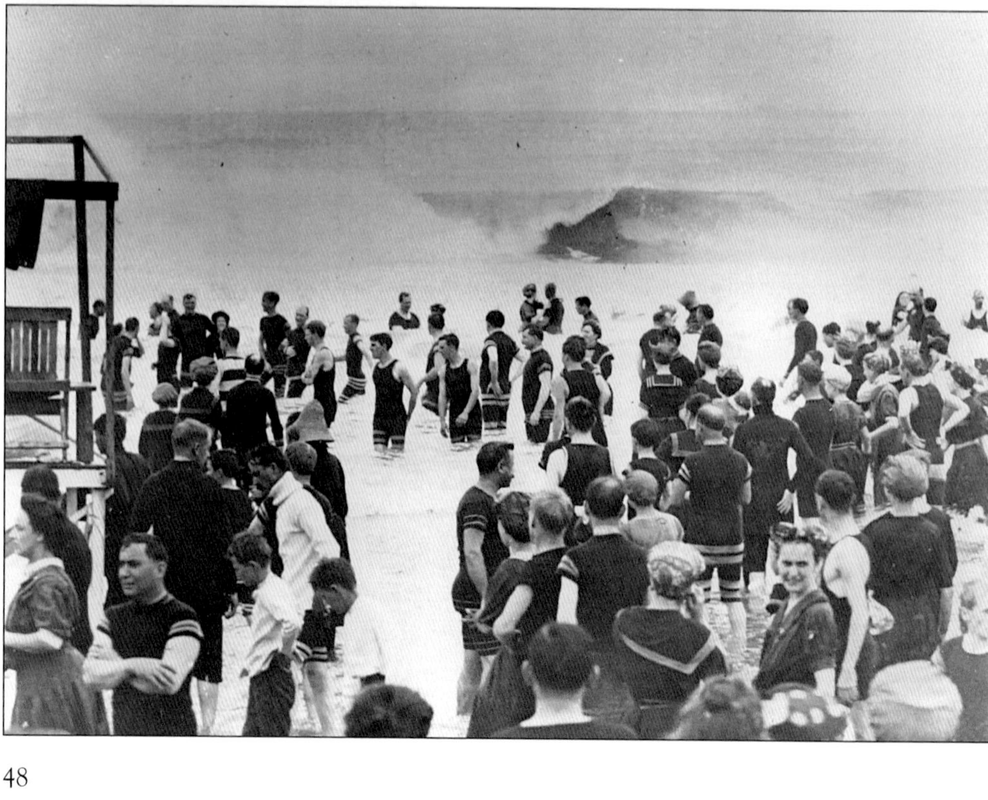

The tools and uniforms of the lifeguard trade advanced very little in a decade. Guy Schaffell, at right in 1915, worked the beach in front of the Brighton Casino at Indiana Avenue. He and his comrades gave the city's beaches a shining reputation for safety. Despite huge crowds, Atlantic City averaged less than one drowning per year for decades. Crowds were especially dense near the amusement piers, as below in 1905. The ocean was such a novelty that one 19th-century convention annually featured a surf-splash, where attendees linked arms and waded out in one unbroken line. (ACFPL, ACFPL.)

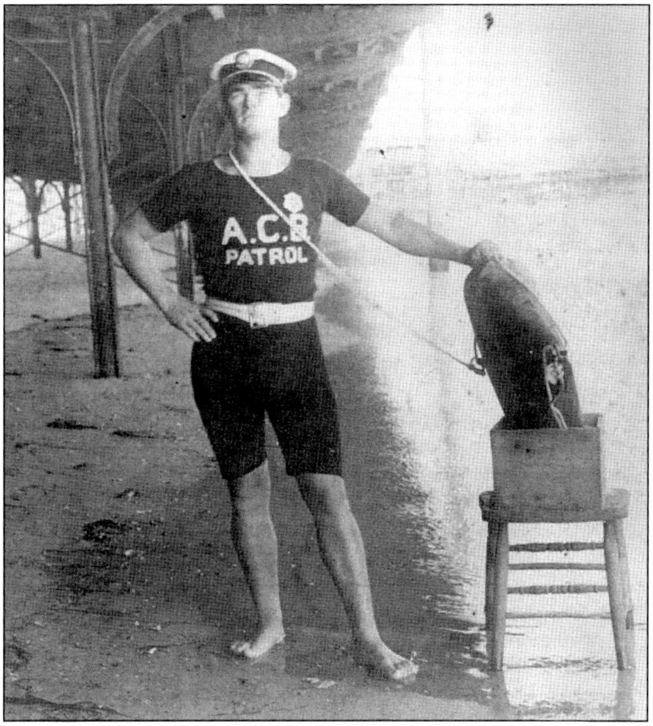

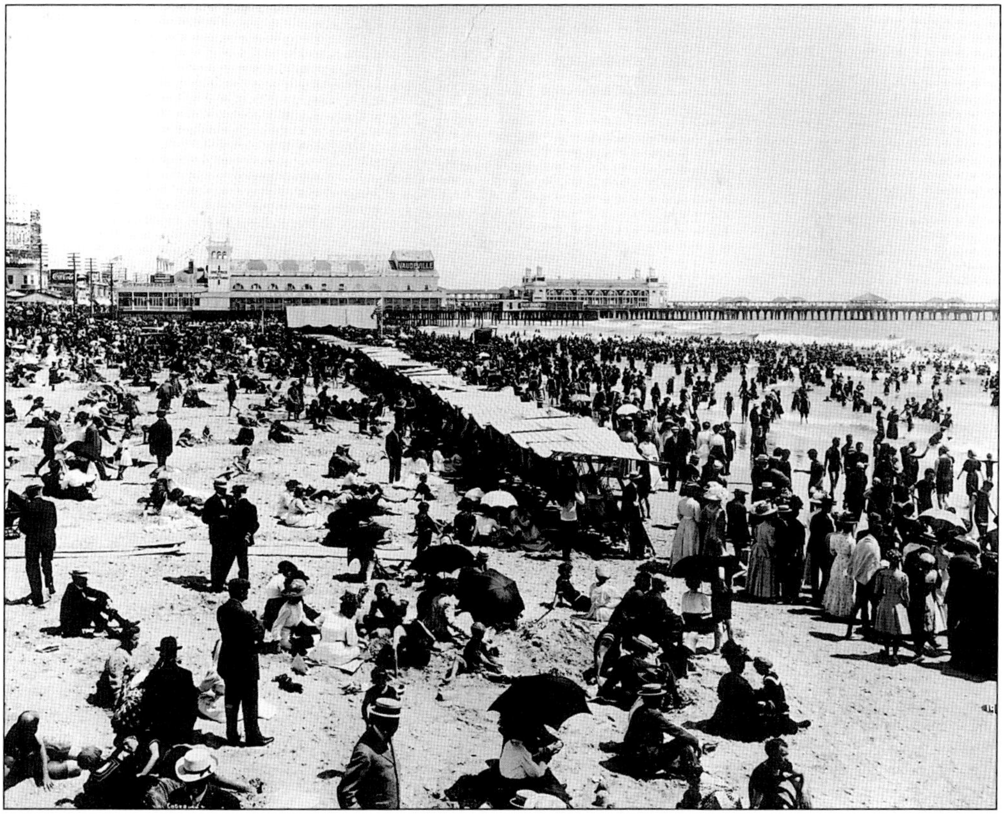

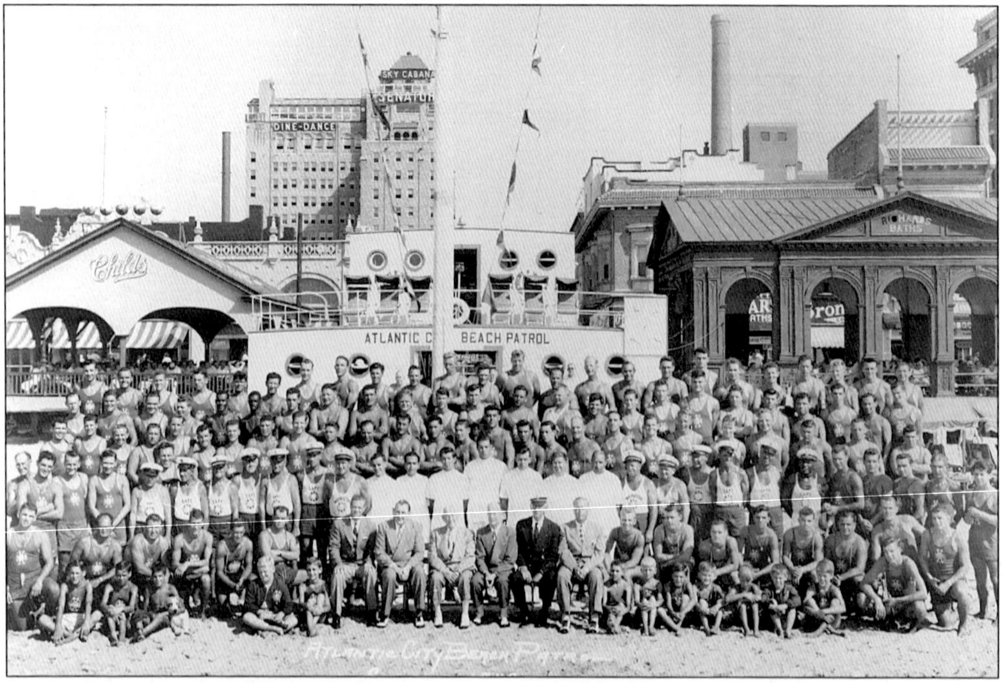

The Atlantic City Beach Patrol was always close to the hearts of city leaders, seen above in the middle of the front row in 1949. Technically speaking, the ACBP was integrated. However, its African-American members were usually consigned, as were all black bathers, to a patch of sand derisively called Chicken Bone Beach. Located at Missouri Avenue, Chicken Bone Beach became a New Jersey State Landmark in 1997. One of its patrols in the 1930s, below, stands in front of George Walls's bathhouse. (ACFPL, ACFPL.)

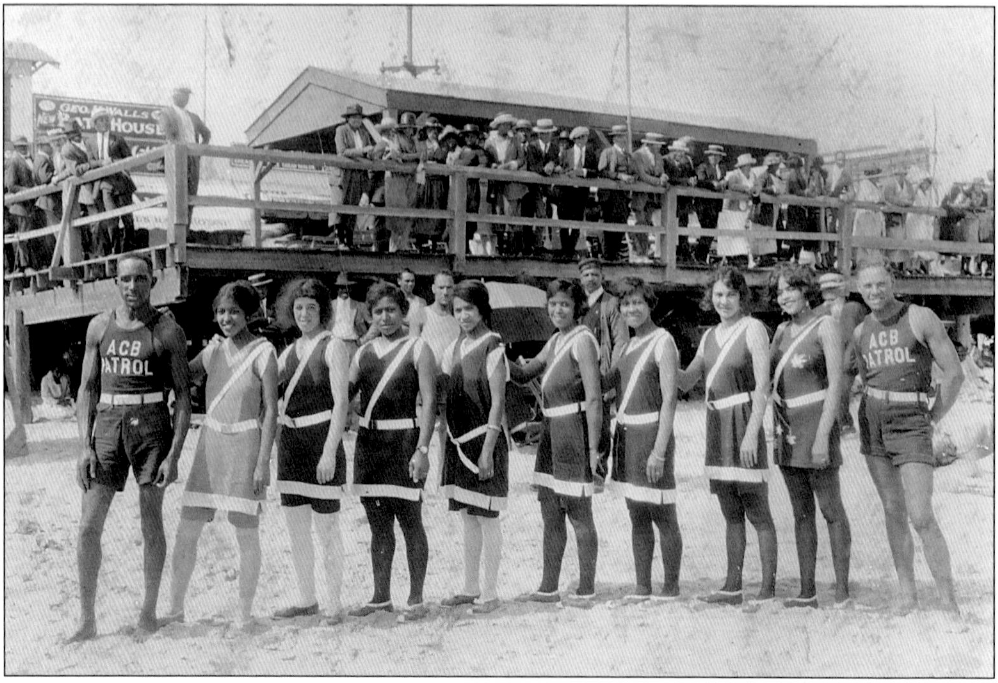

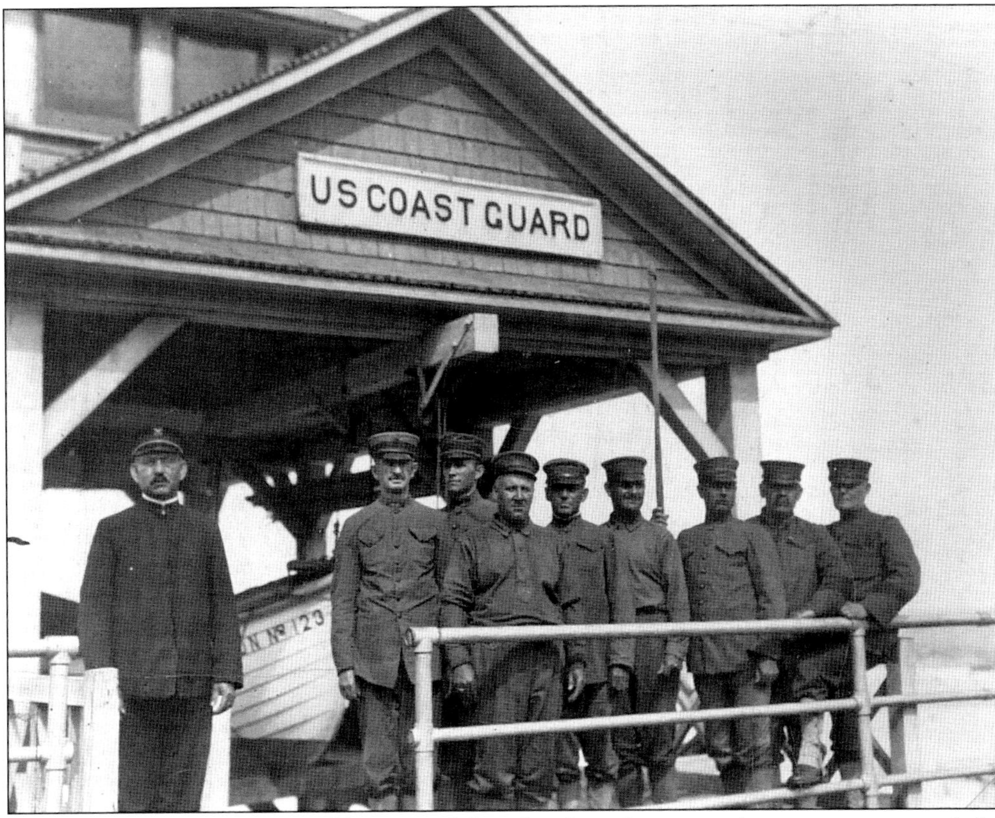

Rescuing the crews of ships offshore was left to local residents or volunteer services until the U.S. Coast Guard assumed the duty in the 1880s. The crew of the Atlantic City Coast Guard Station, above in 1920, had to be a sturdy lot. Horses pulled a heavy rescue dinghy to the water, where crew members pushed it through the shallows and rowed out to sea, as demonstrated below. Until the early 19th century, floundering vessels were as likely to be greeted by privateers seeking salvage as by saviors. (ACFPL.)

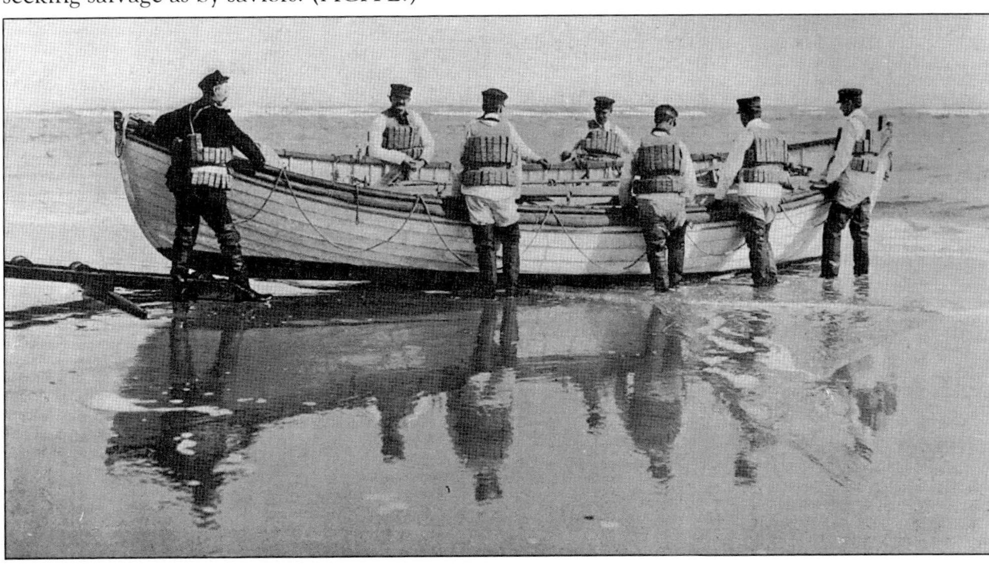

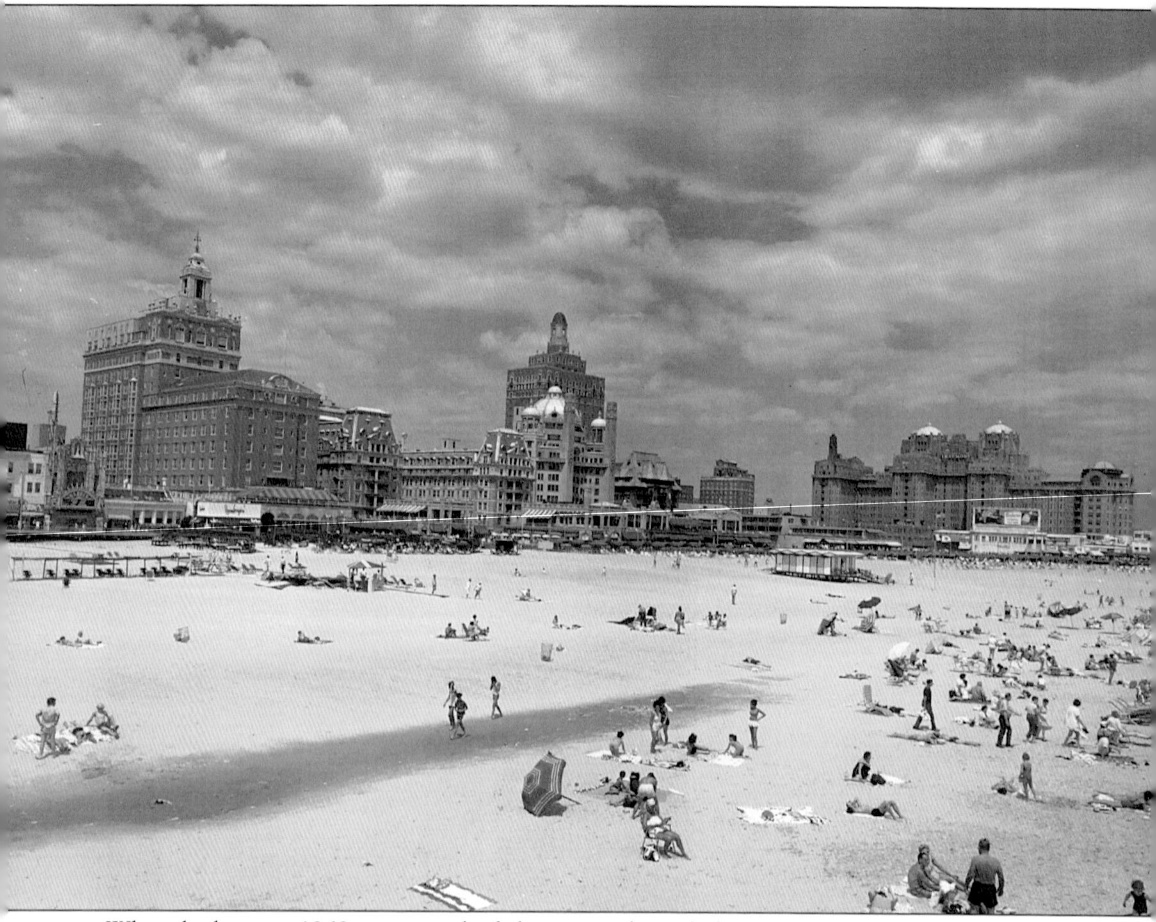

When bathers in 1962 grew tired of the sea and its shifting moods, they could admire the Atlantic City skyline from the beach. The grand hotels were stone and brick monuments that replaced scores of picturesque wooden structures from 1910 through the early 1930s. Whether wood or stone, the hotels coaxed the well-heeled off the beach and into an experience modeled on European resorts. (Conectiv.)

Four

Grand Old Ladies

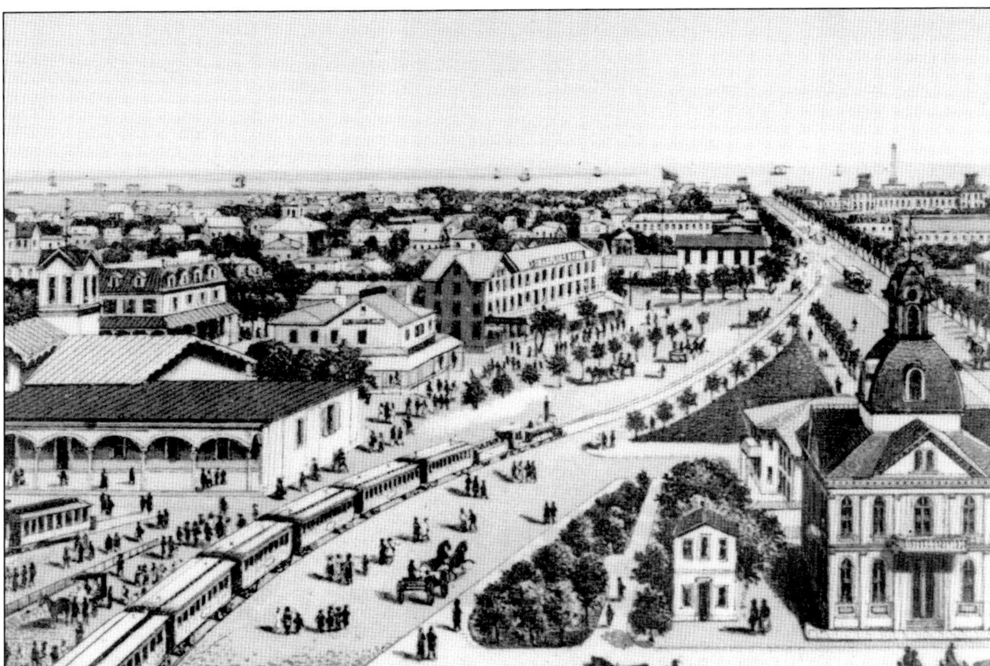

Less than 25 years after Atlantic City's first official visitors arrived in July 1854 to spend a day on the nearly deserted beach, this panoramic lithograph, drawn c. 1870, showed startling change. Boardinghouses and small hotels lined the streets, following the railroad tracks to the sea. Two can be recognized—Schaufler's, on the left center, and the United States Hotel, in the distance on the right. Atlantic City's foremost preoccupation had already come to be keeping guests in town for overnight, a week, a month, or, if possible, the entire season. As the hotels grew increasingly large, most of their interiors became evermore plush. Hotels served as the centers of activity, and customer satisfaction became the hallmark of the city's hotel services. (JTC.)

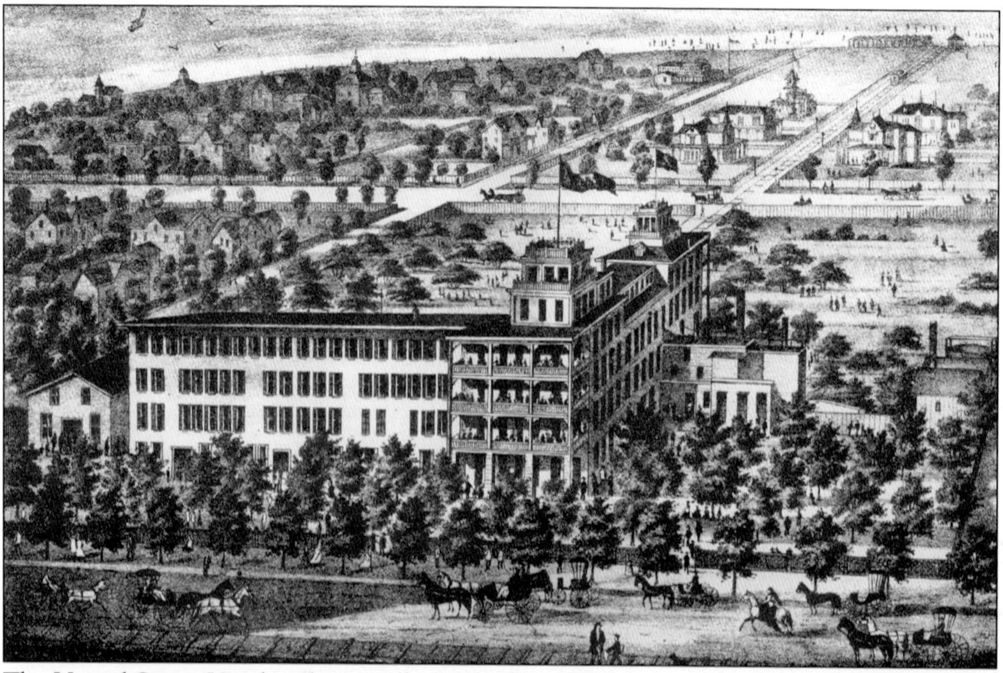

The United States Hotel, only partially finished in 1854, was a reality when the *Woolman & Rose Atlas of the Jersey Coast* published this engraving in 1878. The four-story wooden hotel and its grounds occupied the full block between Atlantic, Pacific, Maryland, and Delaware Avenues. Huge rooftop lookouts offered an acclaimed ocean view. This was the city's first grand hotel. (JTC.)

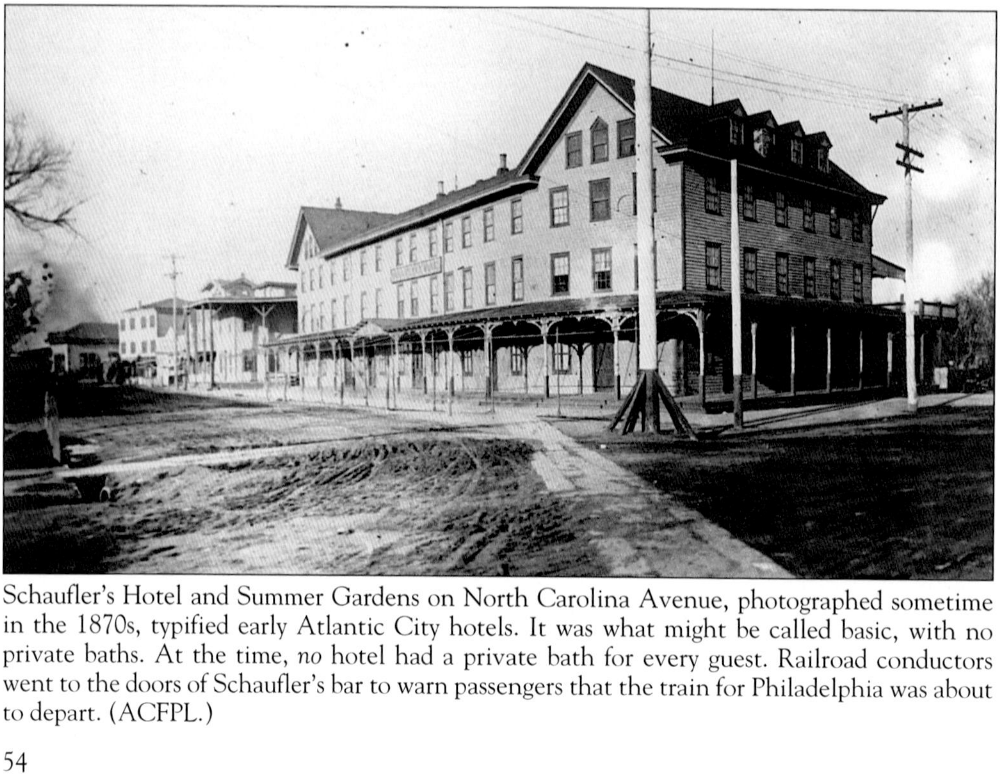

Schaufler's Hotel and Summer Gardens on North Carolina Avenue, photographed sometime in the 1870s, typified early Atlantic City hotels. It was what might be called basic, with no private baths. At the time, *no* hotel had a private bath for every guest. Railroad conductors went to the doors of Schaufler's bar to warn passengers that the train for Philadelphia was about to depart. (ACFPL.)

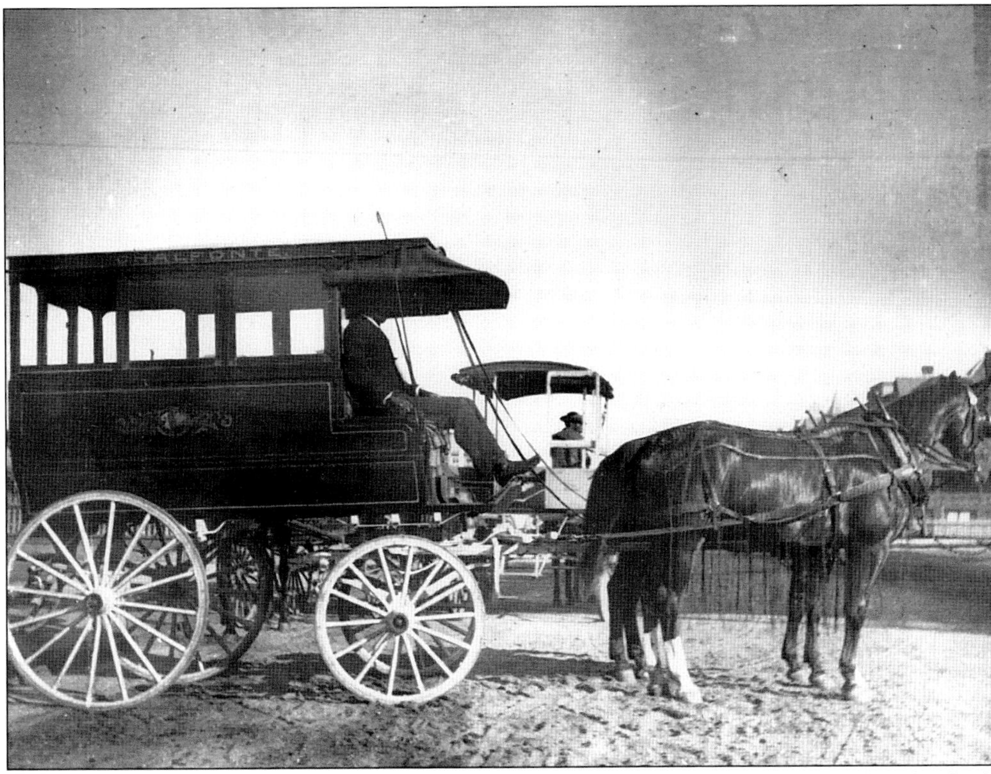

Horse-drawn carriages from the major hotels, such as this high-wheeled, glass-enclosed vehicle from the Chalfonte House, met arriving tourists at the railroad depot. The Chalfonte, below, on South Carolina Avenue, founded in 1869, seems unprepossessing by modern standards but both its proprietors and its guests thought it was a modern marvel. It must be remembered that, from the start, everything needed for any Atlantic City building had to be brought by boat or train from the mainland. (ACFPL.)

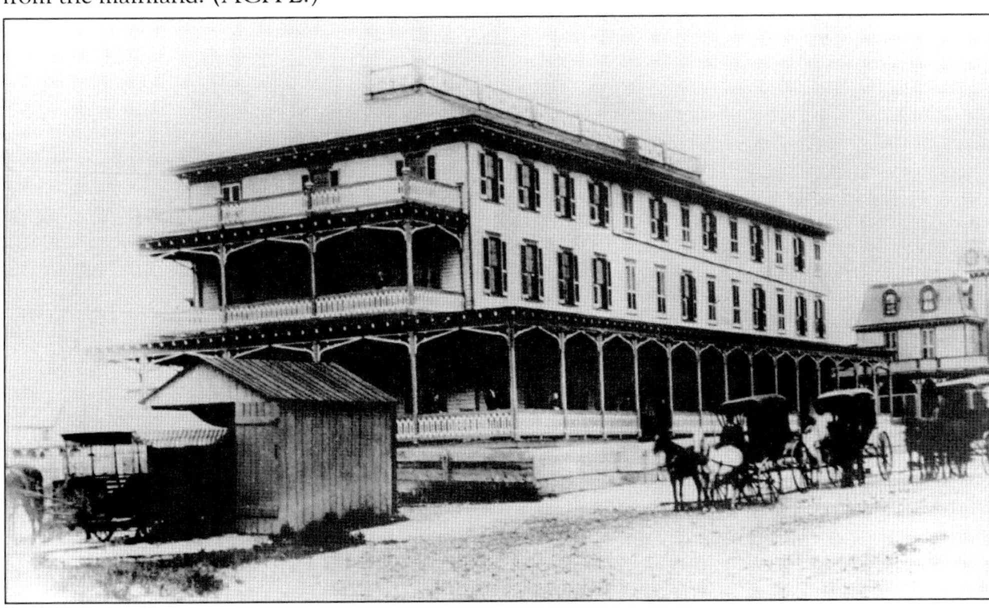

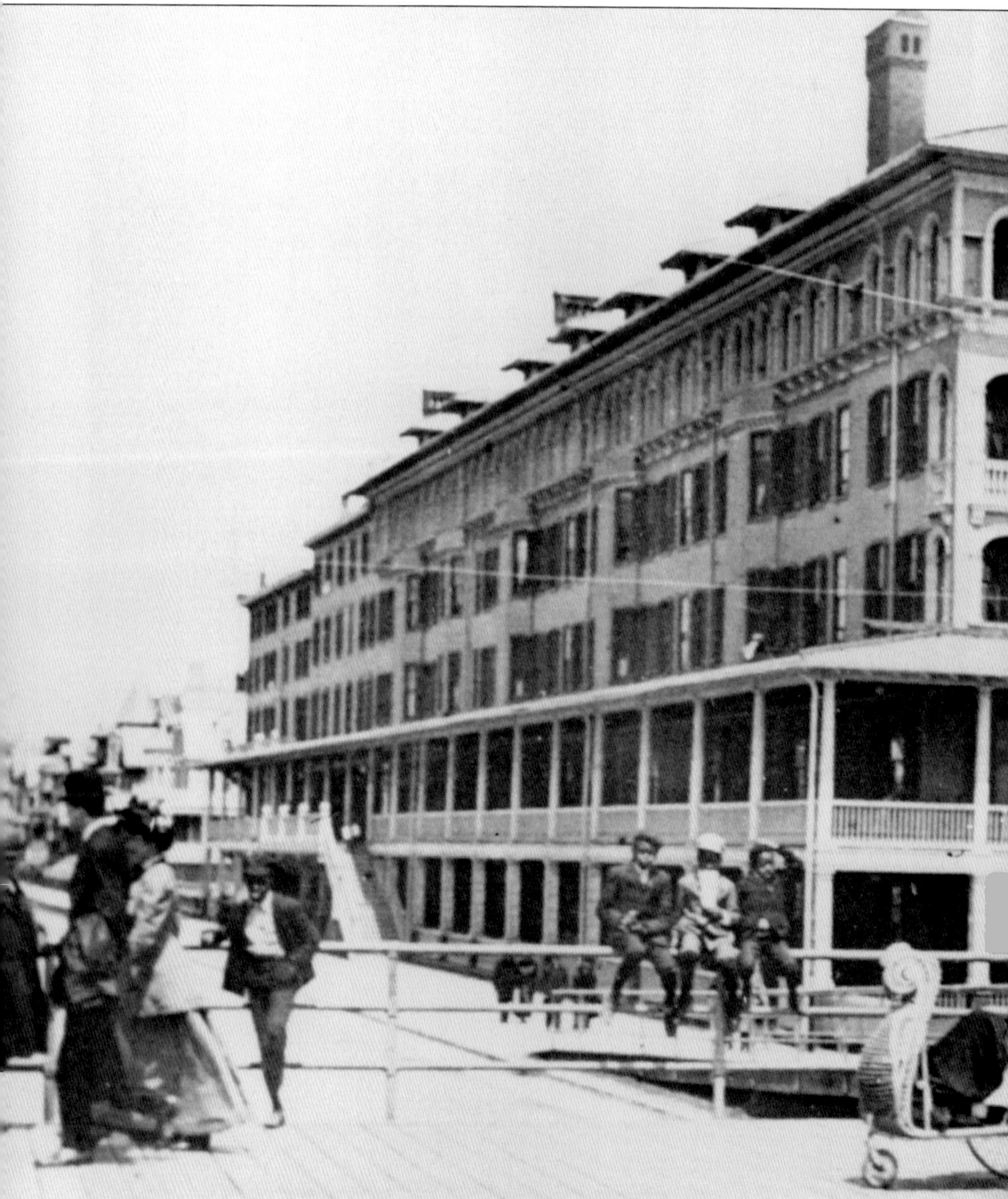

Atlantic City's greatest hotel saga came into being between 1890 and 1900 when two Burlington County Quakers, Henry Leeds and J. Haines Lippincott, bought Haddon Hall (above) and the Chalfonte House (page 55) and merged them under the name Chalfonte-Haddon Hall. Both had been early boardinghouses (Haddon Hall established 1868; Chalfonte opened 1869). The wooden Chalfonte became a ten-story brick building in 1904. Lippincott and Leeds then added two eleven-story brick wings to Haddon Hall during the 1920s. By 1950, the dual brick buildings

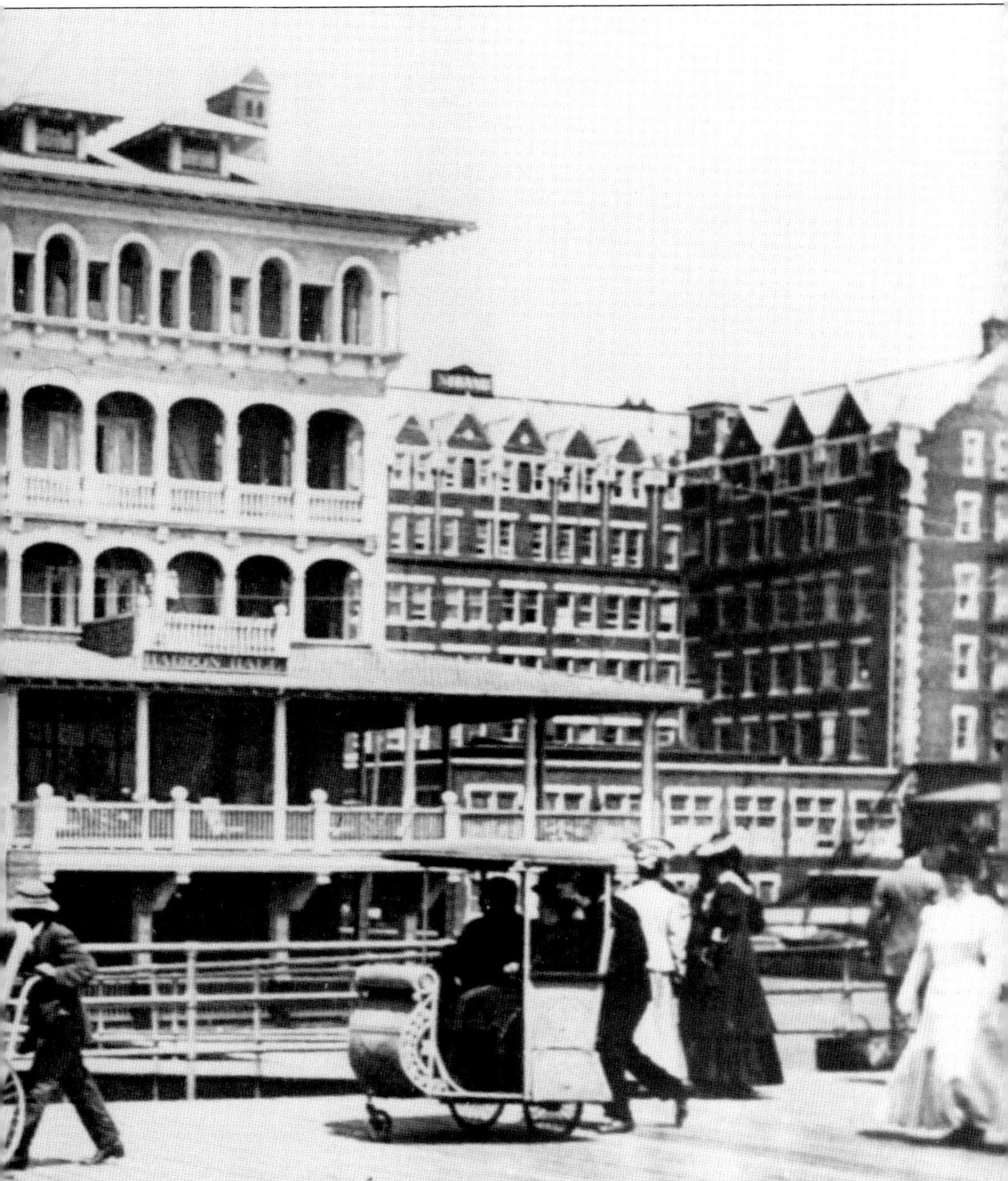

on either side of North Carolina Avenue were said to be "the largest resort hotel in the world." The management at the time boasted that fifth and sixth generations of families were returning to noted Chalfonte-Haddon Hall. The twin hotels became part of the modern Resorts International casino, which opened in May 1978 with a full complement of slot machines, blackjack, roulette, and other games of chance. Gamblers flocked to the hotel-casino. (ACFPL.)

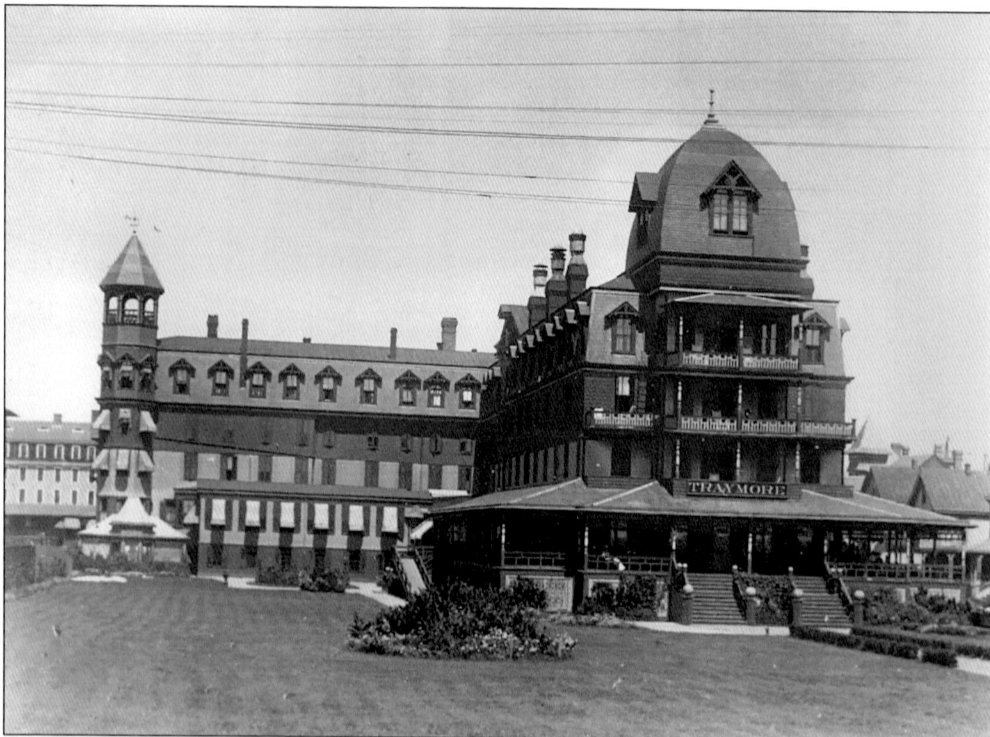

The Traymore Hotel, old and new, offered a fine comparison of the changing hotel architecture and building size in the city. The Traymore, above *c.* 1910, was the very essence of Victorian architecture and elegant aloofness. The new Traymore, below, opened in 1915. It stood 14 stories tall, had 600 guest rooms, and typified the several towering brick palaces erected in the early 20th century. The Traymore's massive size required stabilizing with hundreds of wooden pilings driven deep into the sand. (ACFPL.)

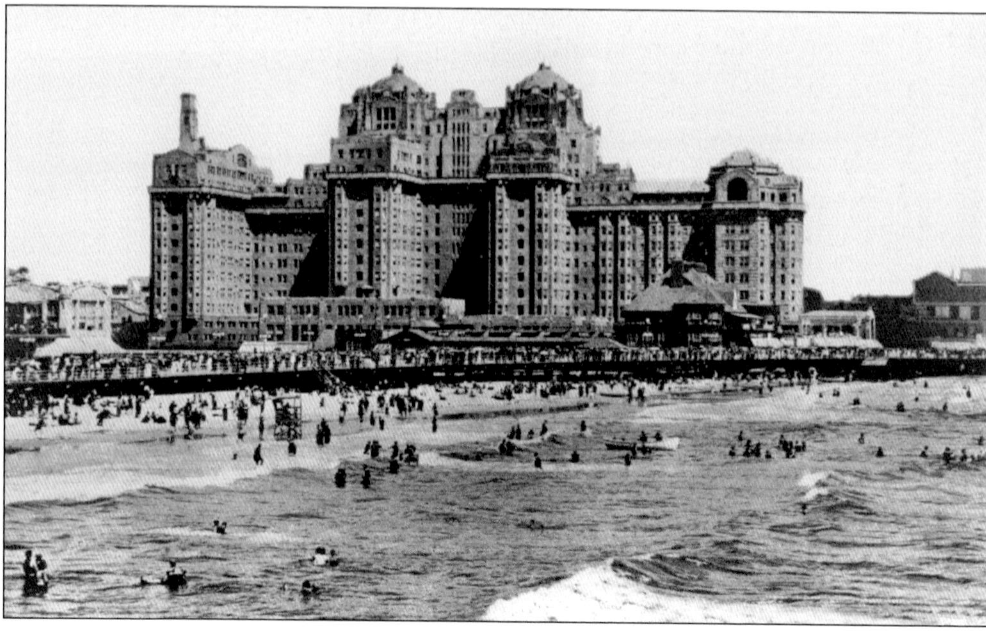

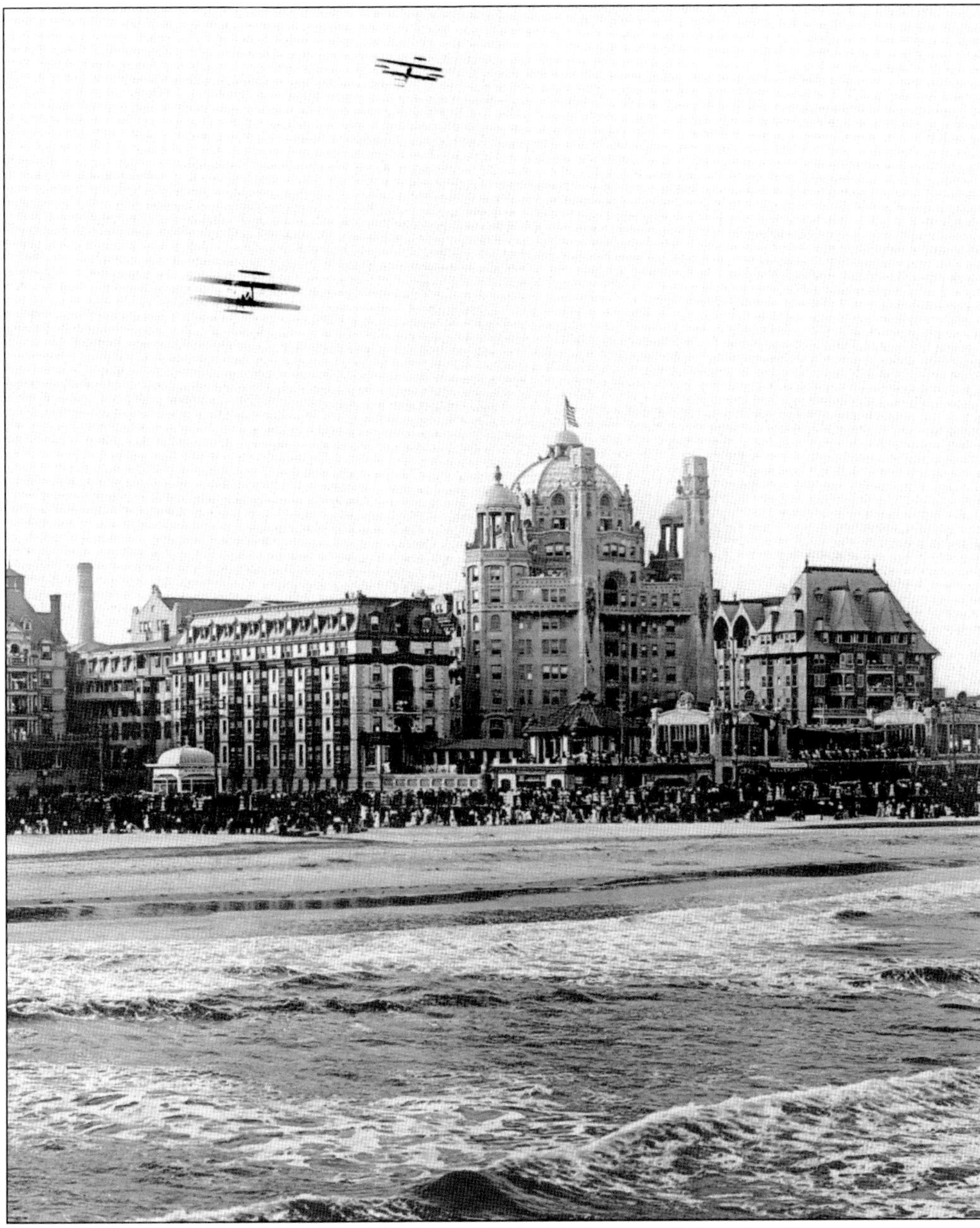

When noted aviator Glenn Curtiss flew over Atlantic City in 1910 in his flimsy single-engine biplane, he came in low over one of the city's newest hotels, the Marlborough-Blenheim Hotel. It was the first hotel in the world built with reinforced concrete. World-famous inventor Thomas A. Edison, who perfected the process of pouring concrete walls for large structures, came often to the city to watch progress. (ACFPL.)

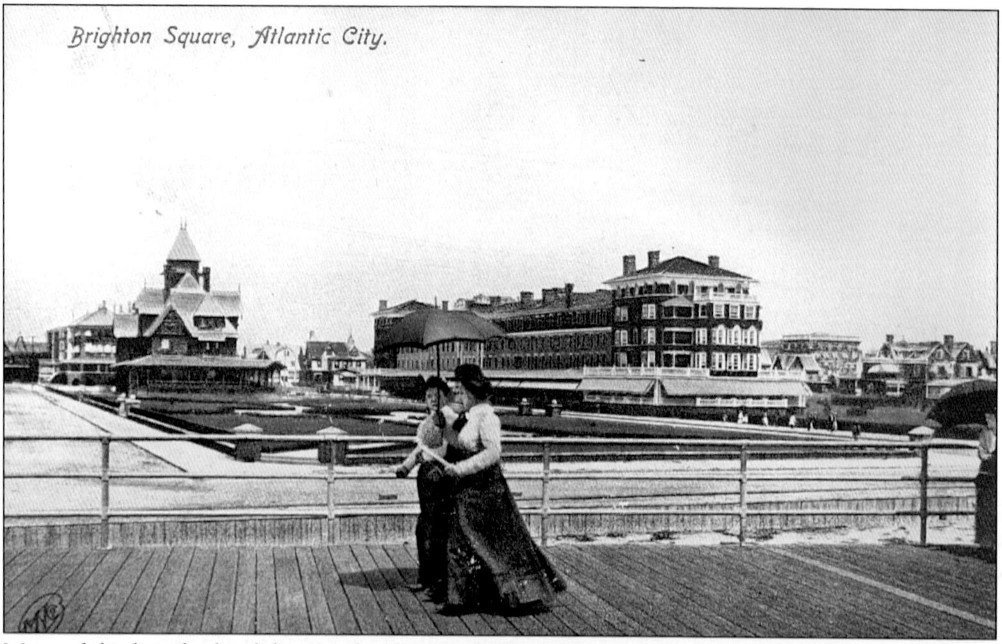

Most of the hundreds of thousands of visitors who came to Atlantic City each summer before WWI seldom stepped inside the posh major hotels. There seemed to be joy enough in walking the Boardwalk under black silk umbrellas. Two long-skirted young women, above, strolled the Boardwalk past Brighton Square. Nearby, they could vicariously enjoy the wealthy people who frequented the very popular Brighton Casino, below center. (ACFPL.)

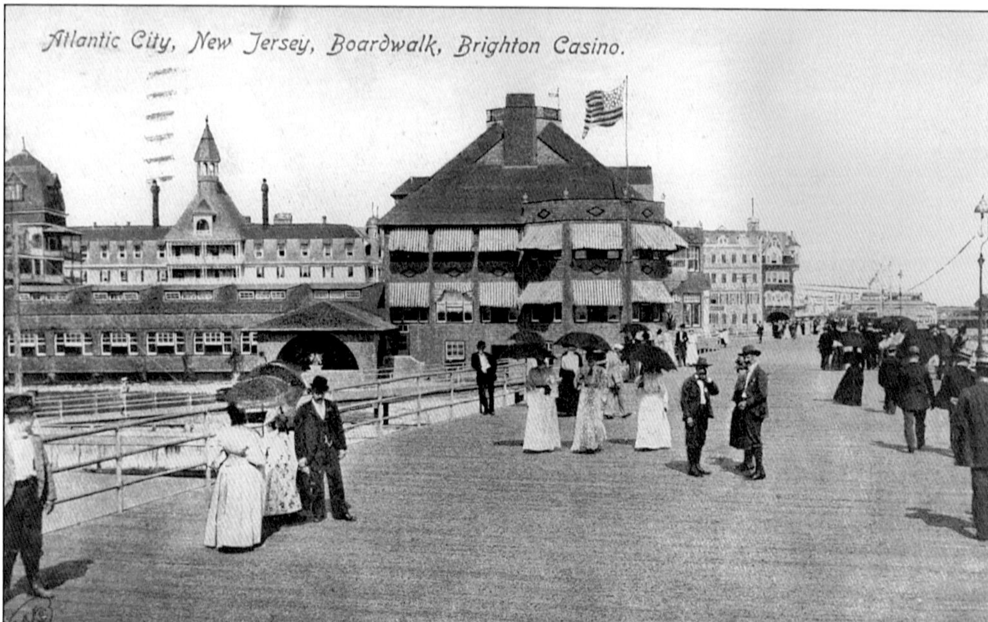

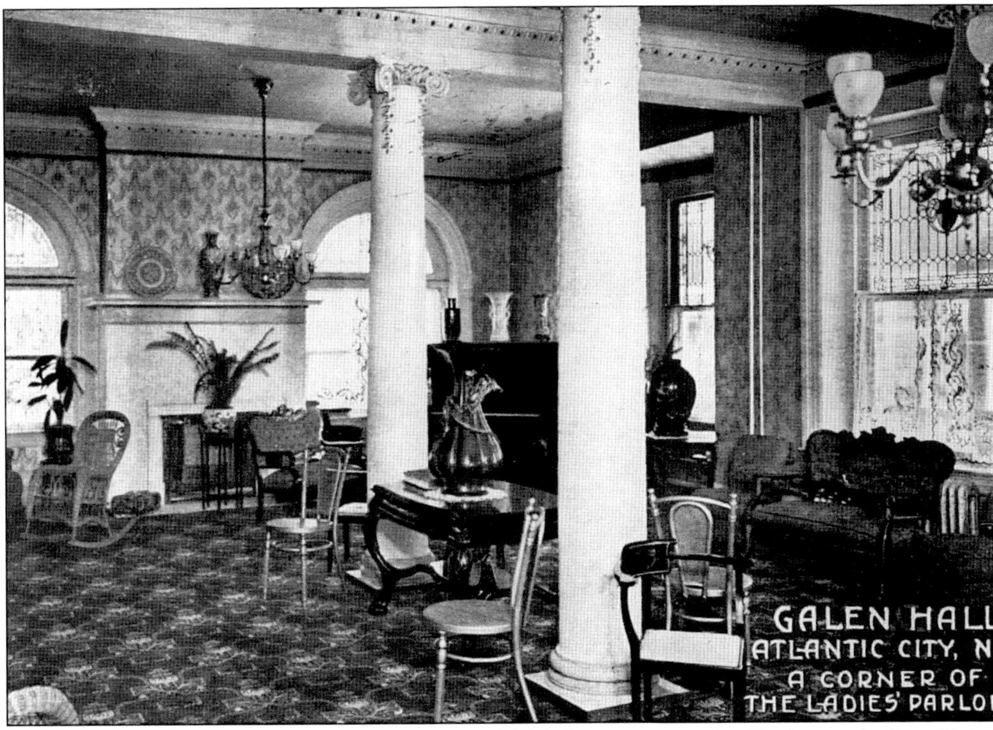

Philadelphia ladies dressed in their finest would likely stop in at this "ladies parlor" in Galen Hall to join in discreet afternoon tea. The stout pillars were decorative to lend a classical touch. Only guests of Craig Hall, below, could be admitted to late afternoon, non-alcoholic gatherings in the Arbor atop the hotel. This was a popular Atlantic City gathering place. (ACFPL.)

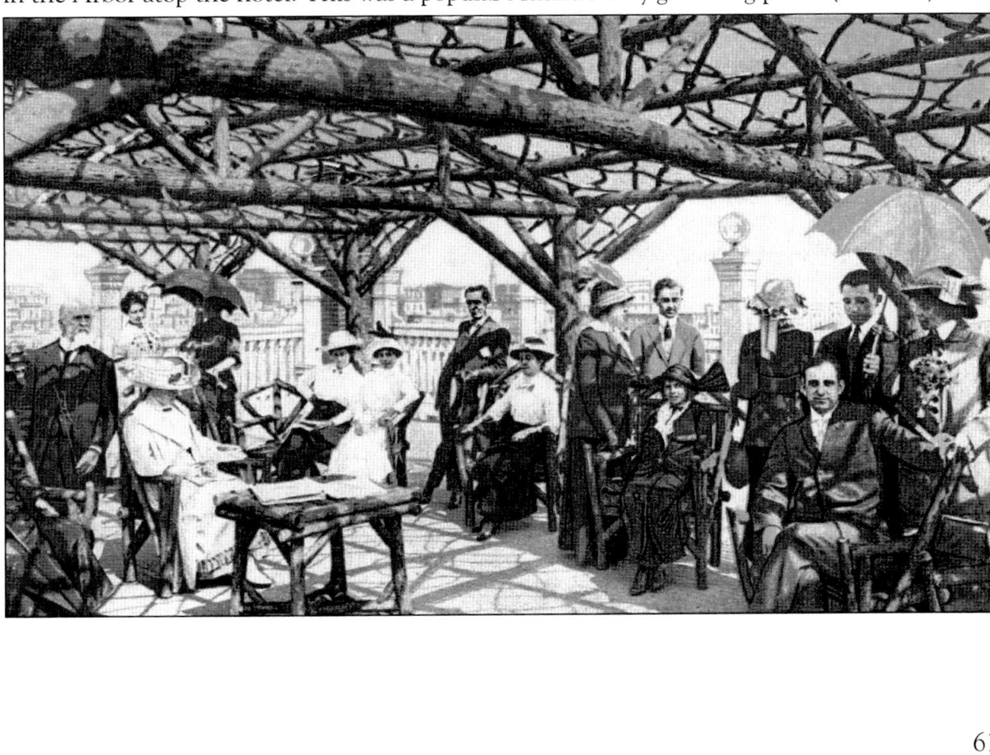

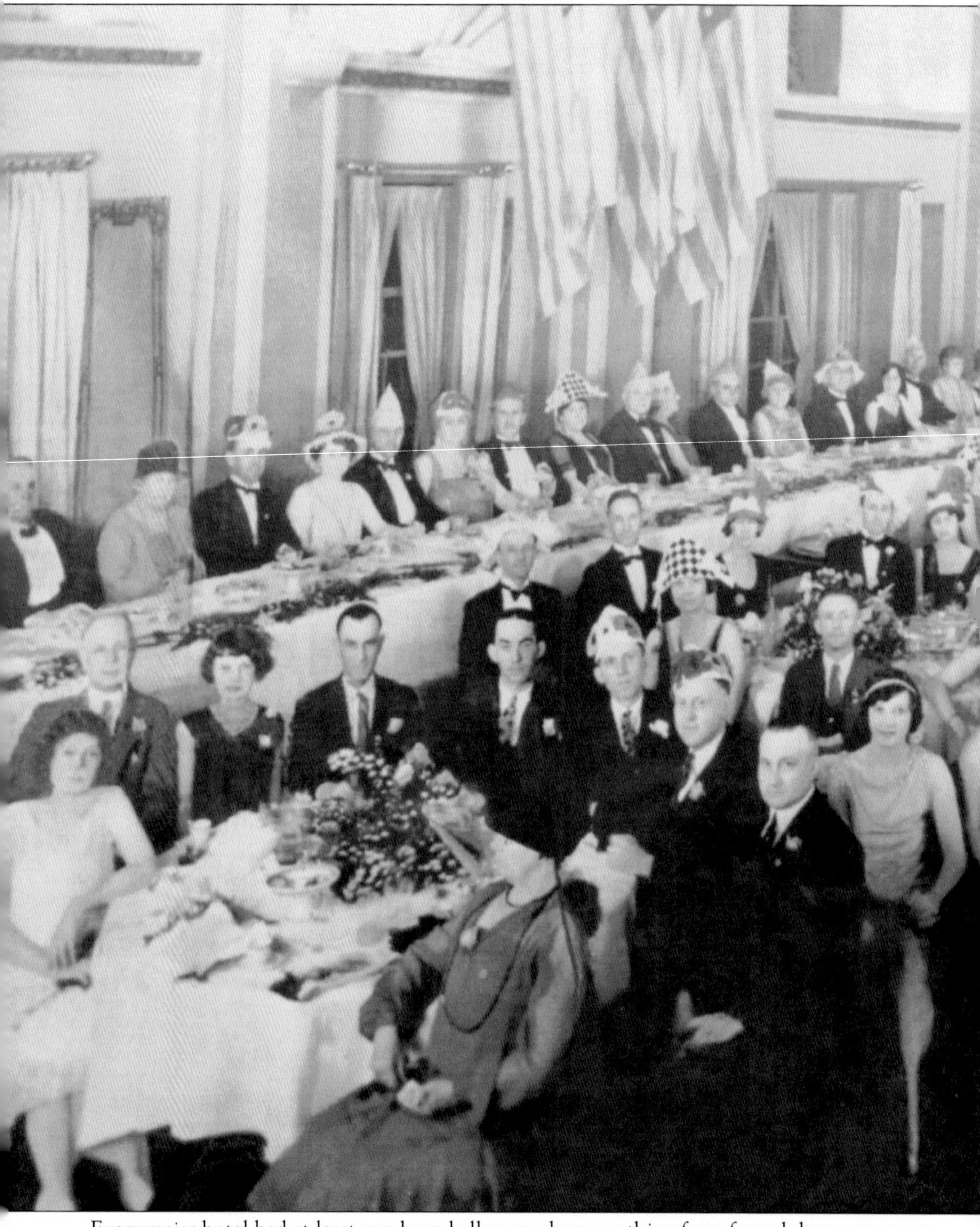

Every major hotel had at least one huge ballroom where anything from formal dances to group gatherings might be staged. This is part of the American Gas and Electric Company crowd that filled the Hotel Traymore's grand assembly room on May 20, 1926. They had come from all over the nation to participate in the American Electric Light Association convention. The

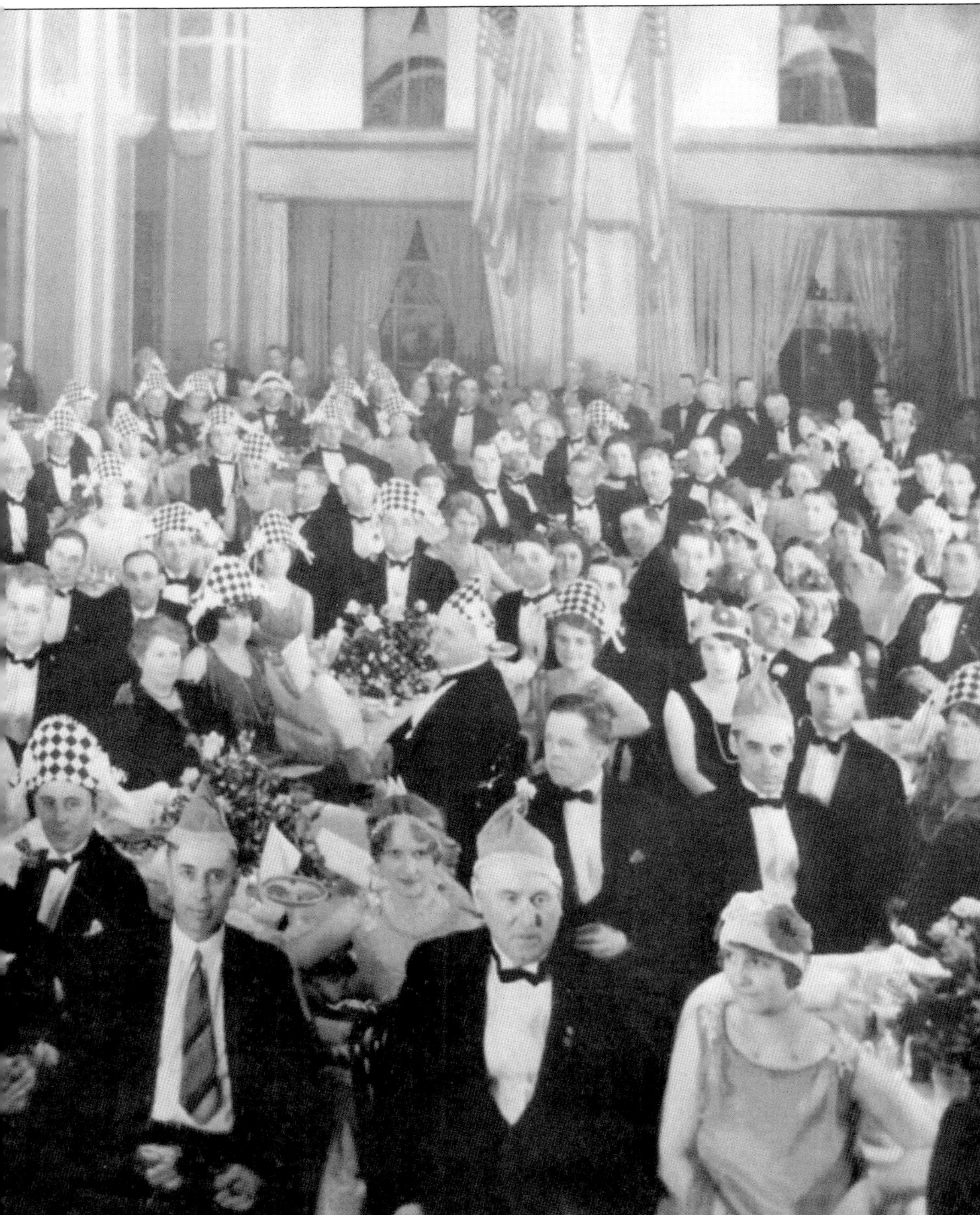

Atlantic City Electric Company hosted this affair. The reason for intelligent business leaders donning fancy caps is lost in time. Note that only a few women wore hats; many of them went bareheaded, rather daring in the still-evolving 1920s. (Conectiv.)

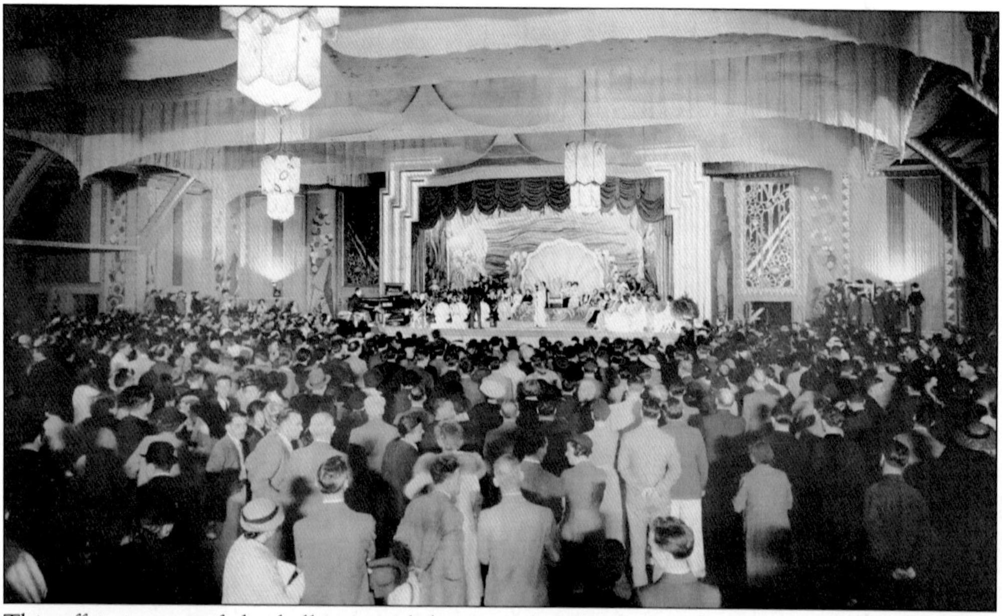

This affair in one of the ballrooms of the city's hotels apparently was a touring "big band" in concert some time in the late 1930s or early 1940s. It is likely that this is one of the very popular swing bands of the day because the crowd is standing, not sitting, as it would be the case for a formal concert. "Big bands" attracted such large crowds that there was no room for dancing. (ACFPL.)

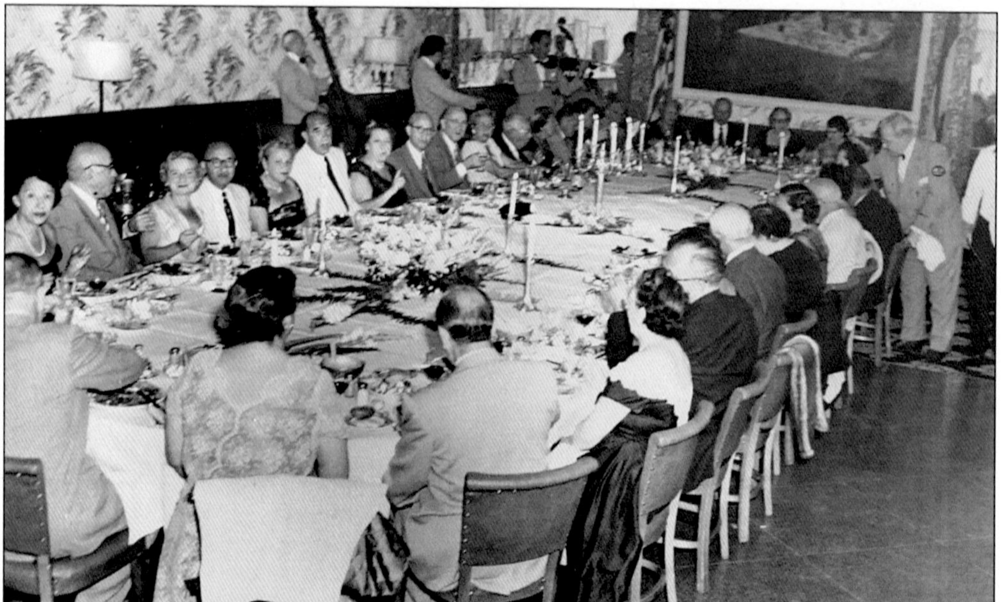

A quite cozy 1948 dinner party gathers in the Hotel Shelburne's "Diamond Jim" Brady Room. The room was named for the flamboyant millionaire who often visited Atlantic City and stayed at the Shelburne. Despite his reputation as a big spender, Brady was a teetotaler who had earned his fortune through selling railroad materials. He began buying jewels, especially diamonds, on the theory they would be easy to pawn if he ever ran out of cash. (ACFPL.)

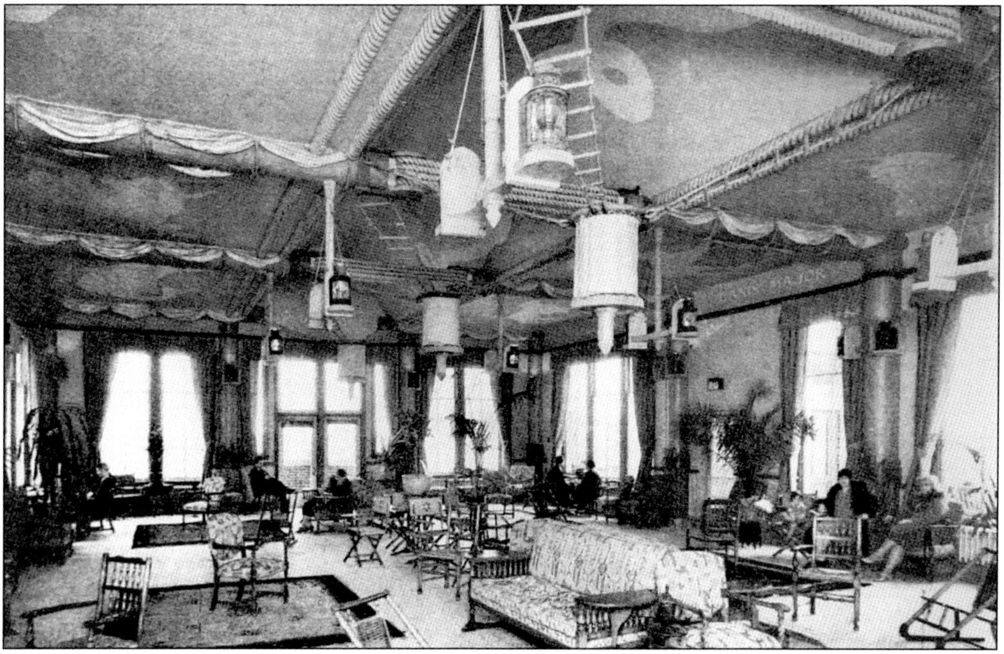

This sedate room with the vaguely nautical theme, above, was the kind of sitting parlor where guests could rest and chat while waiting for formal hotel affairs to begin. Even more sedate was the library on the eighth floor of the Hotel Traymore, below. Writing desks arranged around the perimeter proved very popular for both those who wanted to address postcards and those who wished to write long, thoughtful letters home. (ACFPL.)

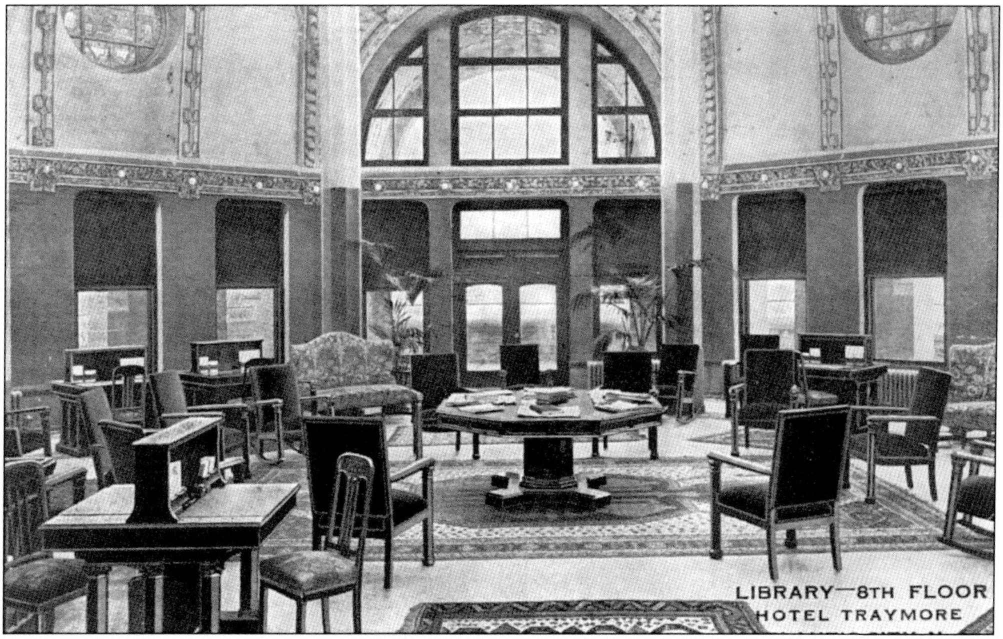

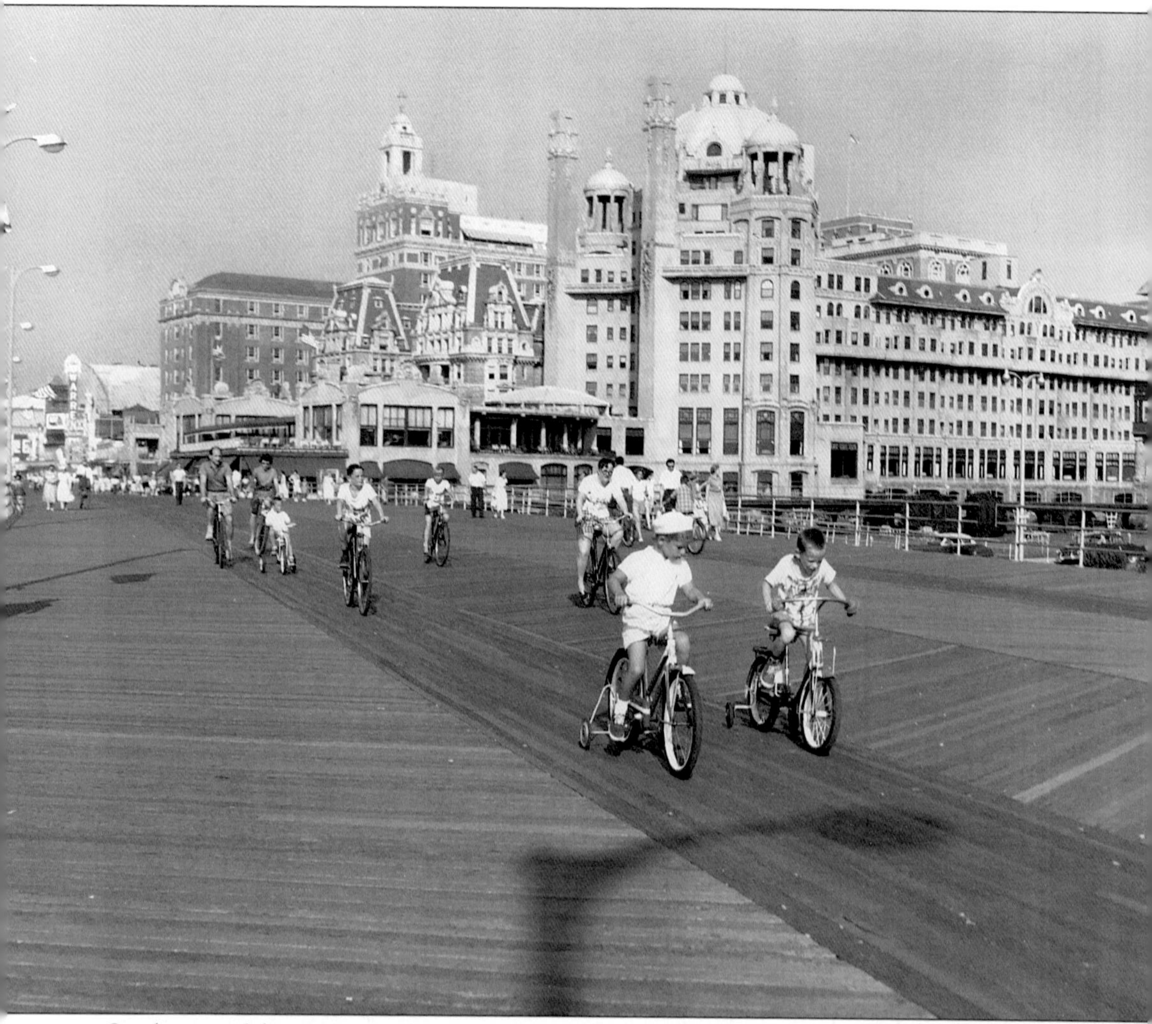

On the eve of the city's transformation into a land of glittering casino buildings, the Boardwalk and its hotels were proclaimed as emblems of family entertainment—a city of Sunday morning bicycling in front of the Boardwalk hotels, including the imposing Traymore. This 1958 picture of serenity would soon disappear to make room for the huge hotel-casino complexes that would rise after gambling was legalized in Atlantic City in 1976. (ACFPL.)

Five

America's Gathering Place

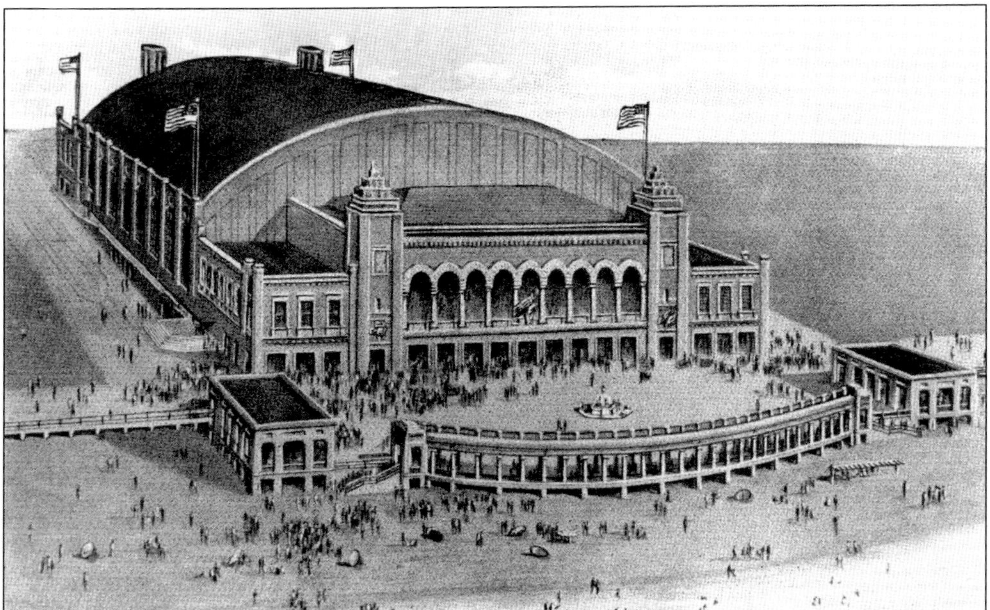

Convention Hall, known by more visitors to Atlantic City than any other place or event, was completed in 1929 to help mark the 75th anniversary of the city's founding. Vice President Charles Curtis led a crowd of 30,000 people in dedication ceremonies. A feature of the day was a mighty salute fired by 16-inch guns of the battleship USS *Wyoming*, anchored well offshore. Since then, the building has hosted nearly every major North American convention. It is said that Madison Square Garden could be placed within the building with a great deal of space to spare. This view is from a postcard of the 1930s. (ACFPL.)

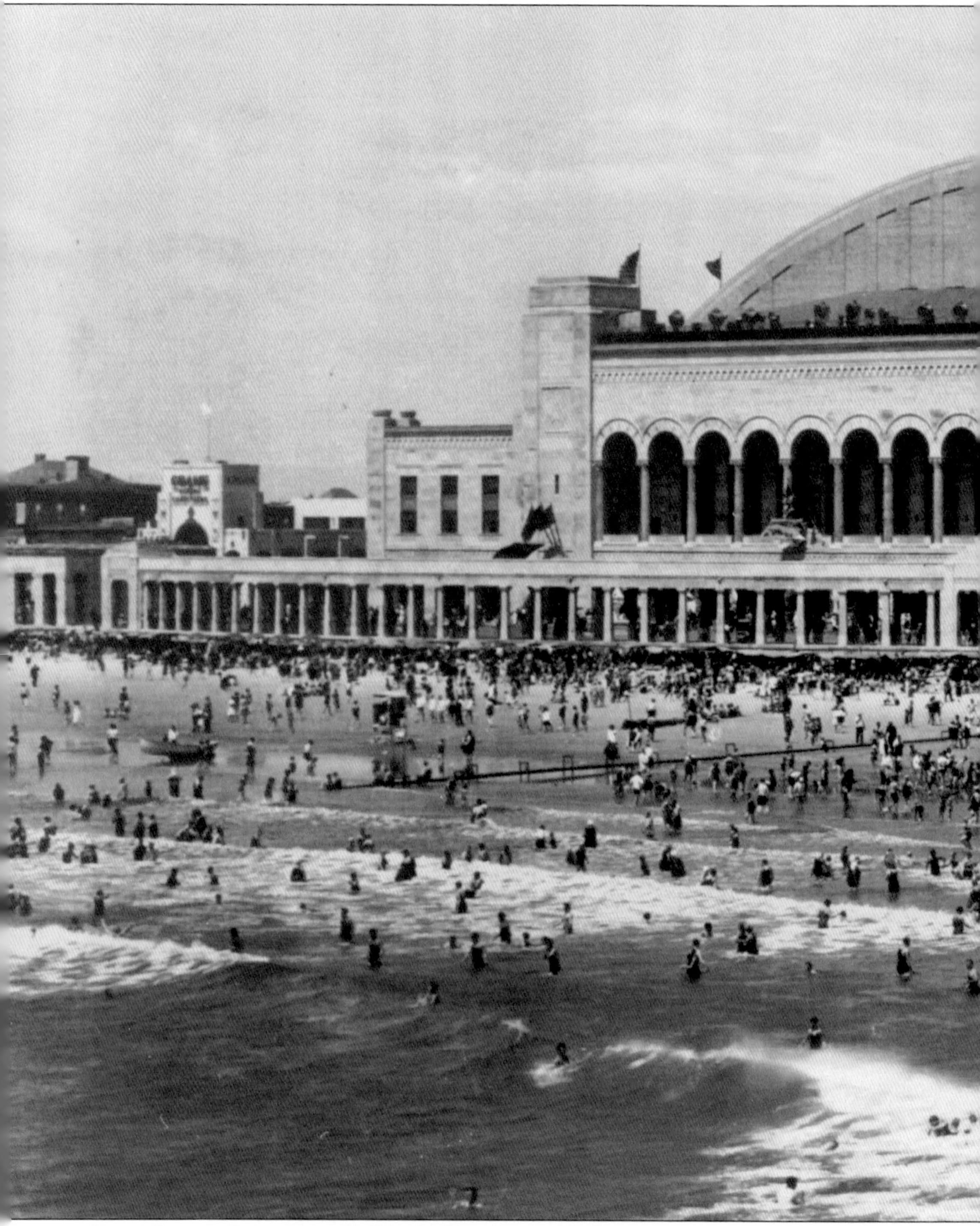

From the sea, Convention Hall looks like the world's biggest Quonset hut, but there never was a Quonset structure to rival this. It stretches from the Boardwalk to Atlantic Avenue and between Georgia and Mississippi Avenues. It occupies seven acres of some of the most valuable real estate in the world. The city's public relations people long have contended that it is the

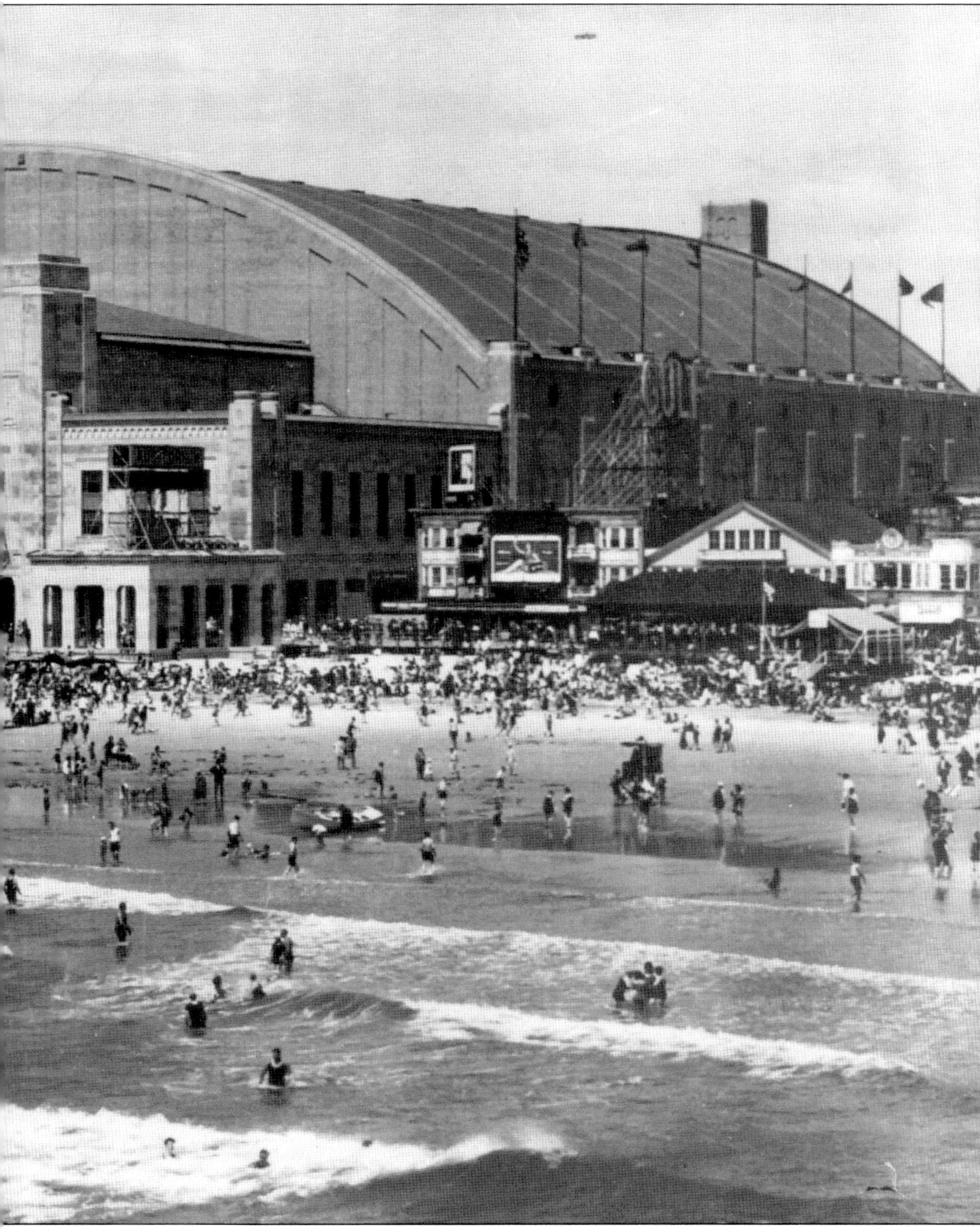

"world's most famous auditorium." It has been the nation's meeting place for years—the place where teachers, doctors, lawyers, scientists, politicians, automobile salesmen, municipal workers, and hundreds of other groups convened. (ACFPL.)

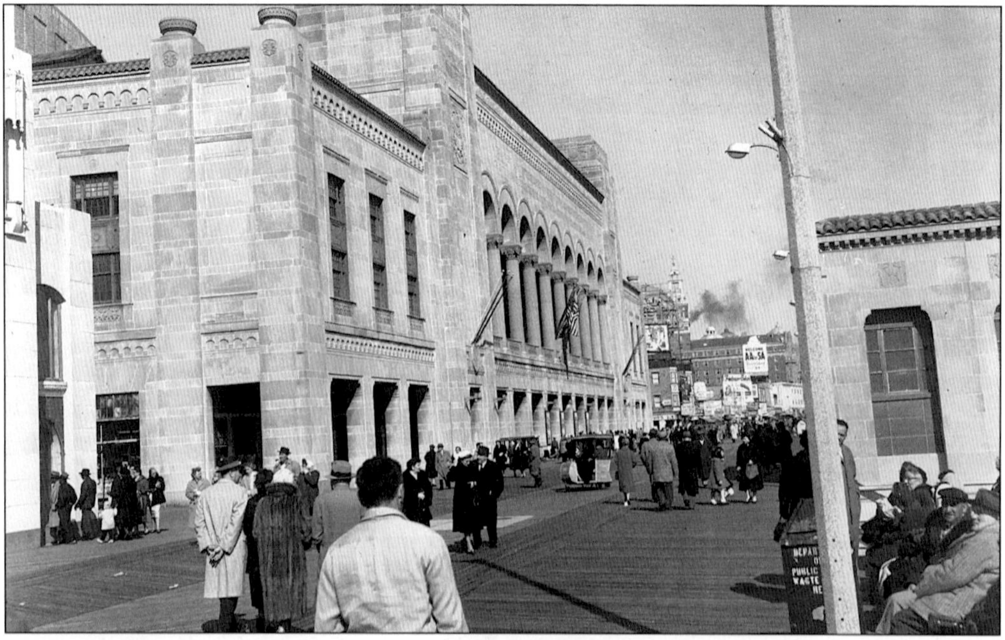

The front of Convention Hall, as it looked in 1960, had changed little since the day it opened. Millions of conventioneers have passed through the big front doors. Inside, the main hall can be converted from a huge exhibit area to a concert hall seating 20,000 to 30,000 people. President Lyndon B. Johnson was nominated here in 1964 in his first campaign to be president. (ACFPL.)

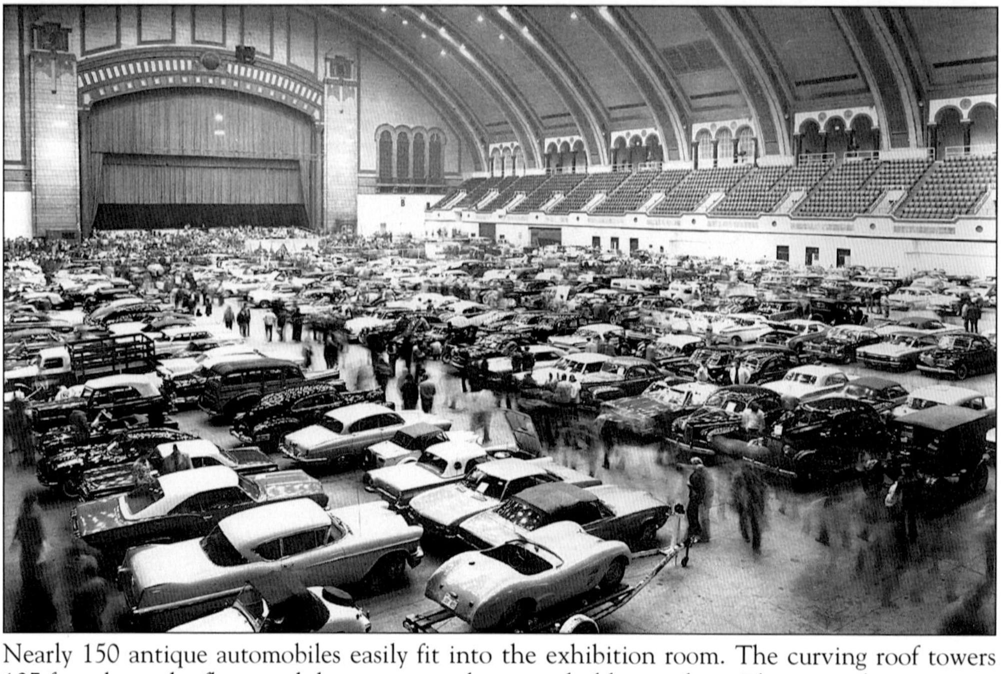

Nearly 150 antique automobiles easily fit into the exhibition room. The curving roof towers 137 feet above the floor, and there are no columns to hold it in place. The astonishing room is 488 feet long and 288 feet wide. All of a convention's meetings can be held in the building if the group so desires. (ACFPL.)

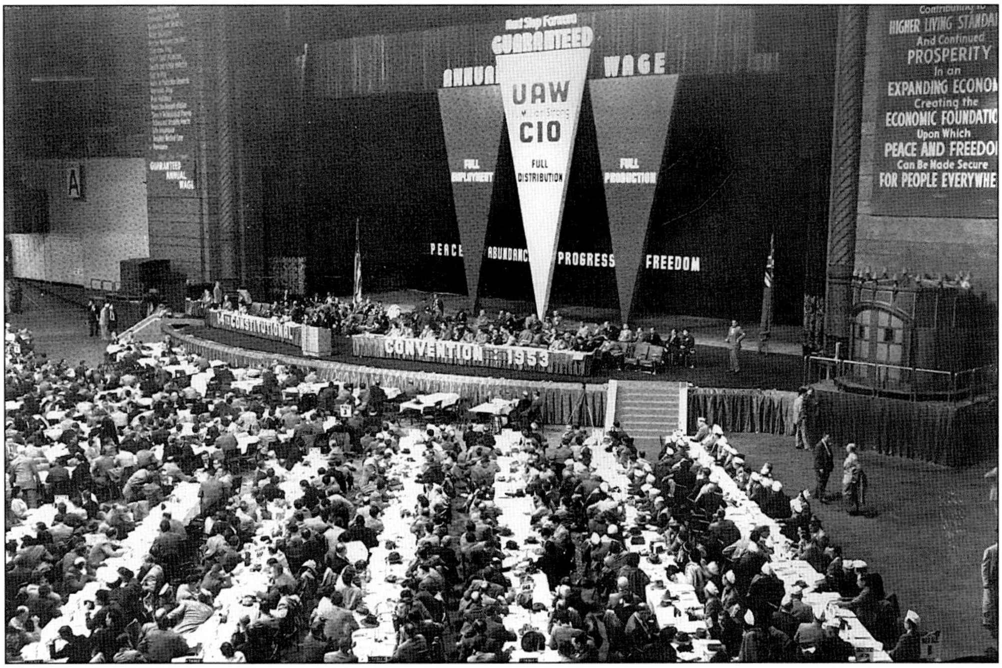

Long tables stretched out from the platform at the UAW-CIO national constitutional convention in 1953. In this unusual arrangement of delegates, the tables afforded attendees places to take notes or keep printed materials together. Note that many delegates used the tables as the place to rest their hats. (ACFPL.)

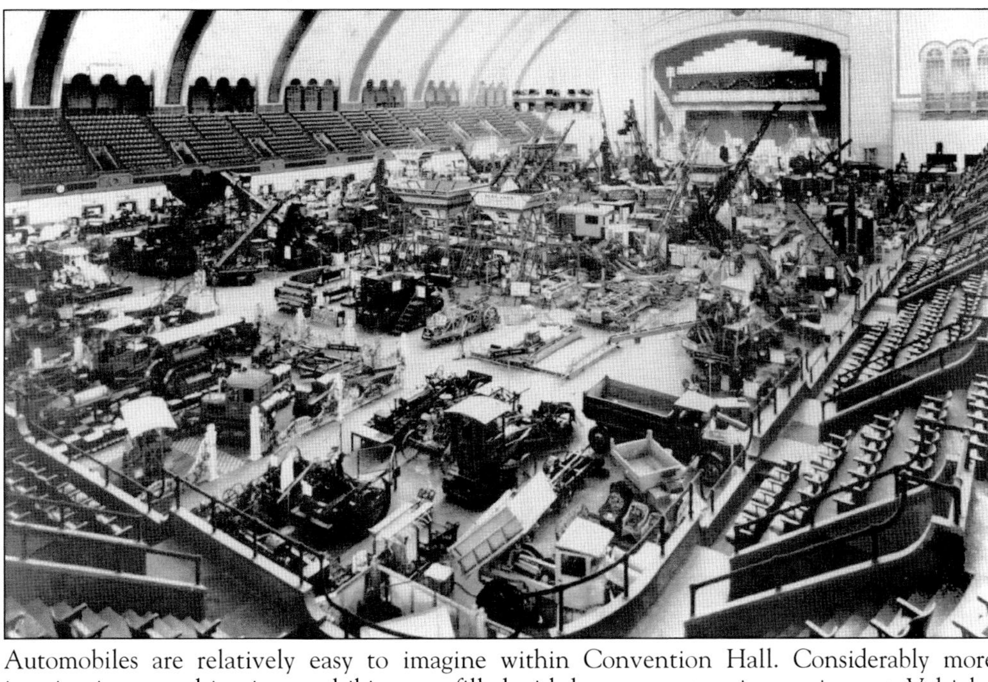

Automobiles are relatively easy to imagine within Convention Hall. Considerably more imagination-stretching is an exhibit space filled with heavy construction equipment. Vehicles range from work boats to earthmoving equipment, from cranes to small tractors, and from dump trucks to road scrapers. (ACFPL.)

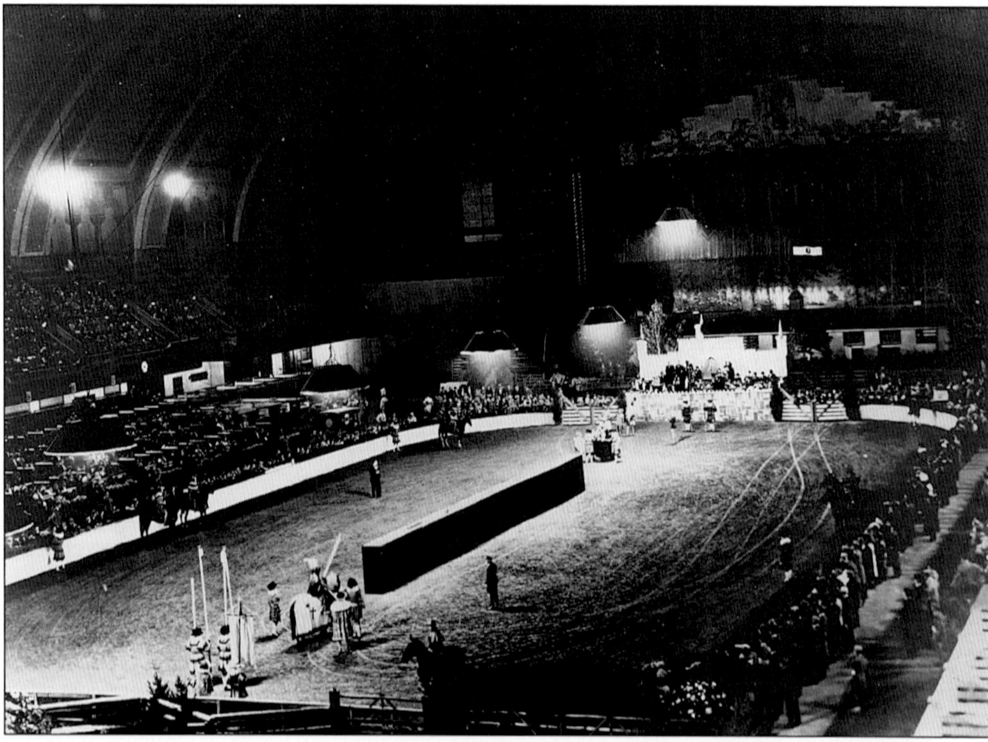

Sports are an important part of Convention Hall activities. The jousting meet in 1932, above, was the first indoor surface to permit horses in an indoor jousting tournament. The city's beloved Seagulls hockey team, below, played its 1930s and 1940s home hockey games on artificial ice within the hall. The ice has also been used for the well-known Ice Capades. (ACFPL.)

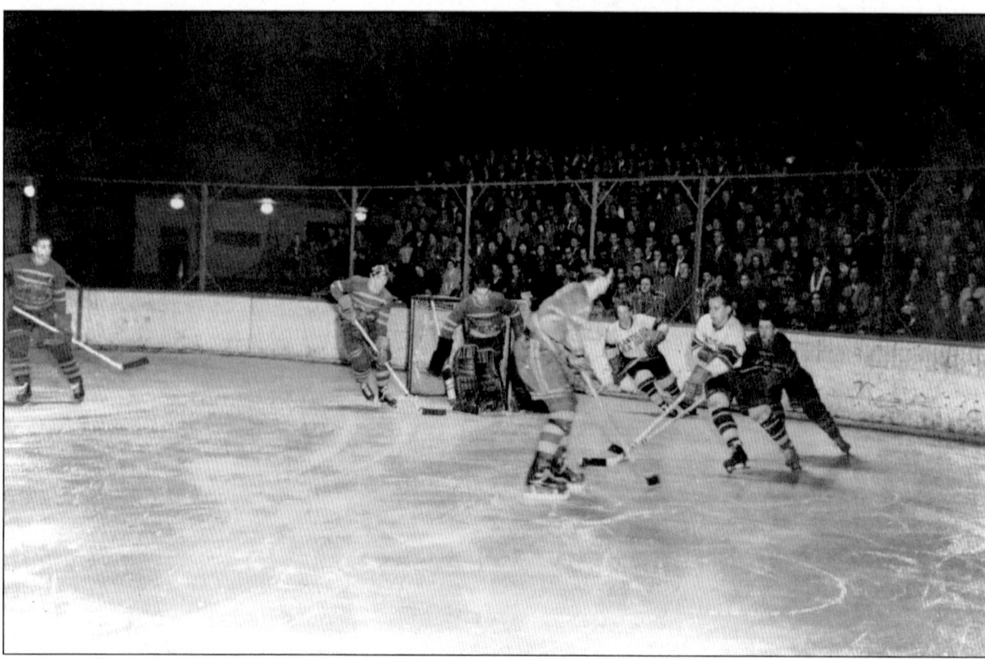

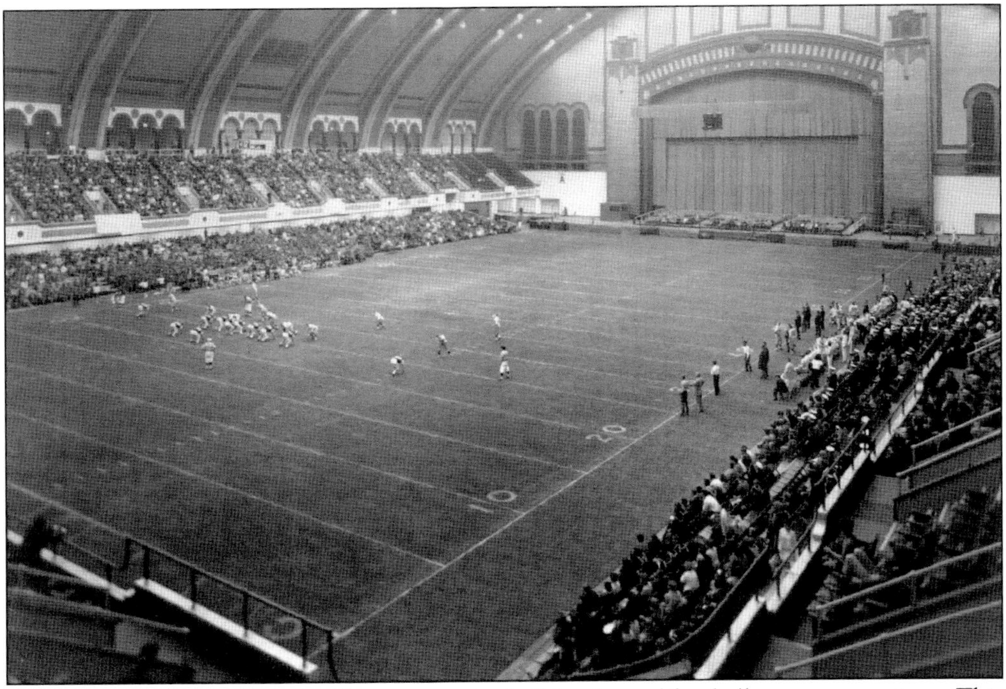

In addition to jousting (rare) and ice sports, the hall has hosted football games many times. This game between two area high school teams was played in the 1960s. Note that there was not enough room for 10-yard end zones, causing officials to move the ball back 10 yards whenever a team advanced close to the goal line on either end of the field. (ACFPL.)

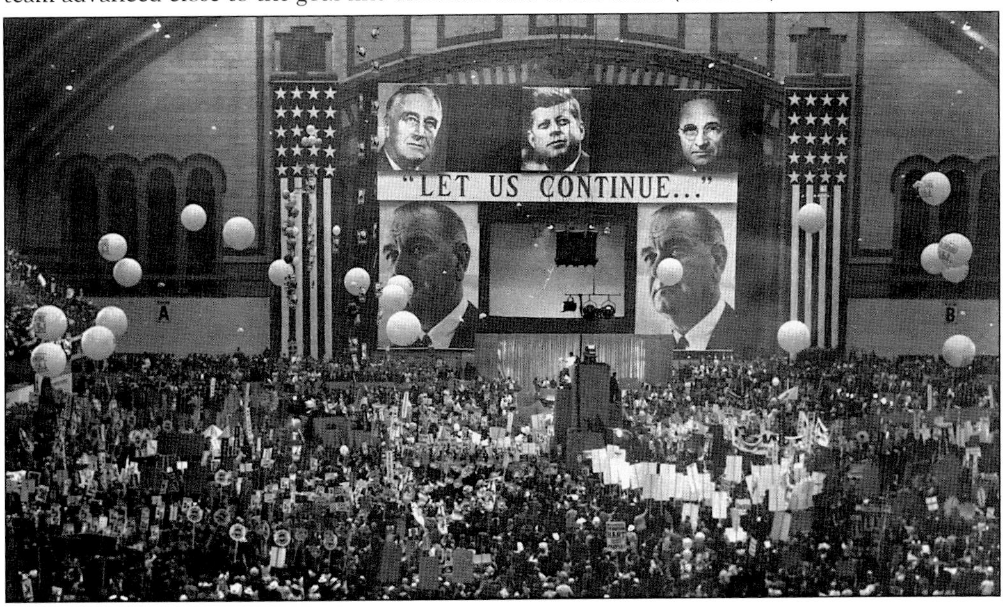

The Democratic Presidential Convention in the summer of 1964 focused attention on New Jersey, Atlantic City, and Convention Hall. The huge throng of delegates, media people, advisers, and others tested the auditorium's capacity. Democrats rode the tide of popular support that befell Lyndon B. Johnson after John F. Kennedy was assassinated in Dallas in November 1963. (ACFPL.)

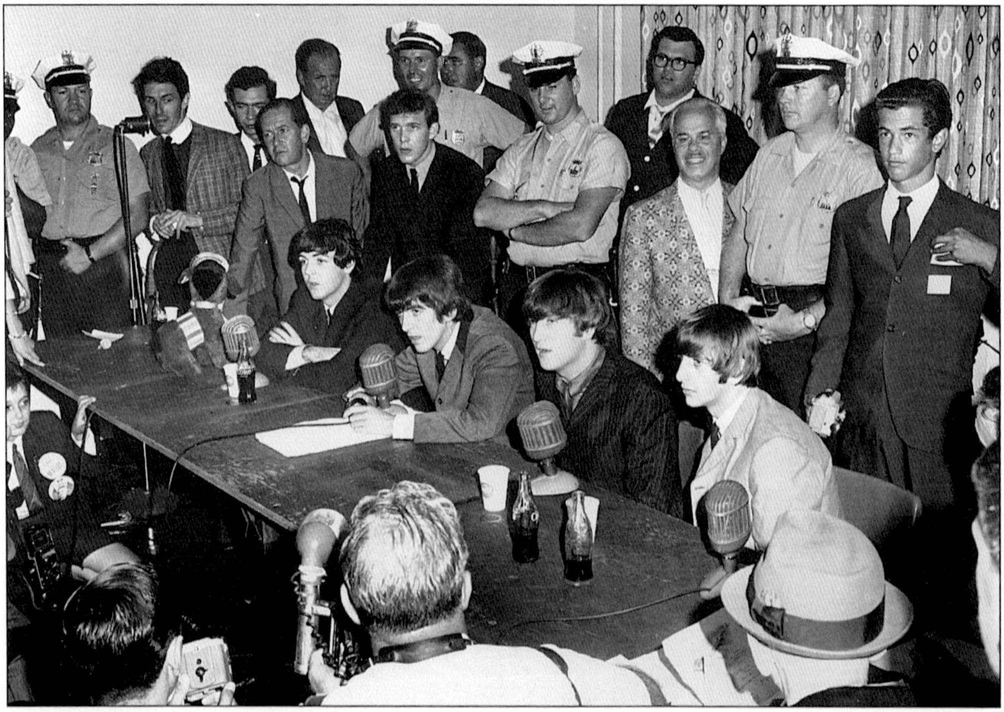

No matter what the measurement—size of crowd, demand for tickets, or audience enthusiasm—nothing came close to matching the accord given the Beatles when they came to Convention Hall in 1964. The serious young men from Liverpool first enchanted the press in the afternoon, above, then in the evening enthralled one of the largest crowds ever to jam into the hall, below. (ACFPL.)

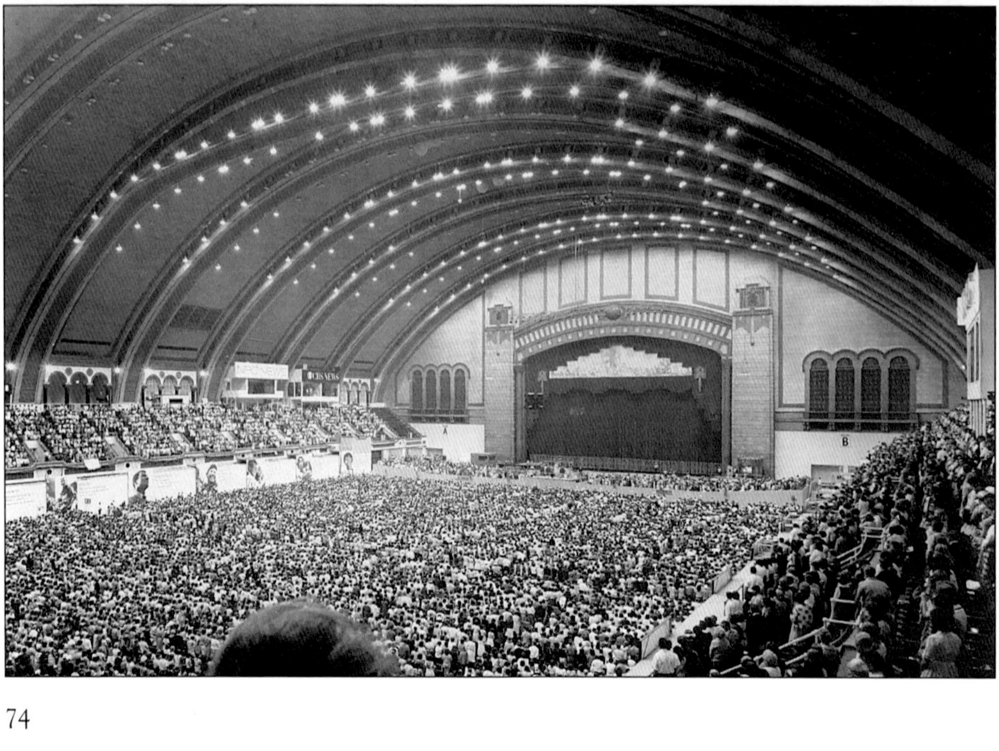

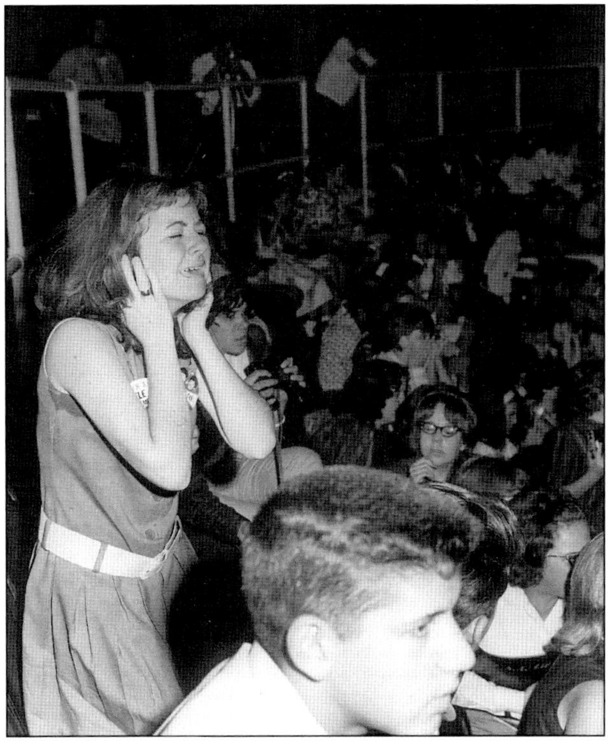

With joy bordering on agony, a Beetles fan wept and emoted as the concert progressed. She became mesmerized by the vibrant harmonies of the group until, midway through the concert, she collapsed. The Atlantic City Rescue Squad responded and led her from her cherished spot in the hall to some fresh air. She was as emotionally spent as if she were leaving a war zone. (ACFPL.)

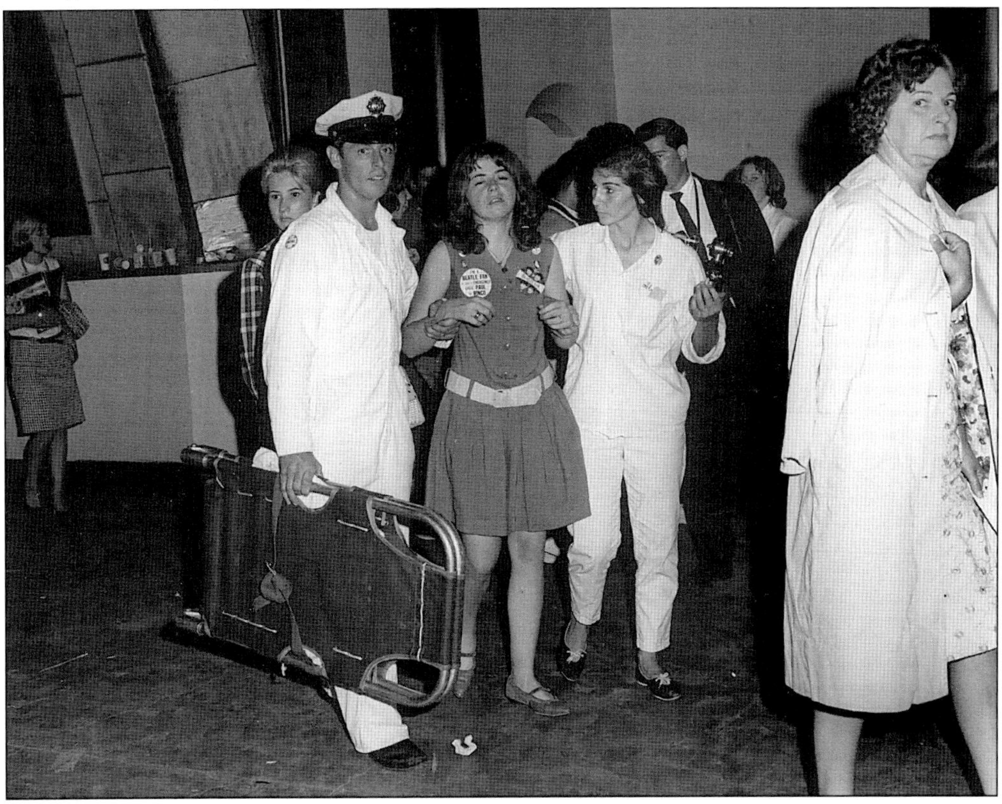

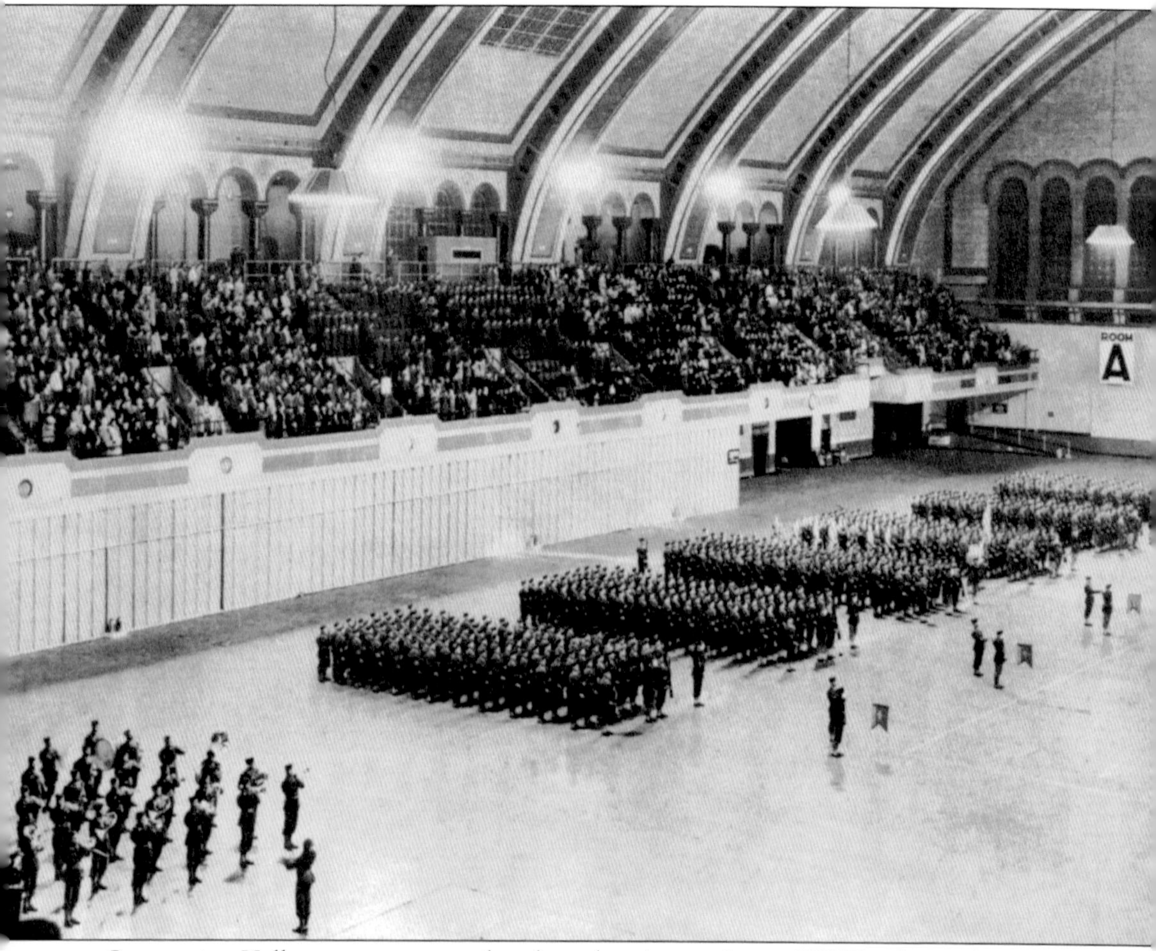

Convention Hall was never a prouder place than it was during WWII, when it became the headquarters for troops training in the city. The giant hall provided space for hundreds of trainees to conduct drills, to engage in calisthenics during inclement weather, and to gather whenever a class moved up or got ready to ship out. Crowds attended such ceremonies to see their favorite sons and daughters graduate or to hear the pulsating military bands. (ACFPL.)

Six

Camp Boardwalk

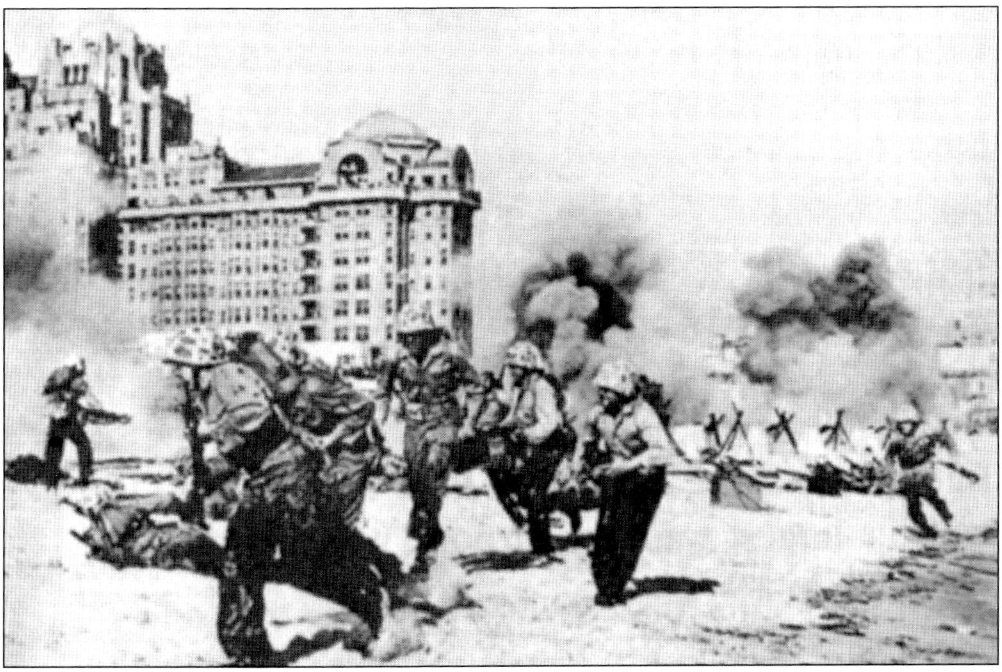

Atlantic City's most dramatic and most transforming performance came during WWII, when the city exchanged its party clothes for military garb. Beaches exploded with simulated warfare. Soldiers and sailors marched on the Boardwalk behind stirring military bands. The city shuttered its windows and dimmed its lights to mask the city from enemy submarines patrolling the ocean just beyond the Boardwalk. The armed services began coming in 1942, and eventually 47 hotels housed men and women from all the services. An estimated 30,000 new recruits arrived each month; eventually about one-half million service personnel trained in the city. Inevitably, as the trickle of wounded returning from distant battlefields became a flood in 1943, the services converted the city's largest hotel system, the Chalfonte-Haddon Hall, into the Thomas L. England Hospital to care for the sick and wounded. (JTC.)

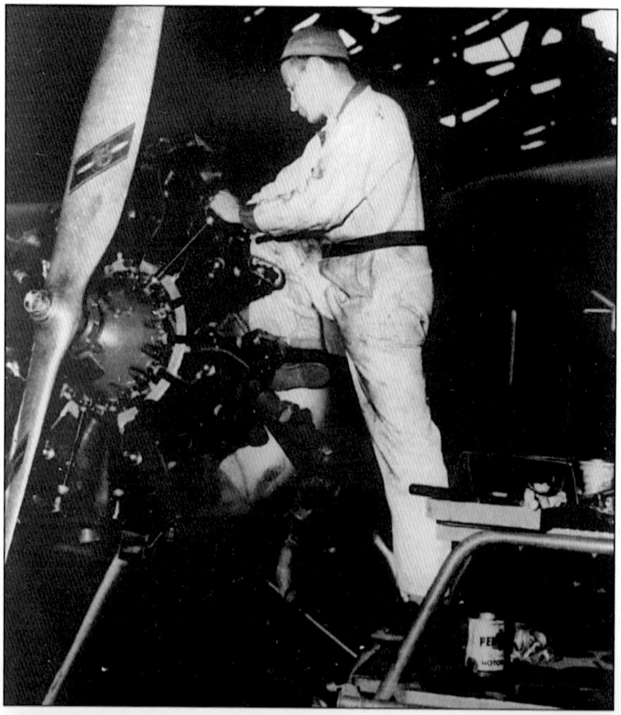

The war effort was widespread even before the troops began converging on the city. A Civil Air Patrol mechanic, left, worked on one of the patrol's small planes stationed at Bader Field. Below, women war workers at S.G. Seyfang Laboratories put the finishing touches on three of the many reconnaissance balloons made in Atlantic City to further the war effort. (ACFPL.)

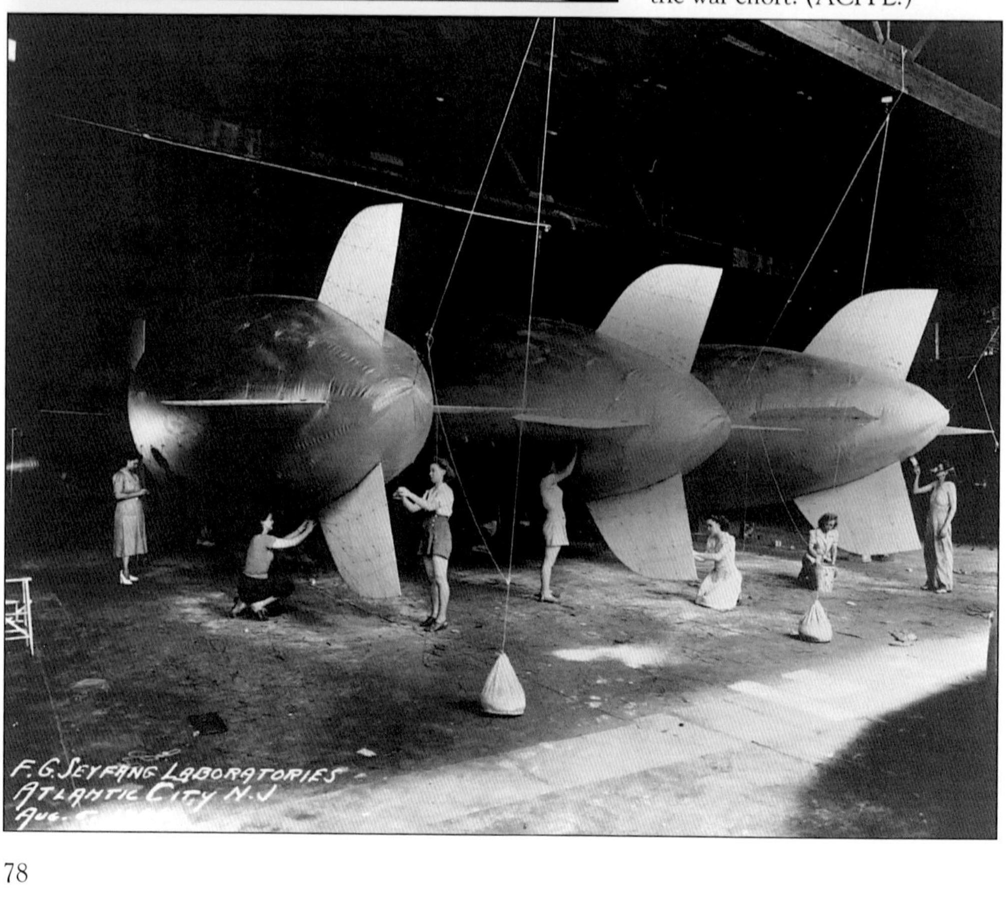

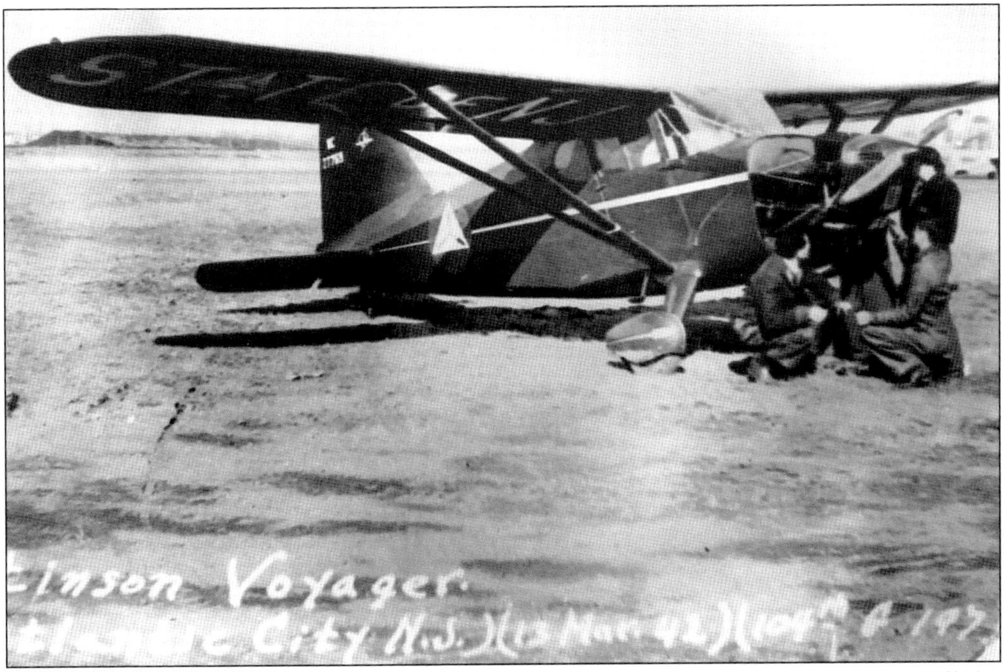

Seeking German submarines, the Civil Air Patrol flew search-and-destroy missions off the Atlantic City shore in this small single-wing, propeller-driven Stinson. Two unsung heroes of the local CAP unit were Ben Berger of Denver, Colorado (below, left), who died in a plane crash at Bader field on Easter morning, 1943, and Johnny Haggin (below, right), who sank a German submarine off Atlantic City. The submarine threat was very real; about a dozen ships were sunk off the New Jersey coast during the war.

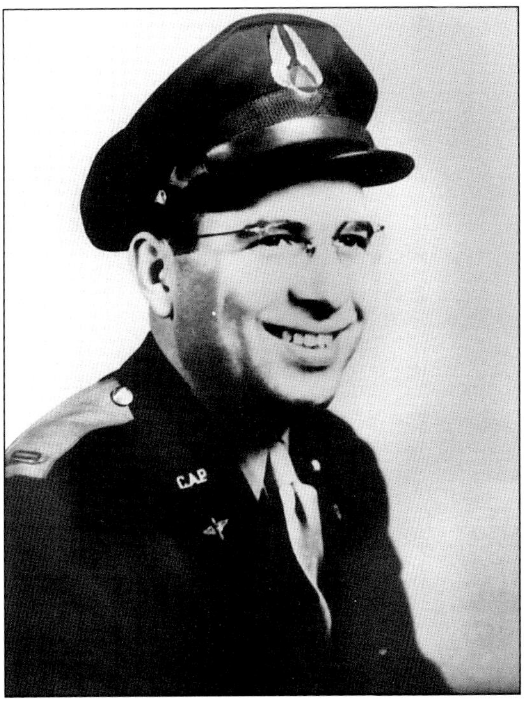

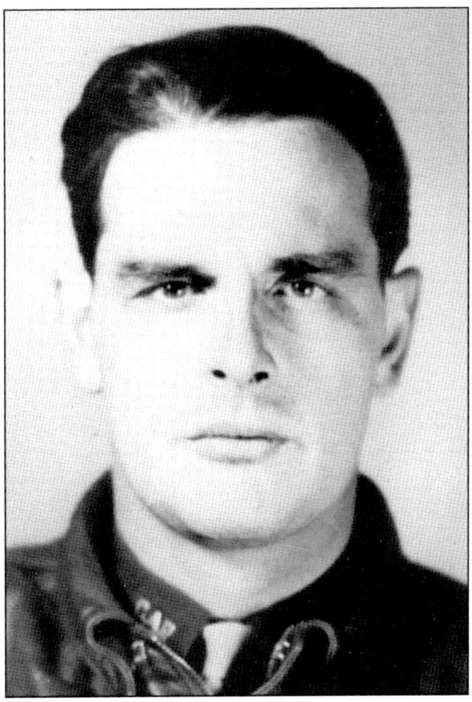

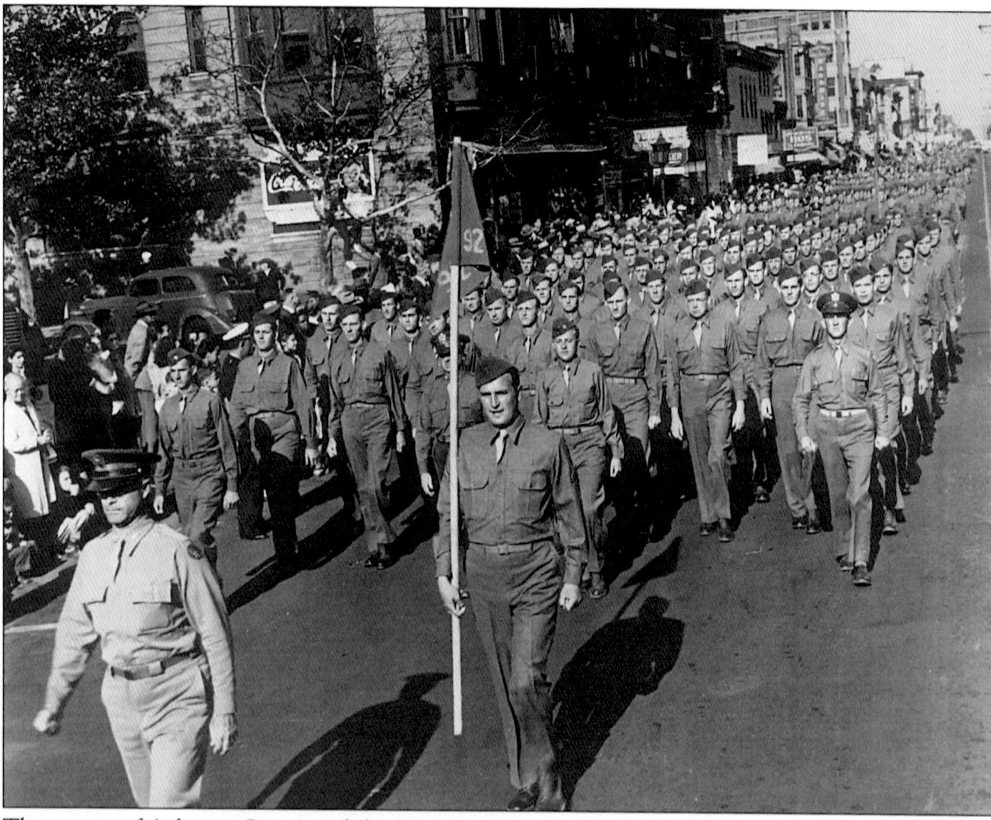

The streets of Atlantic City—and the Boardwalk—resonated every day, seven days a week, with the rhythmic sounds of marching feet. Some of the stepping out was behind military bands, but more often, the marchers provided their own cadence by singing popular songs to a military beat. The 92nd company of an Air Corps regiment, above, was in perfect stride on Atlantic Avenue. Equally in stride, a contingent of the Women's Army Auxiliary Corps (WAAC) is seen below, pacing its way along the Boardwalk by singing. (ACFPL.)

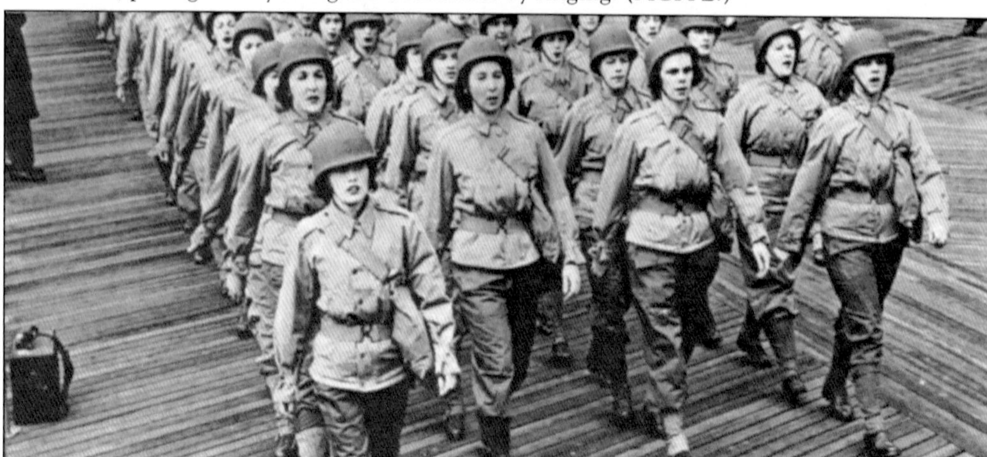

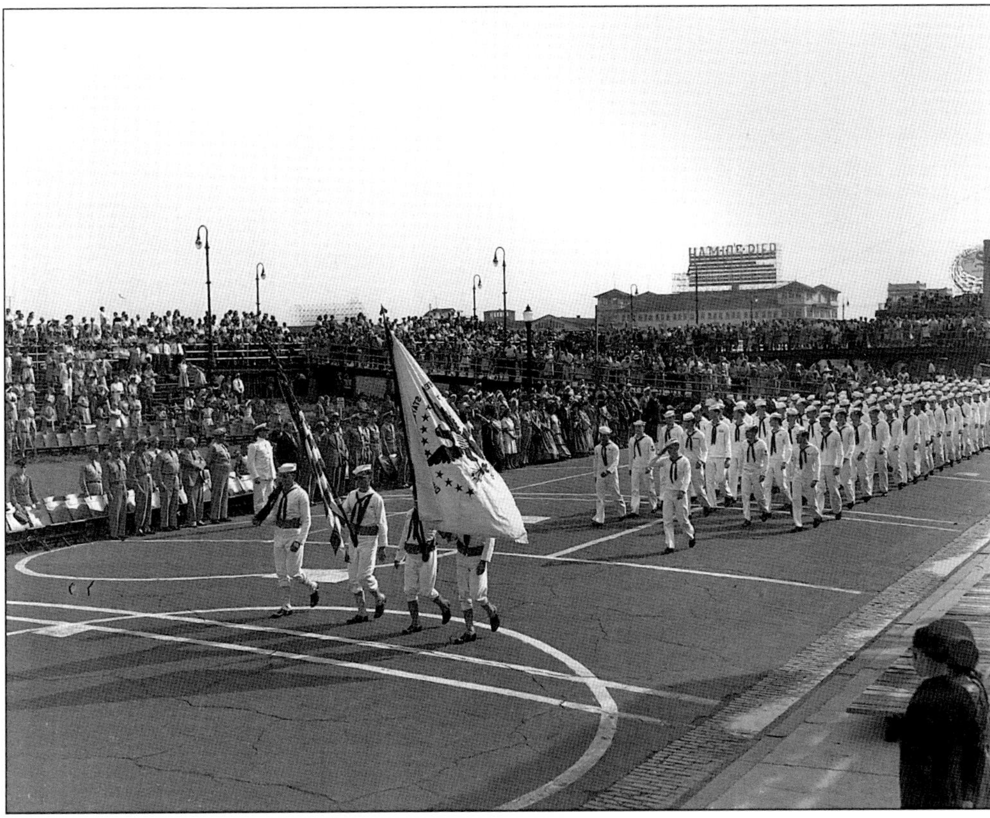

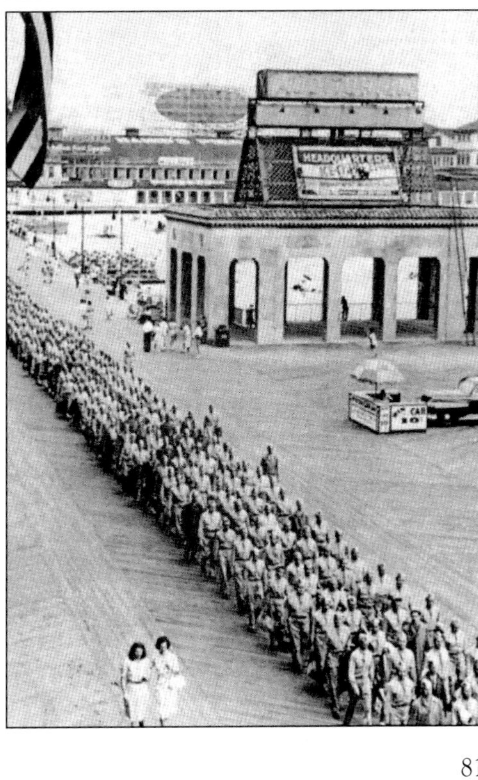

Sailors, sometimes not known for precision marching, were in impeccable cadence on Atlantic Avenue in a military review, above. Note the crowds of spectators lining the Boardwalk in the rear and the ramps leading to the walk. The long khaki line of soldiers marching back to their hotels after the evening meal, right, made every effort not to notice the two young women to the side of the line of march. No unescorted girl under age 18 was allowed on the Boardwalk after 9 p.m. (ACFPL.)

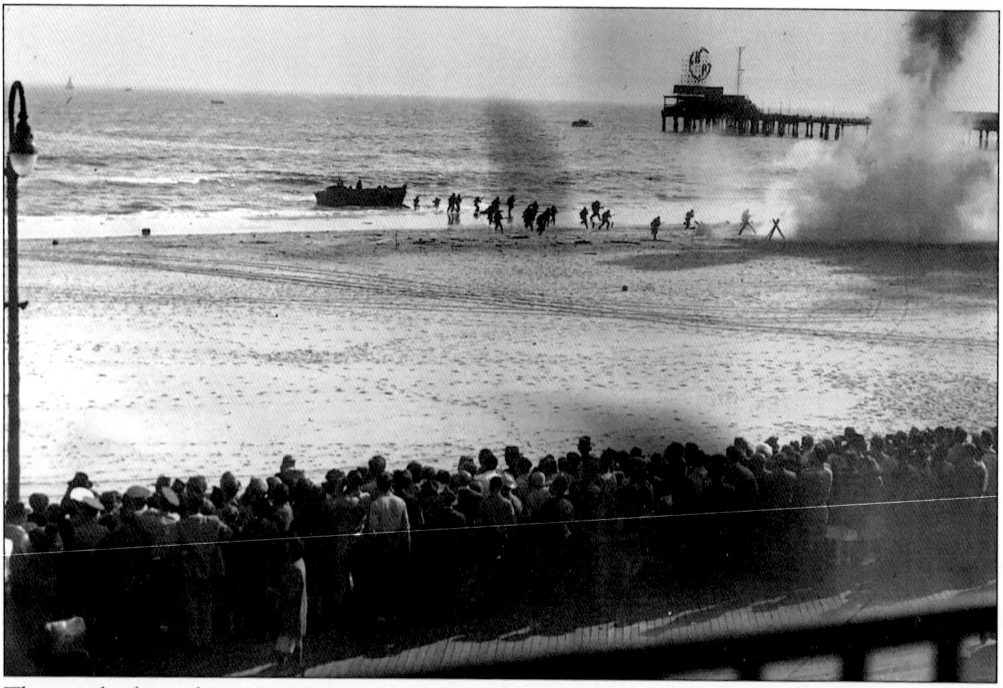

This might have been Iwo Jima, Guadalcanal, or Saipan. Indeed, some who here stormed the beach at Atlantic City, above, eventually went ashore on such distant sands. Boardwalk crowds gathered to watch the mock assaults, complete with exploding bombs and the rattling of machine guns. After securing designated posts, four hungry officers, below, were among the thousands of soldiers who sampled field rations on the beaches and in the grassy sedges west of the city. (ACFPL.)

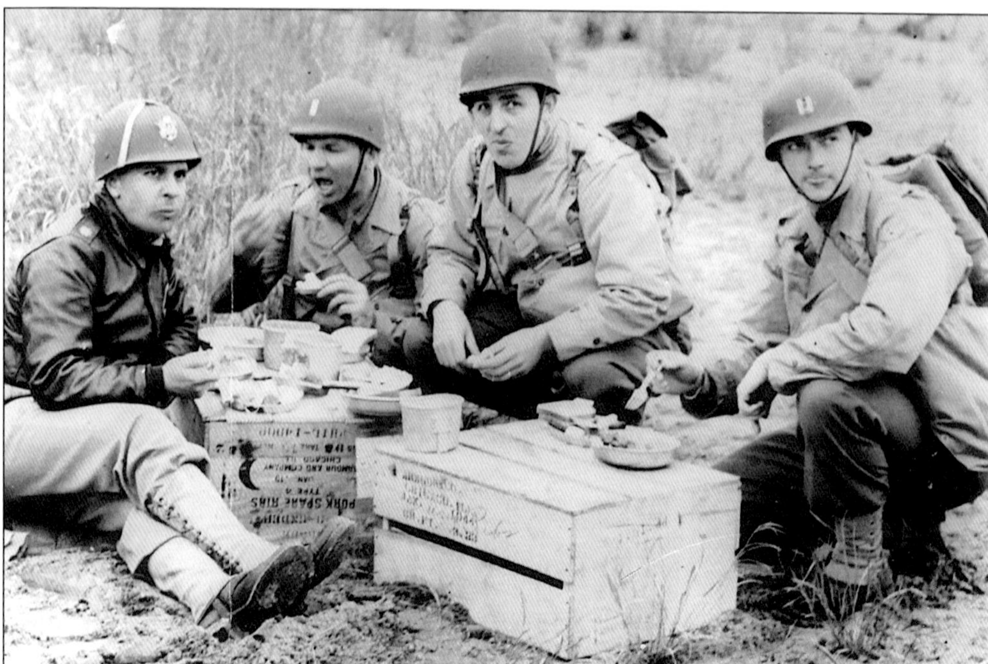

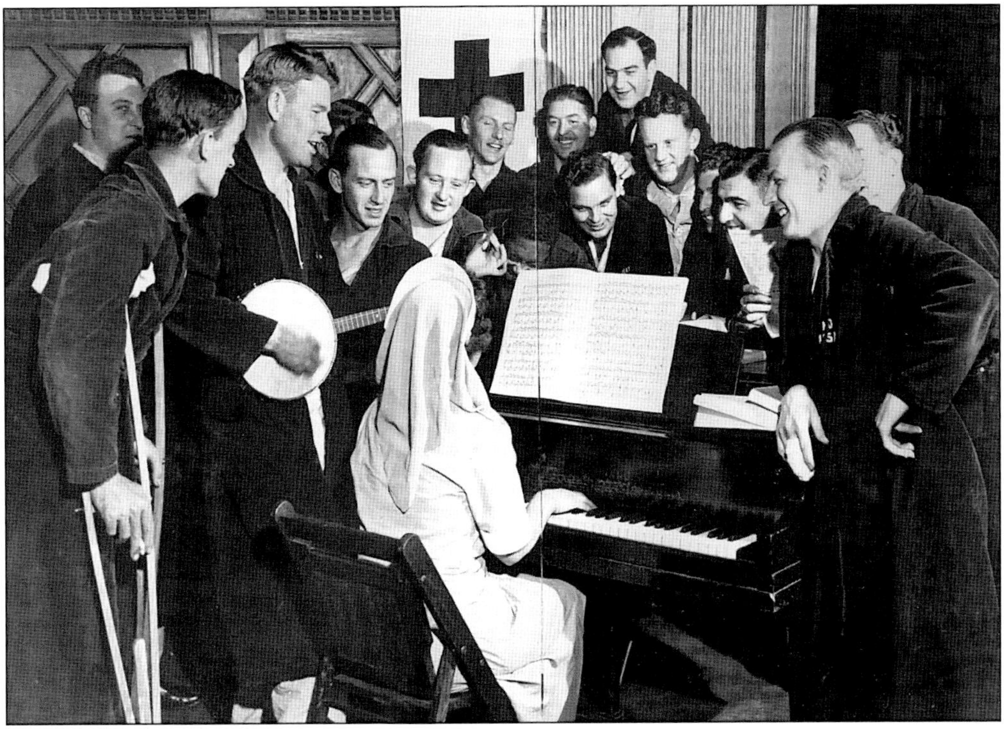

Injured servicemen, who had been sent home after being wounded in body or mind, gathered around a piano, above, to sing while a nurse played nostalgic songs. The military life was not all drilling and marching; service personnel also cleaned the hotel "barracks" more strenuously than they had ever had cleaned before. Atlantic City residents took the soldiers to heart and helped while away lonesome hours with USO parties, such as the one below, for African-American troops in the YMCA on Halloween, 1943. (ACFPL.)

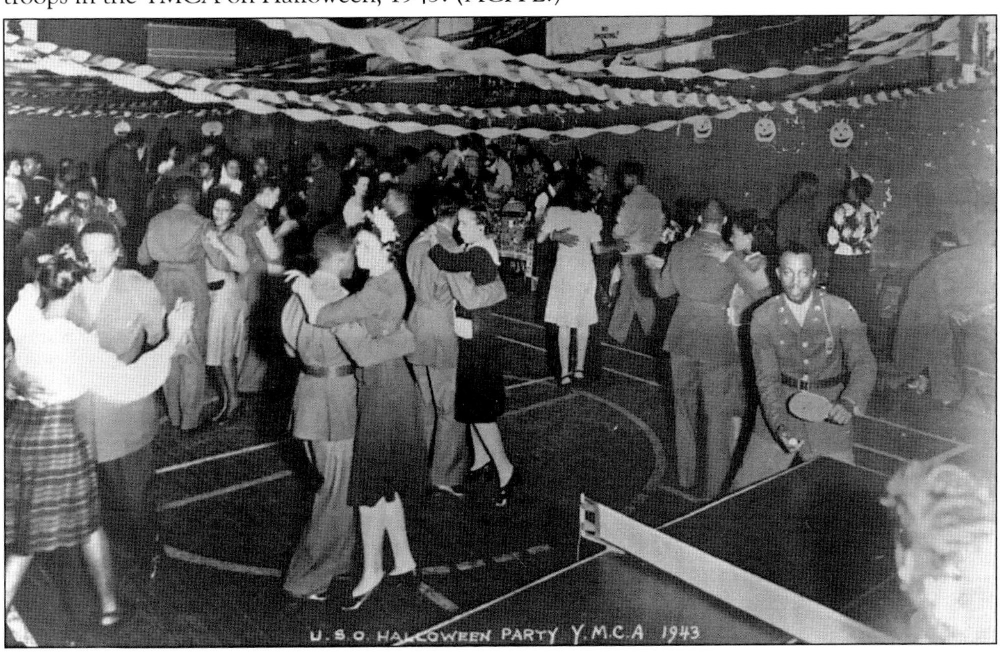

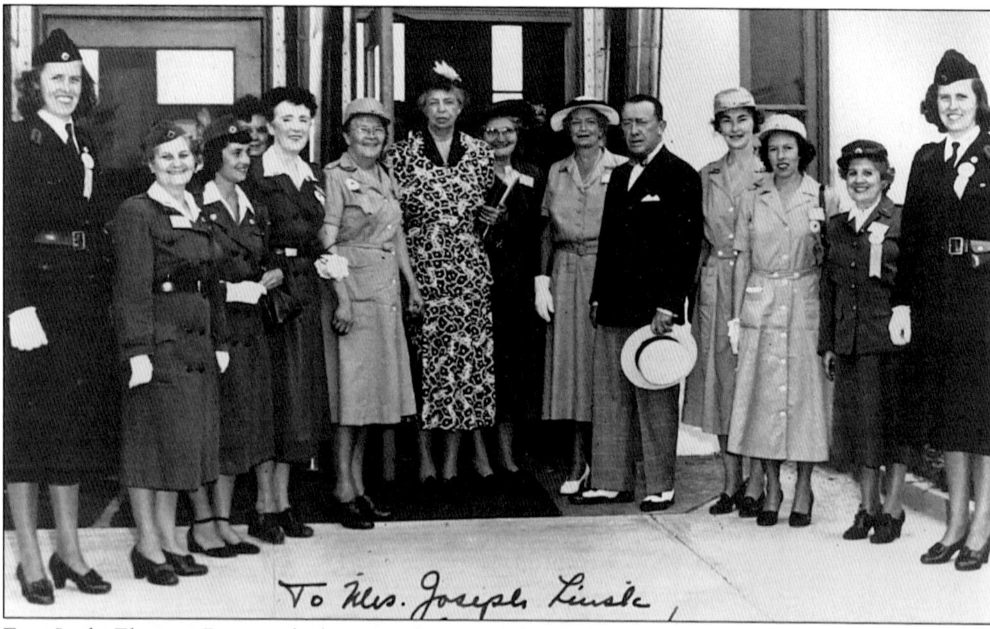

First Lady Eleanor Roosevelt (center above, in the flowered dress) came to Atlantic City to encourage the Red Cross and other volunteers as well as to visit some of the thousands of soldiers at the Thomas L. England hospital for injured servicemen. On any given day, as seen below, soldiers would wait in line at the hospital for inoculations, one of the most disliked chores for troops anywhere. (ACFPL.)

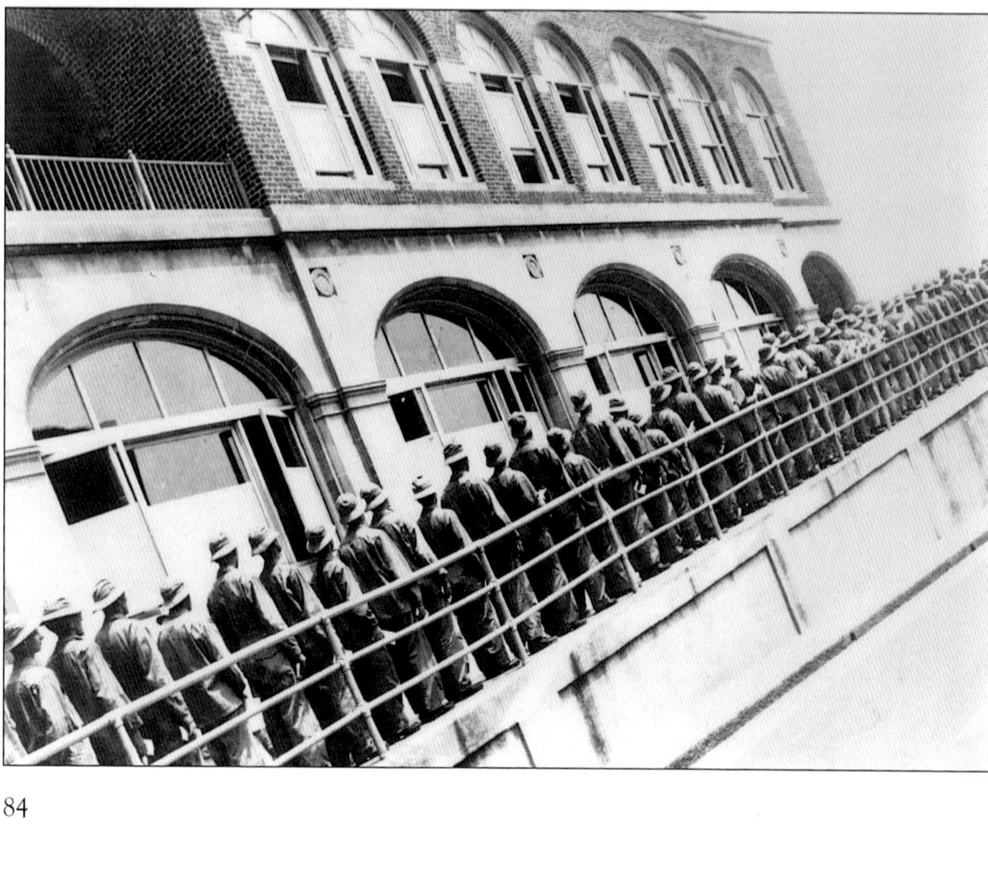

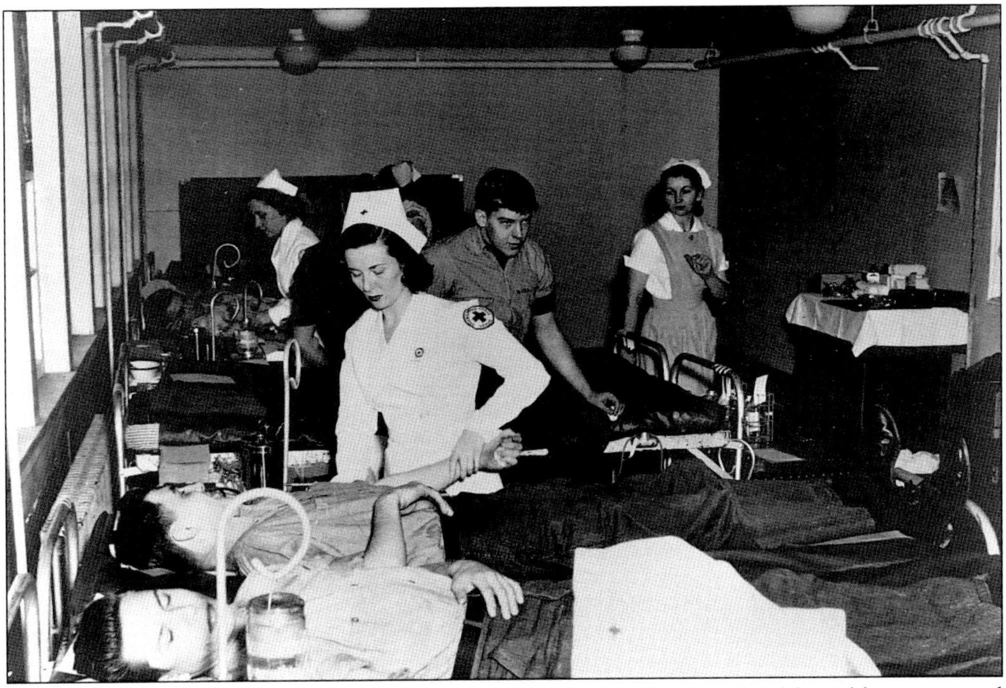

Recognizing the constant need for blood at the T.L. English Hospital, healthy soldiers streamed to the blood donation center in one of the hotels. It was a chance to help the war effort and an opportunity for soldiers to see a pretty young nurse up close. On sunny days, as seen below, patients at the hospital would sit on comfortable chairs and watch able servicemen drilling on the Boardwalk. (ACFPL.)

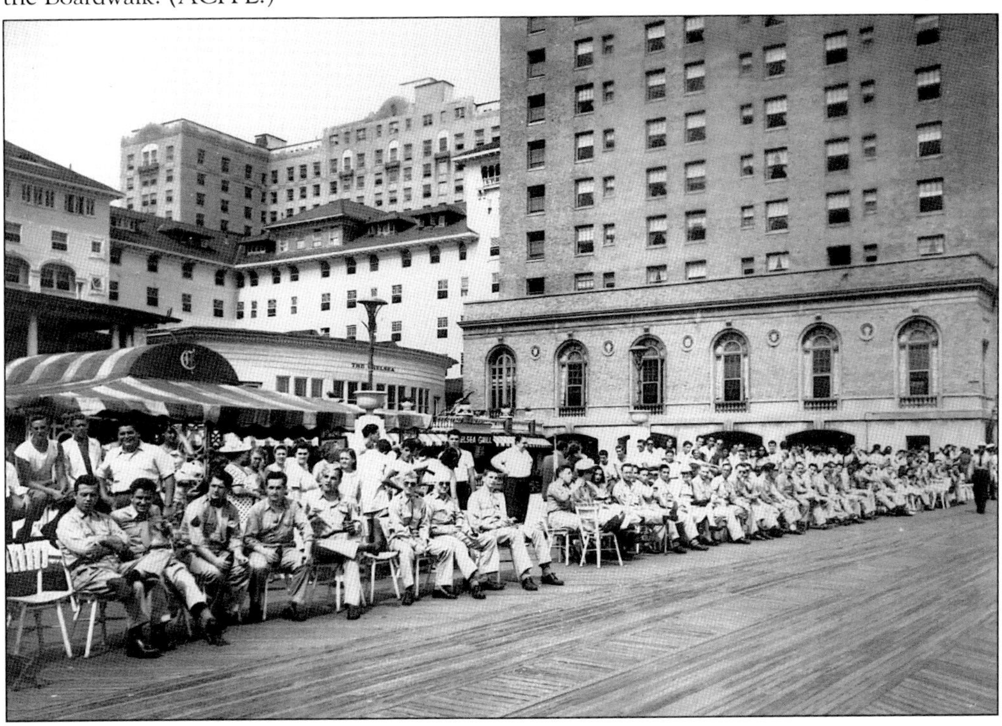

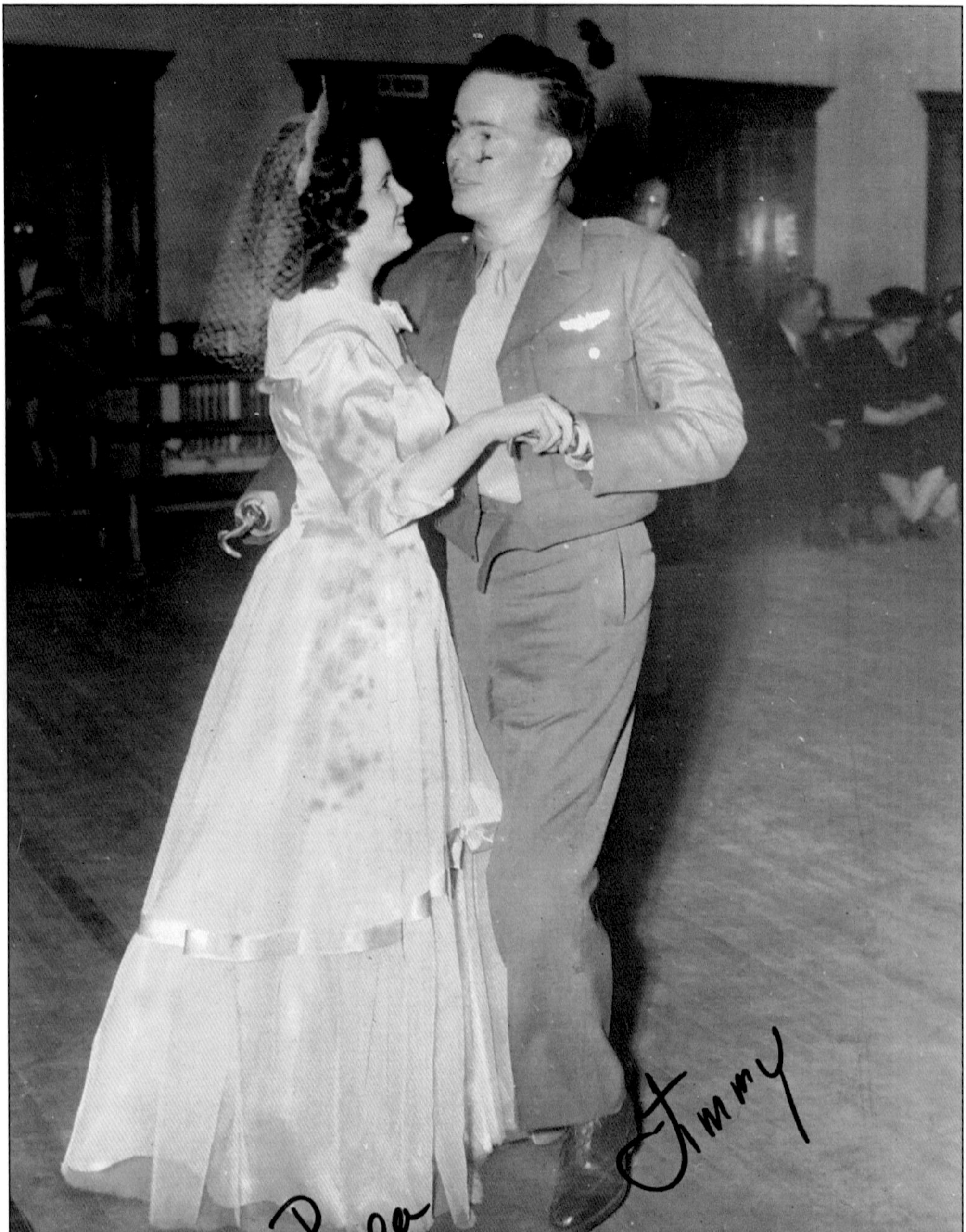

This handsome veteran, Jimmy Wilson, had known so much of war that he had lost both arms and both legs. Yet, in the midst of enough adversity to kill most men's spirits, he met, wooed, and married a lovely young woman, Bea Hilsec. They danced at their wedding in an Atlantic City hotel ballroom. Quite naturally, they honeymooned in the city. (ACFPL.)

Seven

There She Is!

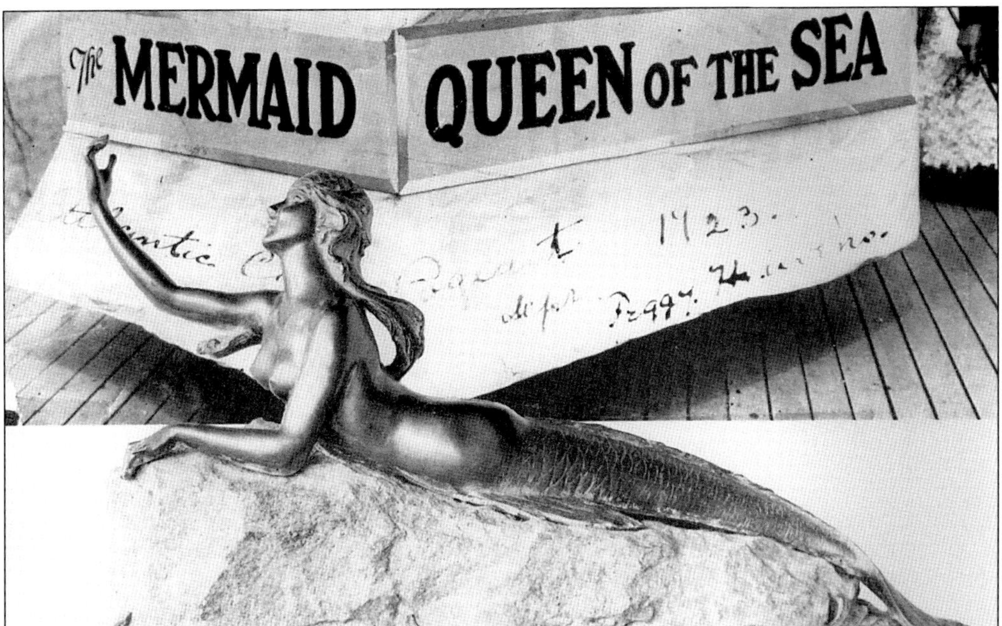

No young American woman is more glorified, admired, and envied than Miss America, who, since 1921, has reigned supreme among all American beauties. The show was started to promote Atlantic City and to extend the tourist season beyond Labor Day. After choosing a winner, show officials would emphasize the tape measure specifications of the contestants in press releases. The first winners were given the "Golden Mermaid," seen above. After nearly 20 years of on-and-off success (the show was closed between 1928 and 1935), the affair officially became the Miss America Pageant in 1940. Millions of dollars have been raised to provide scholarships for Miss America and other contestants. Miss Americas, in turn, have raised millions of dollars for their favorite charities. Brains and talent now are said to be more important than the ability to round out a bathing suit, but Miss America must always be lovely first; brains and talent are happy extra dividends. (MAO.)

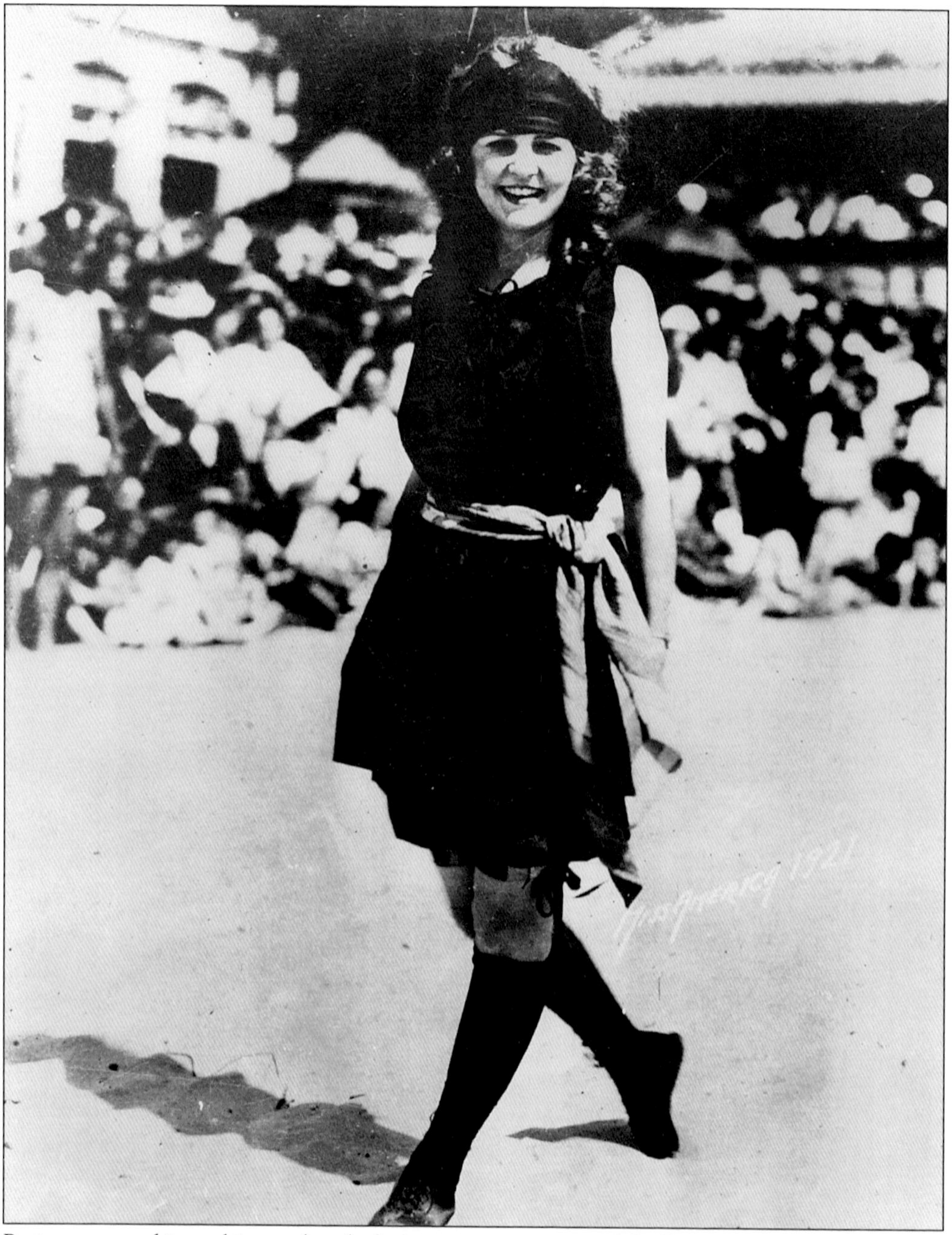

Petite, pert, and just a bit naughty, befitting a young woman of the Roaring Twenties, Margaret Gorman of Washington, D.C. was chosen in 1921 as the first "most beautiful girl in America." Miss Gorman, age 16, wore a loose-fitting, black bathing suit and showed dimpled knees above rolled-down, black stockings. She had to post a $5,000 bond to assure that she would return the trophy, which could be retired by the first woman to win it three times. (JTC.)

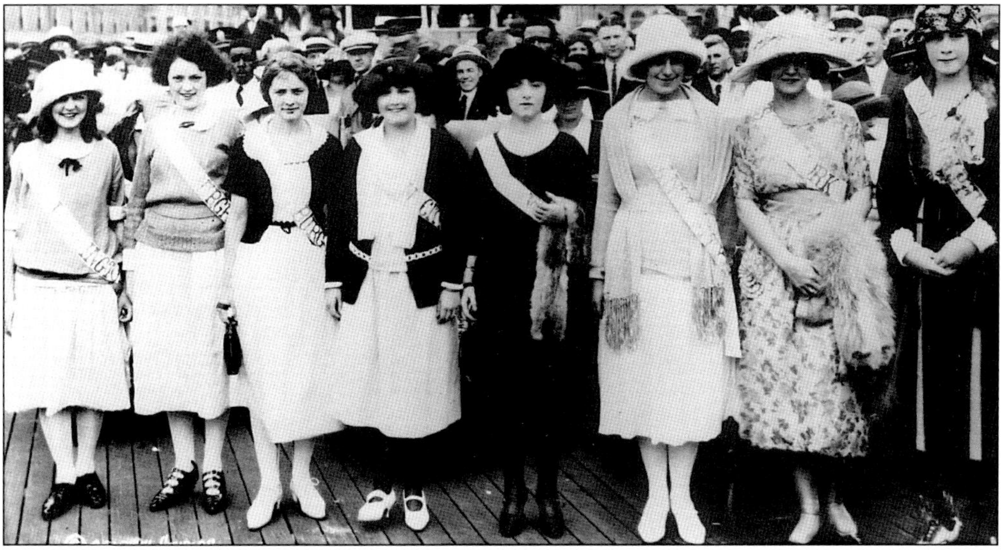

Style and modesty in 1921 demanded hats. Two brave contestants, defying tradition, showed their bobbed hair. The eight young "beauty maids" represented cities—Washington, Pittsburgh, Newark, New York, Ocean City, Camden, Philadelphia, and Harrisburg. Contestants strolled wherever they wished, unlike today's closely chaperoned Miss America candidates. (JTC.)

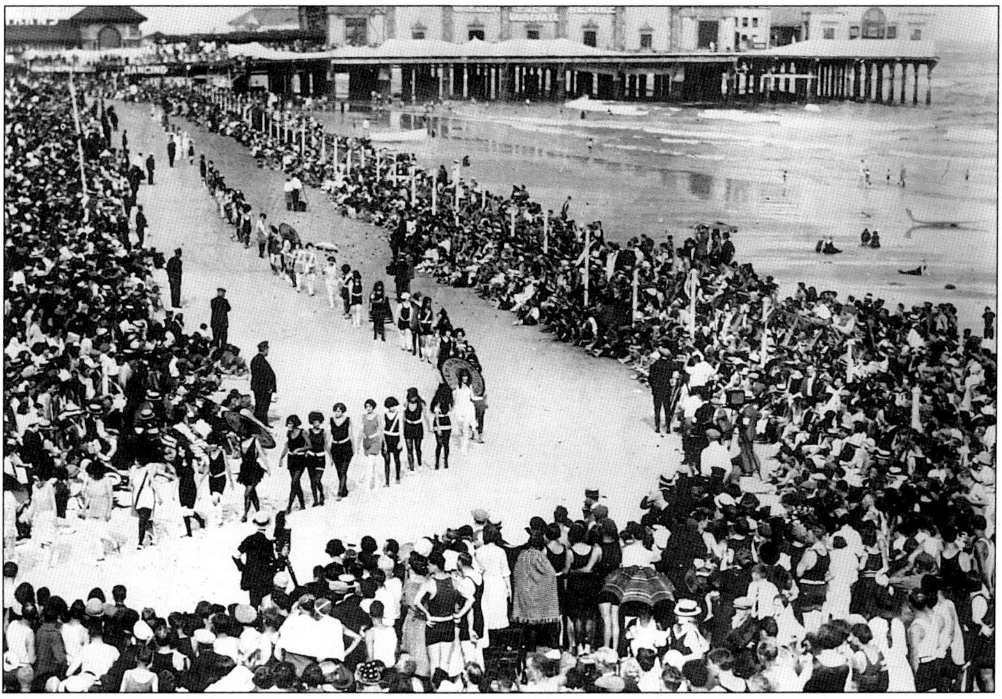

In the second year of the pageant, 57 girls competed for the privilege of posting $5,000 for the Golden Mermaid, which would be given outright to the first young beauty to win it three times. When Mary Campbell of Columbus, Ohio, won in 1922 and 1923, promoters gave her a replica of the trophy and told her never to compete again. This free Boardwalk parade of beauties in 1923 was part of the judging process. The show attracted thousands of spectators. (JTC.)

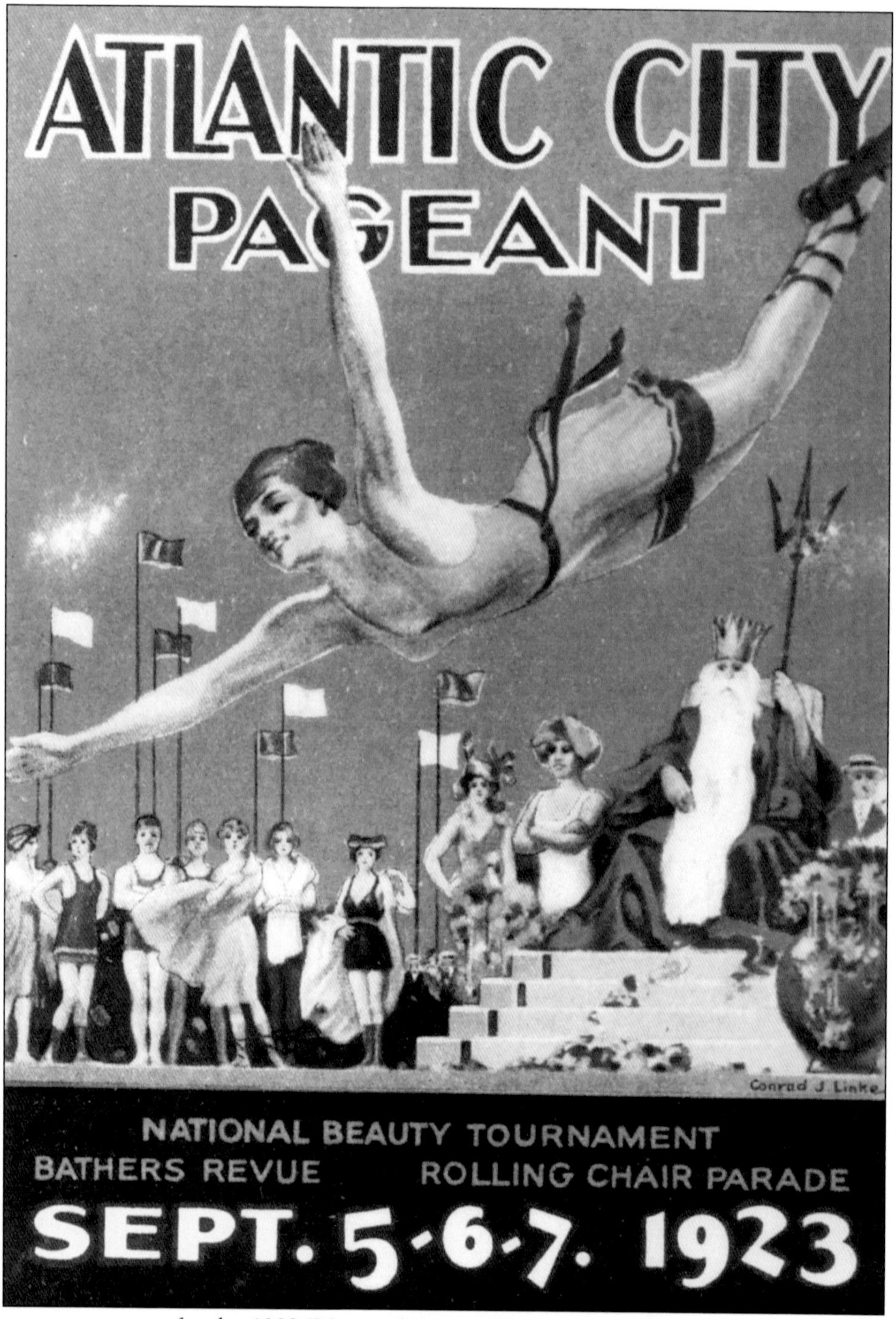

The program cover for the 1923 "National Beauty Tournament" was a bit more flamboyant than the show itself. King Neptune looked on as a presumed contestant dove into the sea. The bathing suits displayed by young women in the background were somewhat advanced for the period. No one cared, since the Atlantic City Pageant was bringing tourists to the resort in droves. (MAO.)

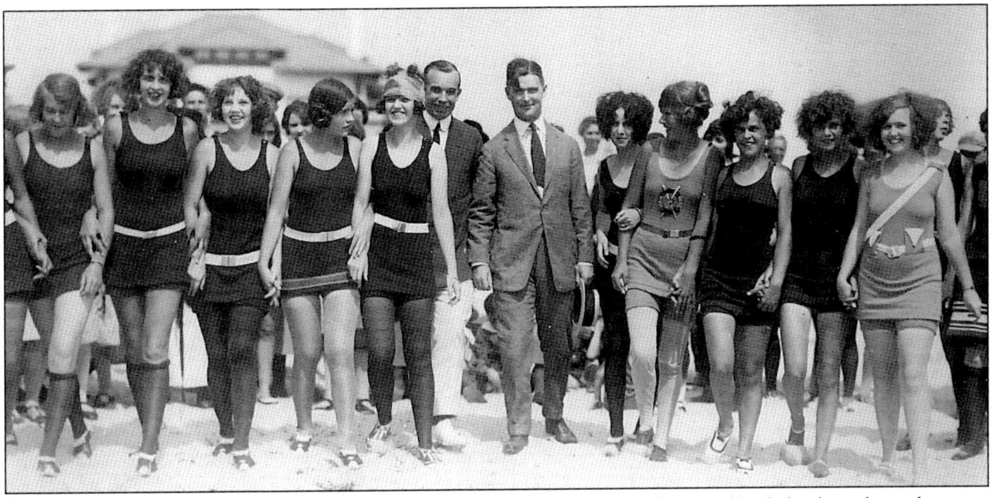

It was far from frolicking, yet it was at least fraternizing when judges walked the beach with some of the 1923 contestants. Forty years later, this would have been considered a grave breach of protocol. When a new and stronger group of promoters took hold in 1940, rules became strict and chaperons were close by when candidates for the crown appeared anywhere in public. (MAO.)

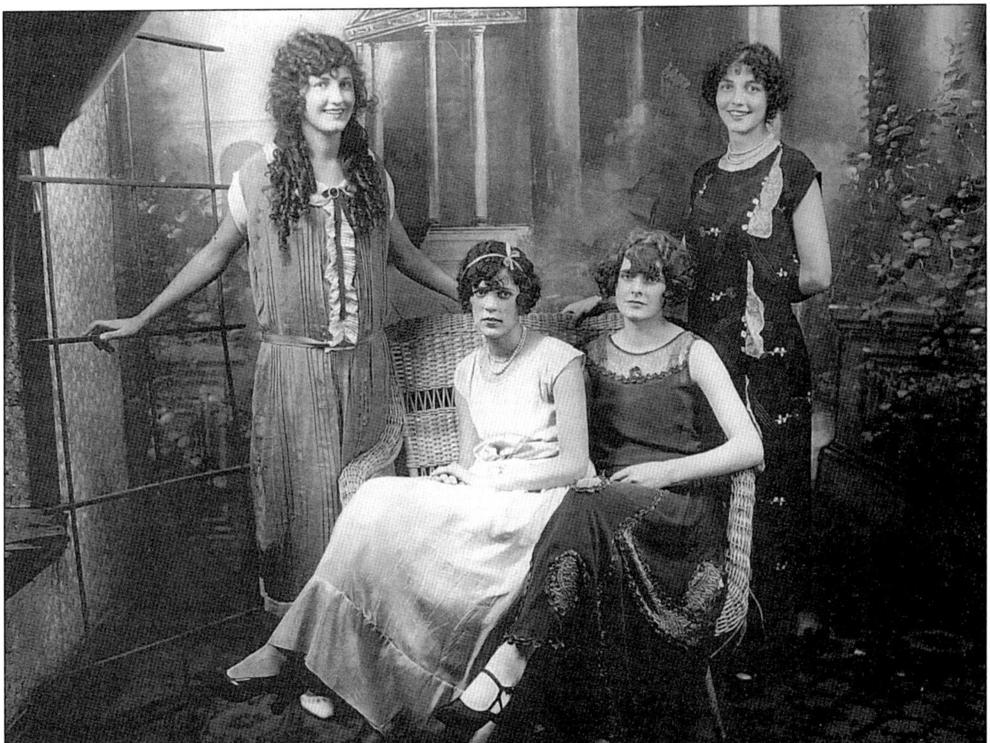

Miss Philadelphia, Ruth Malcolmson, gathered her court of other beauties in 1924 for a photograph after she was chosen Miss America. The setting must have delighted the promoters. Here were several of the nation's most beautiful women sitting in wicker chairs as serenely and as elegantly as if they were West Philadelphian newlyweds meeting for afternoon tea rather than contestants in a national "beauty show." (MAO.)

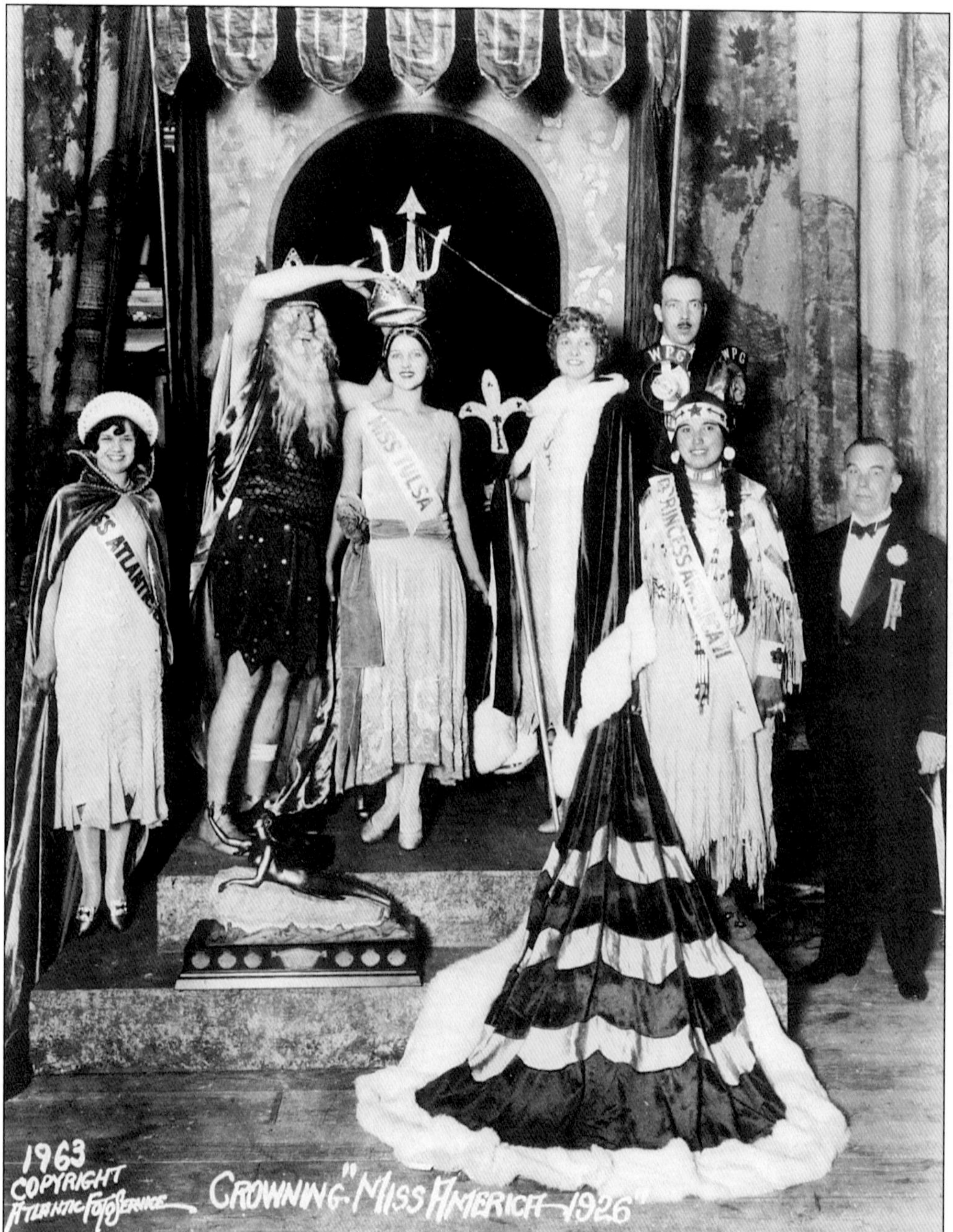

He bore not the slightest resemblance to Bert Parks, who in future days would rule supreme in the crowning of Miss America. But in 1926, King Neptune was acceptable at the coronation. Here, he crowns Norma Smallwood, who took the coveted headpiece back to her home town of Tulsa, Oklahoma. (MAO.)

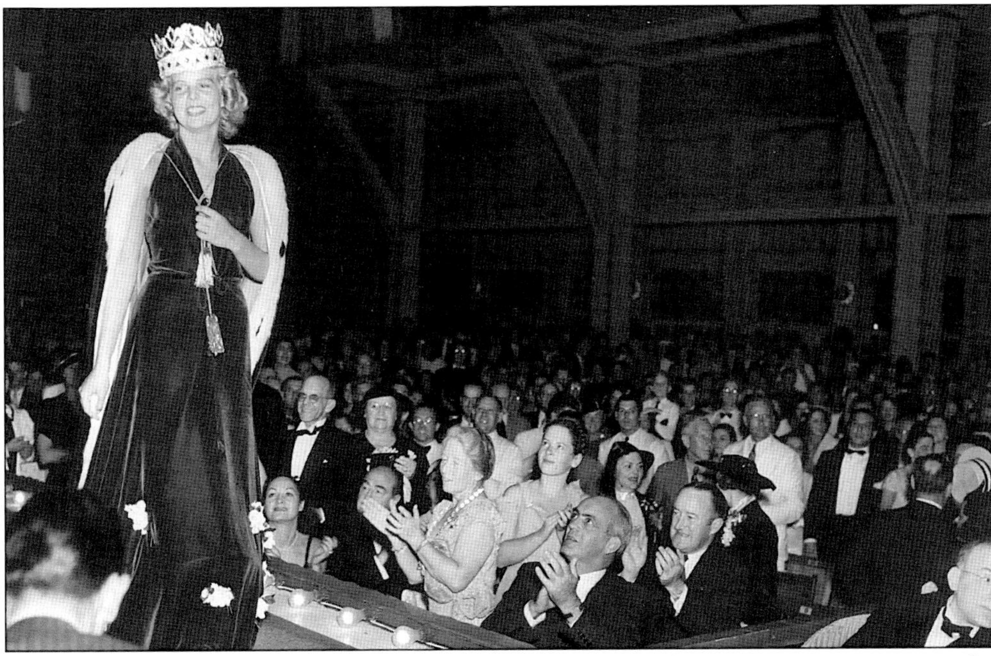

Bette Cooper knew what she wanted in 1937 when she won the Miss America crown, and it was *not* the fame and fortune that went with the title. After this exciting coronation walk, she left Atlantic City in the early morning and went to her home in Hackettstown, New Jersey, refusing to participate in any Miss America activities. Some rules of the pageant were changed to forestall a reoccurrence. (JTC.)

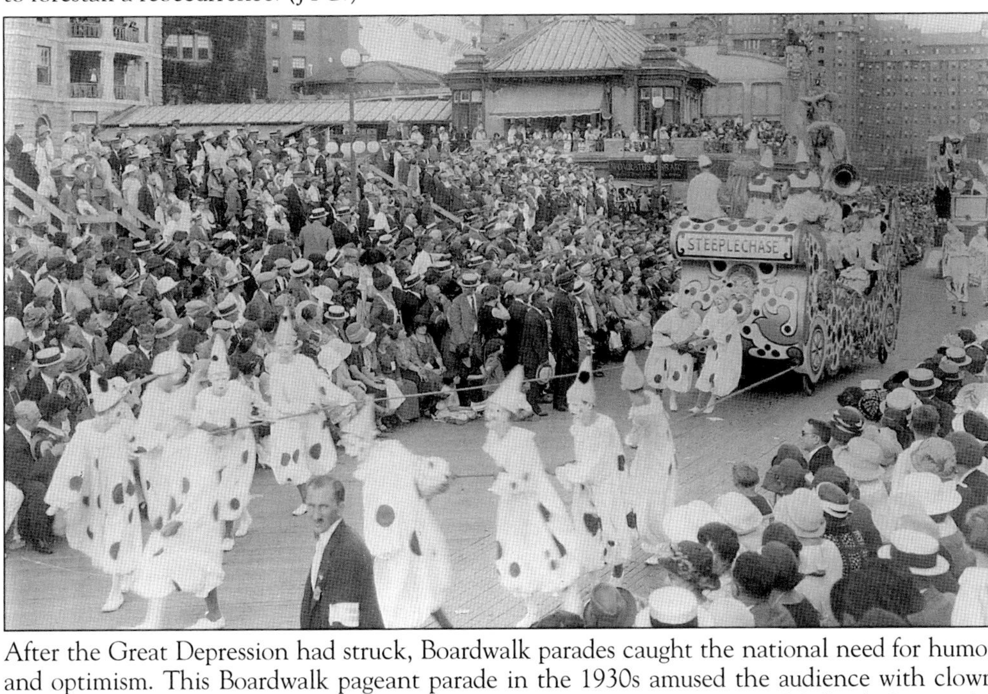

After the Great Depression had struck, Boardwalk parades caught the national need for humor and optimism. This Boardwalk pageant parade in the 1930s amused the audience with clown capers and huge, brilliantly colored floats. The contest, which had endured difficult days in the prosperity of the late 1920s, became increasingly popular after the economy collapsed. (MAO.)

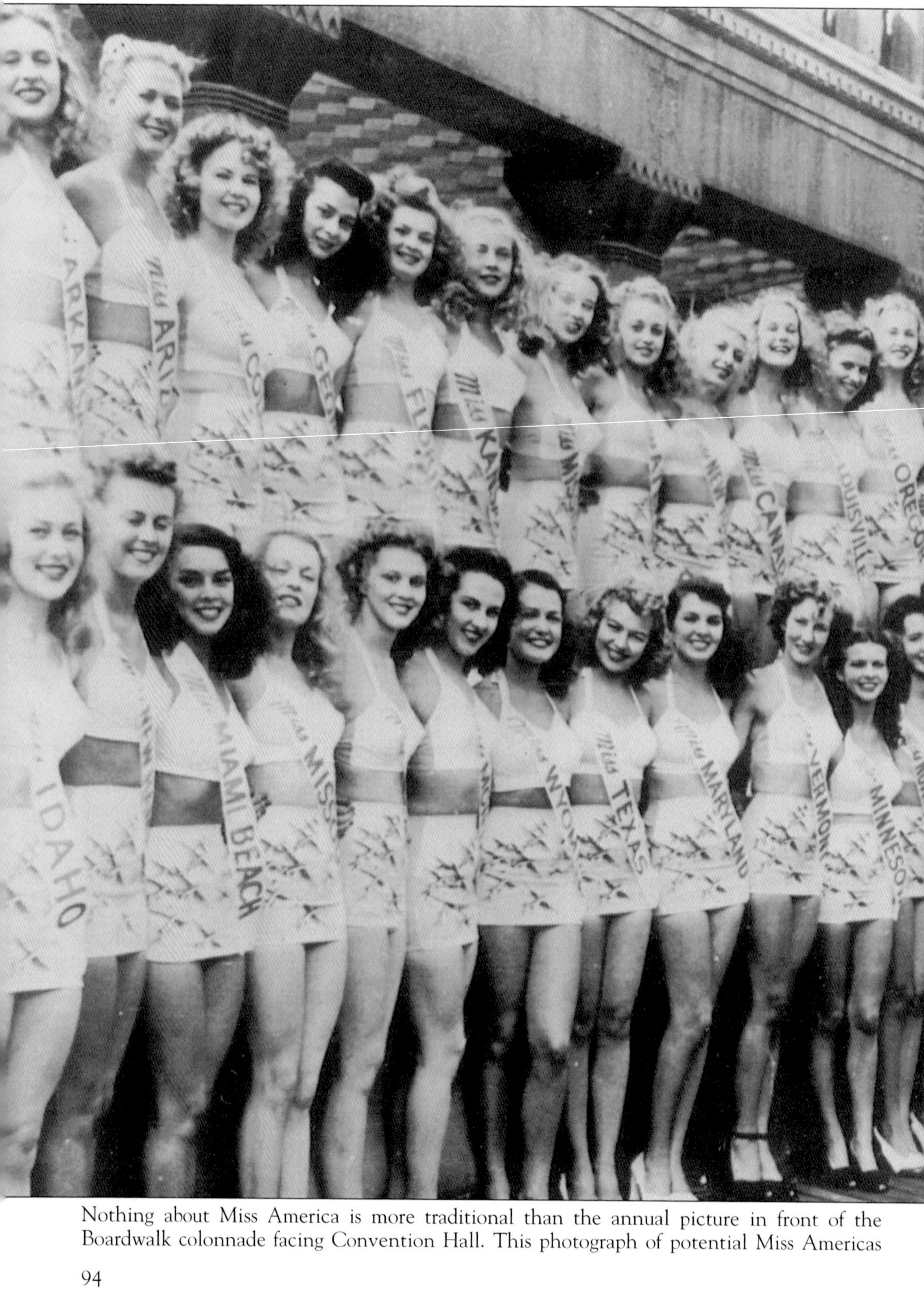

Nothing about Miss America is more traditional than the annual picture in front of the Boardwalk colonnade facing Convention Hall. This photograph of potential Miss Americas

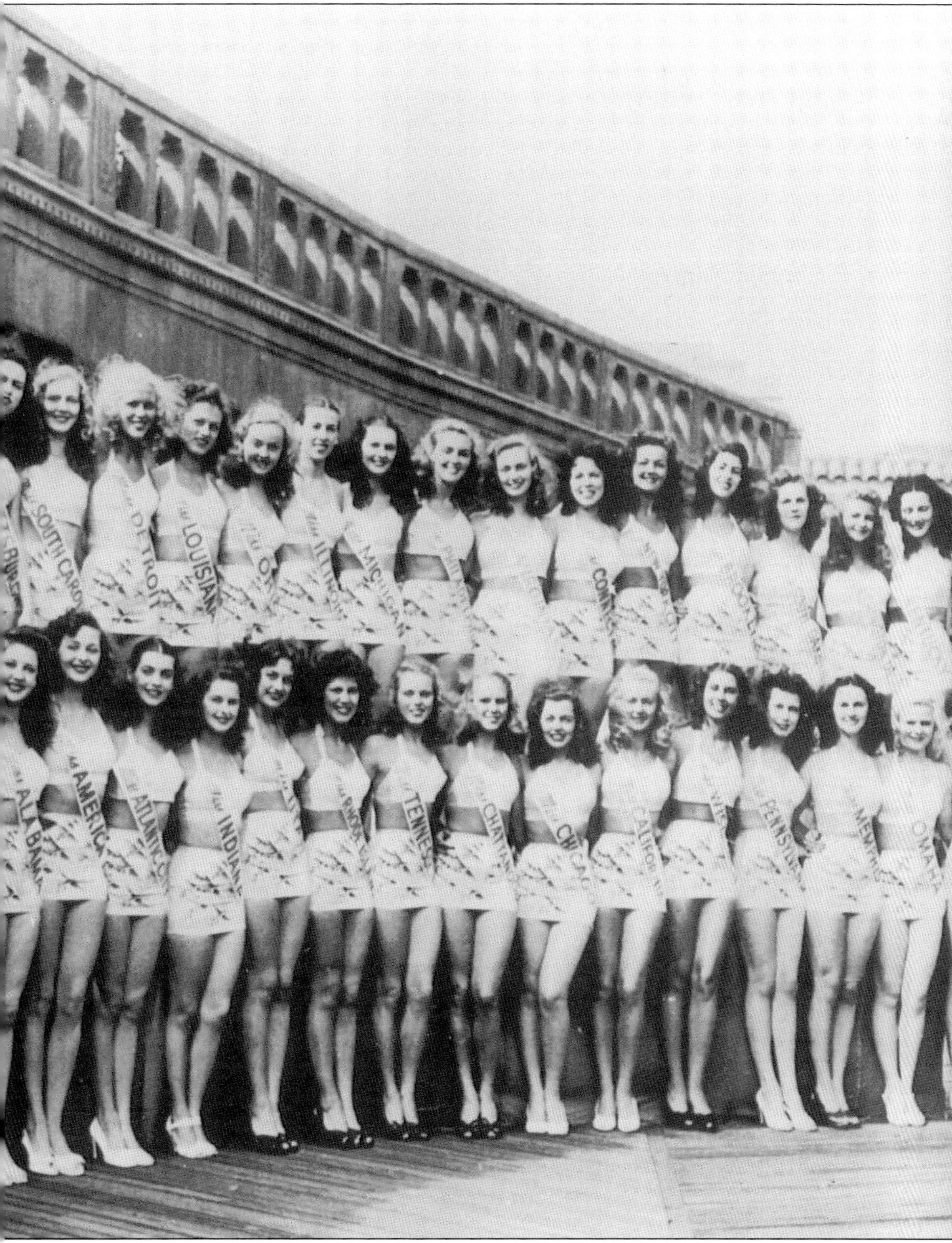

leans more toward body form than the "charm, poise, personality, and talent" that the pageant stresses (MAO.)

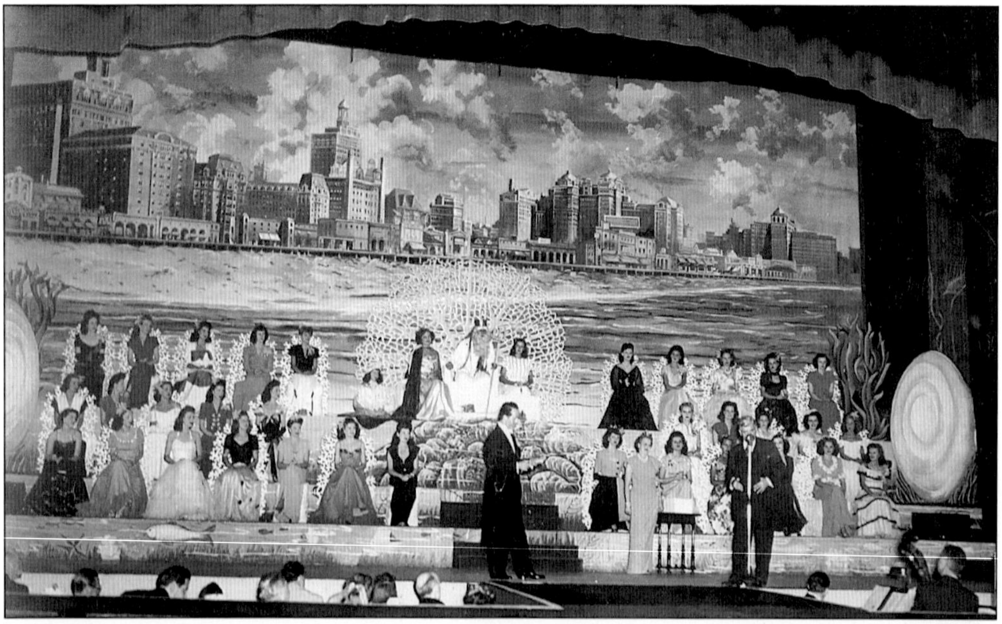

Television created the need for elaborate settings and themes for the Miss America show, as much for the millions watching across the nation as for those present at the coronation. The 1942 contestants performed with a huge backdrop of Atlantic City, above. The 1952 setting, below, lent a patriotic tone to the evening's performance (MAO.)

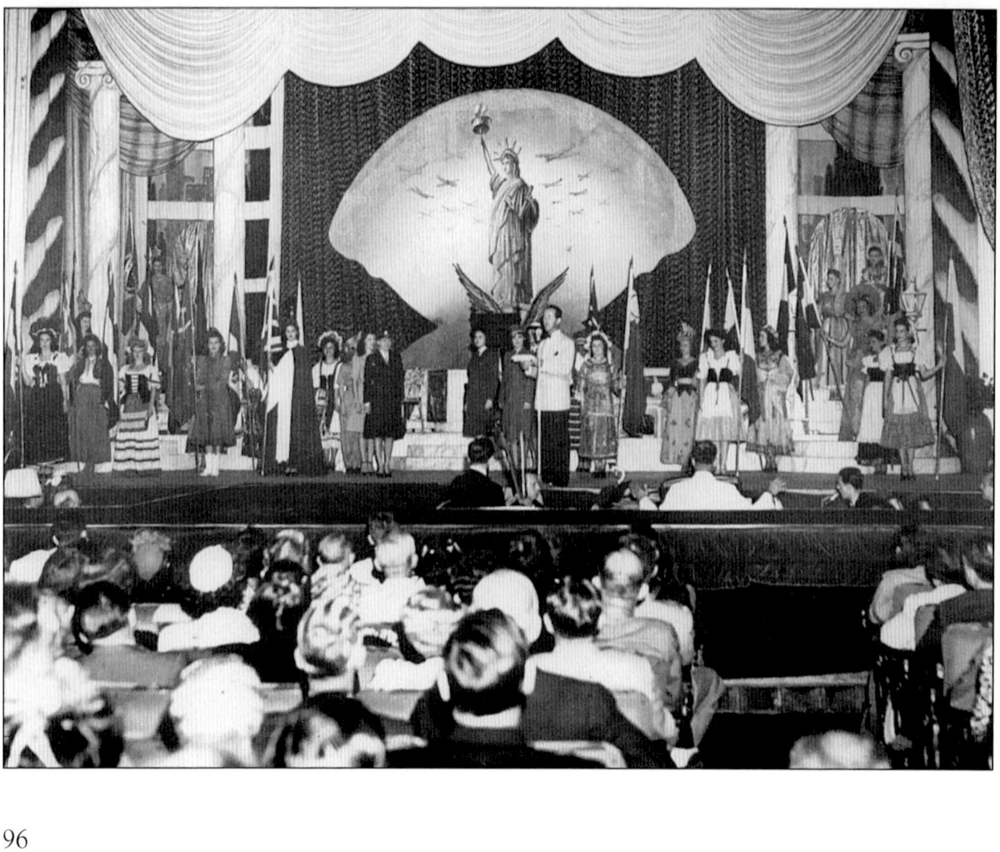

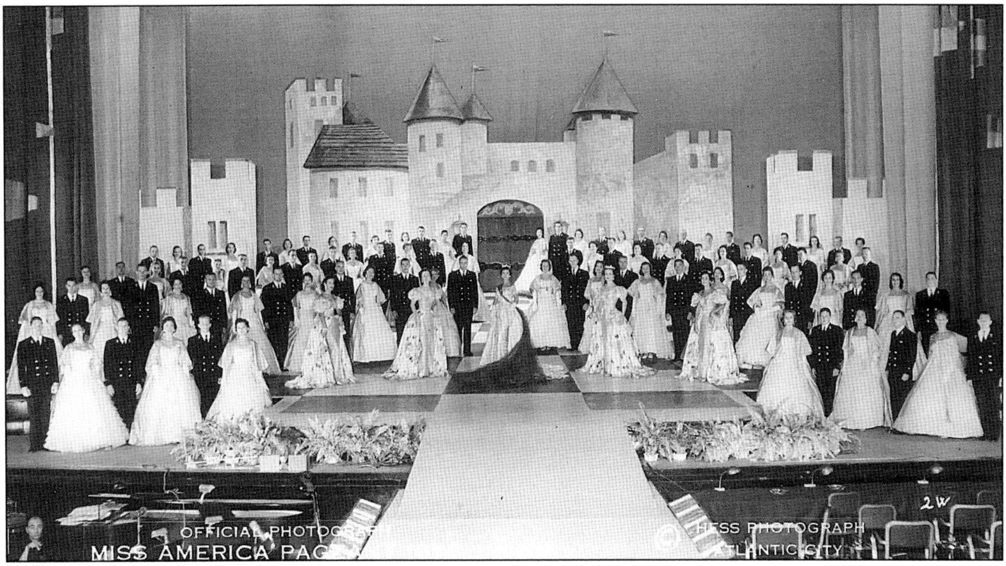

The huge Convention Hall interior comes alive on the night of choosing Miss America. Thousands of people line the side of the runway where the contestants will parade. On stage, above, the hopeful contestants perform whatever singing or dancing program has been written for them. Then, at last, "There She Is!" is performed, as in 1956, below, when Marian McKnight of Manning, South Carolina walked down the runway to greet her Miss America subjects.(MAO.)

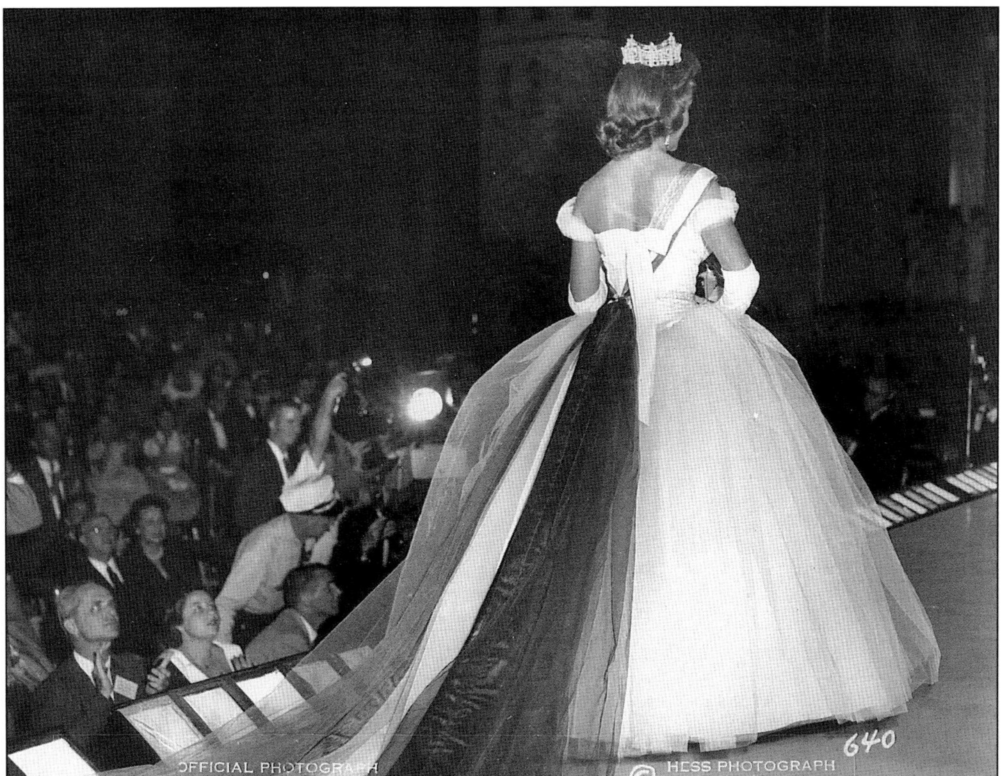

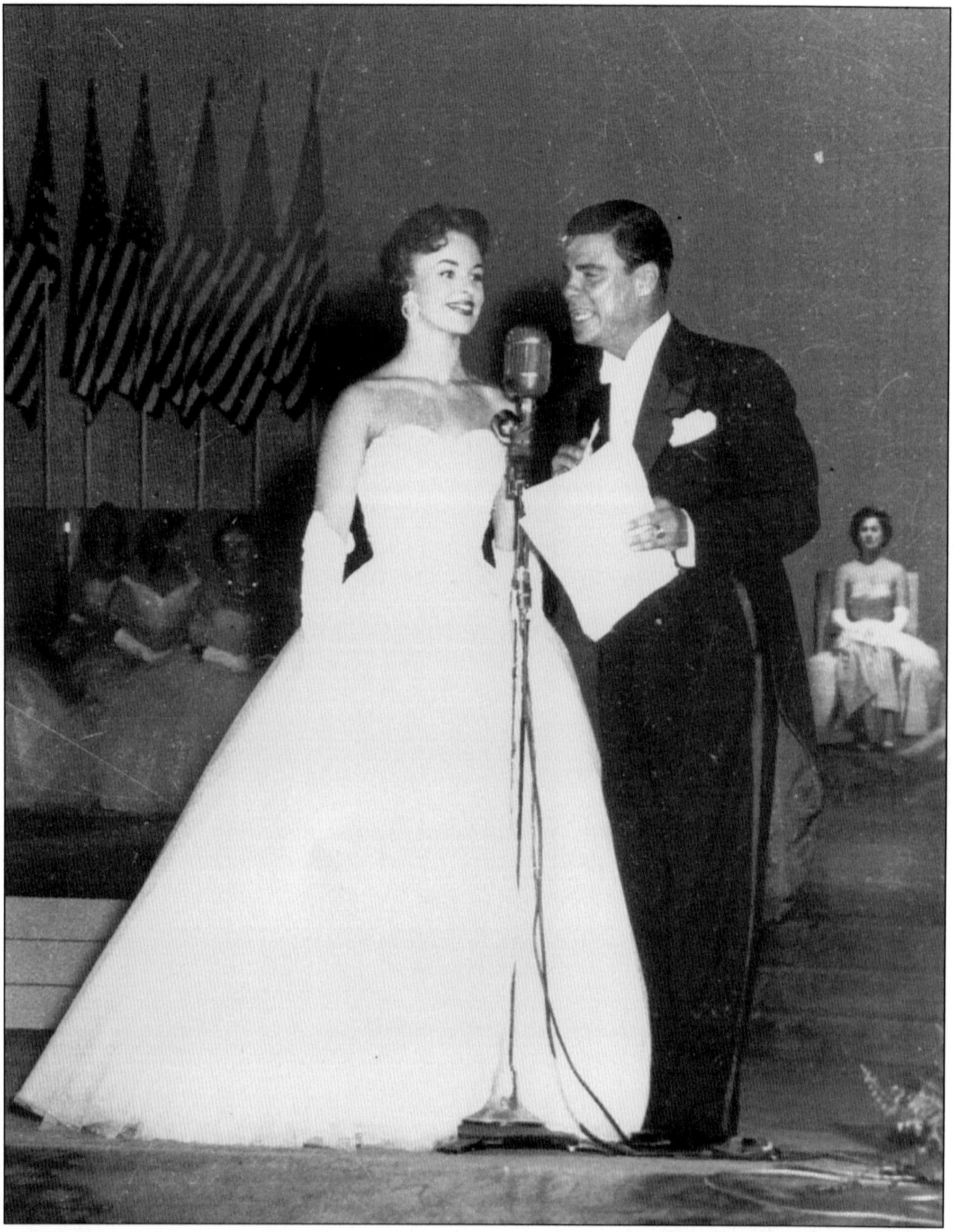

Miss America devotees will continue to insist (at least for a while) that there will never be a master of ceremonies to rival Bert Parks, the host of every show from 1955 to 1980. The song he made famous, "There She Is!" is sung here to Sharon Ritchie of Denver, Colorado, the 1956 Miss America. (MAO.)

Eight

Beyond the Boardwalk

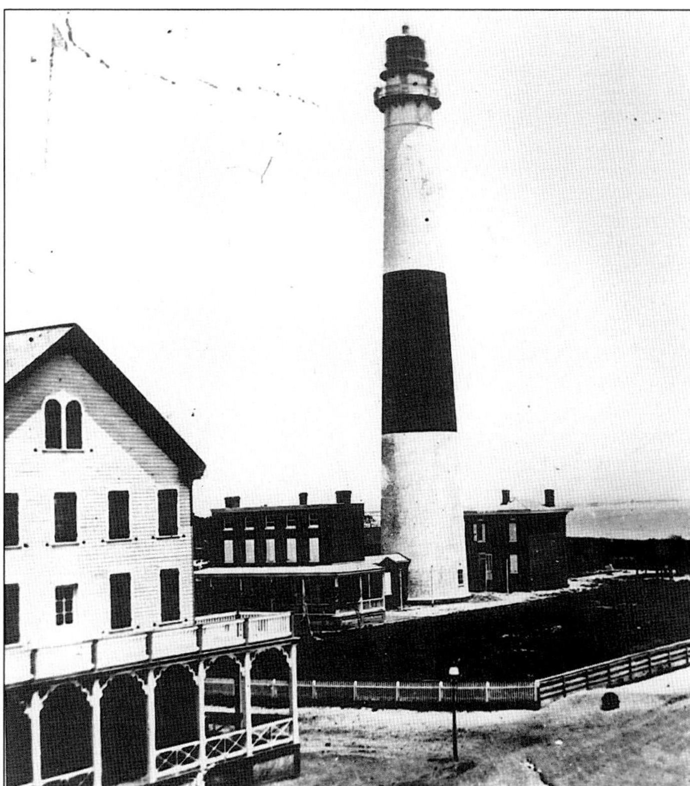

Absecon Lighthouse and its keeper's quarters, shown in 1868, were built in the city's Inlet neighborhood one year before. The lighthouse is the only remaining Atlantic City landmark dating from the city's earliest days. Thanks to the shifting sands of time, it now sits several hundred feet further from the water than when it opened. Originally painted orange and black, the lighthouse was completely restored in 1998–99 and stands as a reminder of all that Atlantic City has experienced since its founding. (ACFPL.)

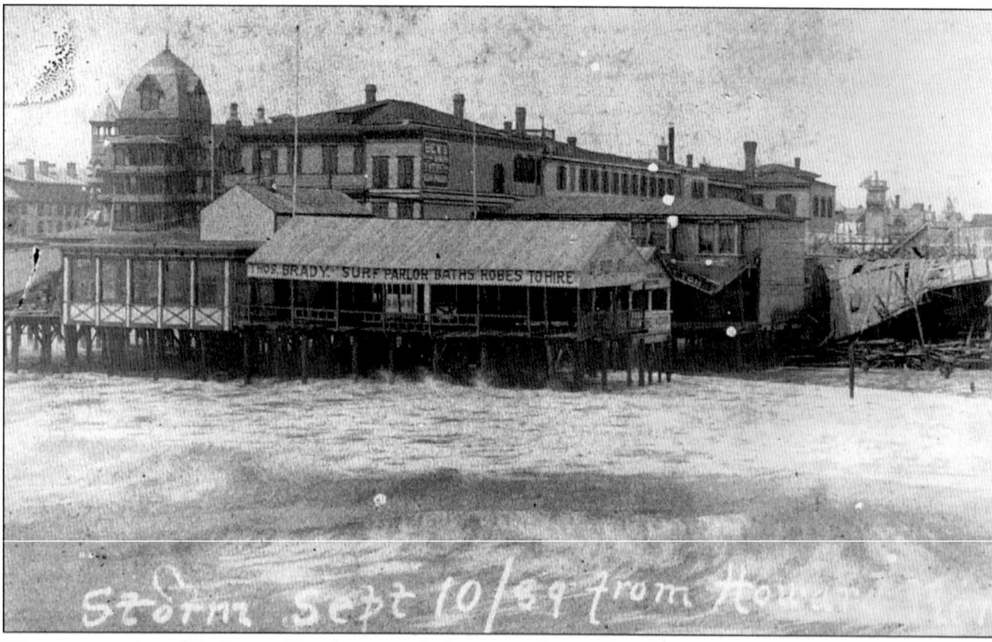

Water was one of Atlantic City's natural enemies. Once development had removed the barrier dunes, the city suffered through every storm, including the hurricane of September 1889. The hurricane ravaged the business district, inundating avenues running to the beach and destroying the city's second Boardwalk, including Brady's Baths, above. (ACFPL.)

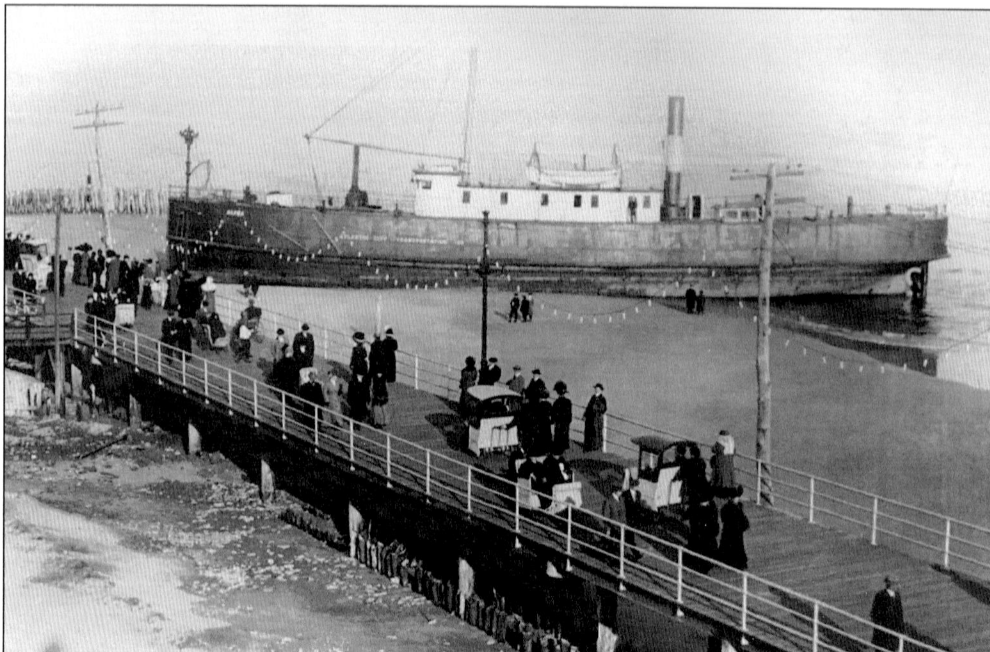

A 1910 storm stranded the *Alpha*, above, within feet of the Boardwalk, where it became a free Atlantic City attraction. When the brig *Strandet* was beached in the 19th century, its captain had charged admission to tour the wreck. Not until the city began dune restoration in the 1970s did flooding abate to any degree. (ACFPL.)

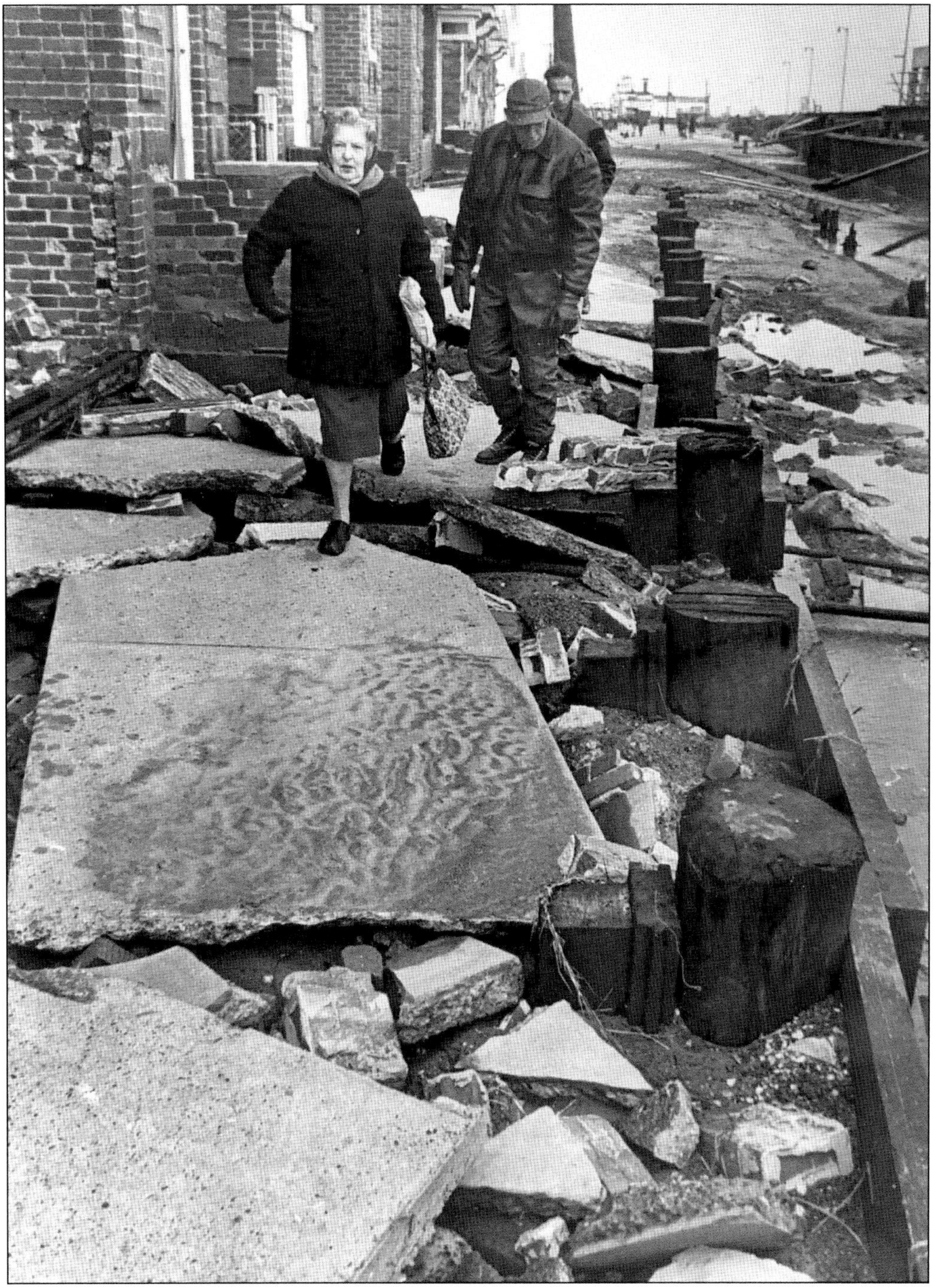

The September 14, 1944 hurricane wrecked Heinz's Pier and removed a section of Steel Pier. Then, in March 1962, a "nor'easter" tore up blocks of sidewalks and streets, submerging almost every ground-floor establishment in Atlantic City in water and sand. The city needed more than a year to clean up and repair the damage. The storm destroyed more of the city than another storm in March 1984 and Hurricane Gloria on September 26, 1985. (ACFPL.)

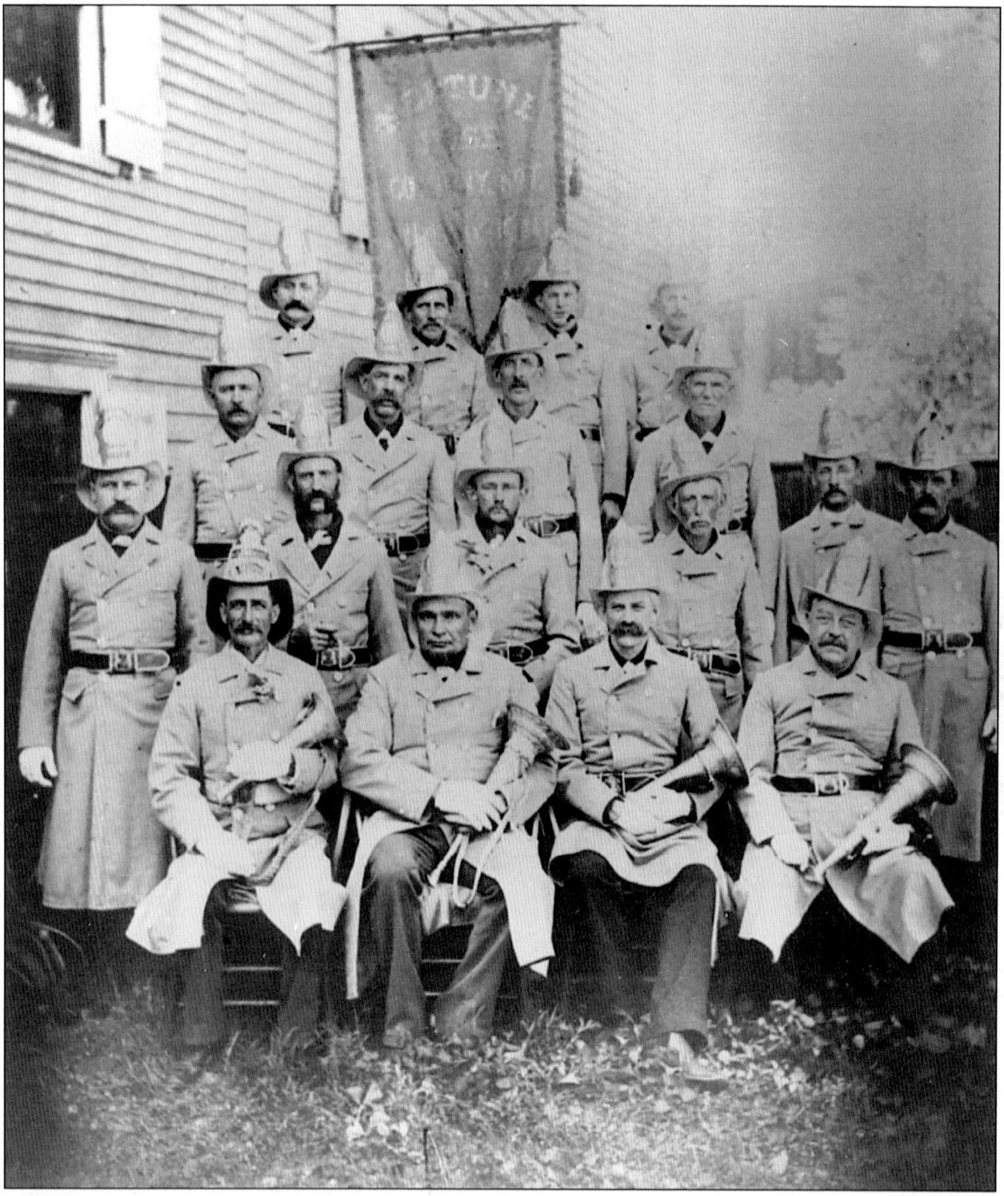

If water was one enemy, fire was another in a city built entirely of wood. Fire brigades soon organized, and the Neptune Hose Company, seen above in 1897, was one of the city's oldest, having been founded in 1882. When they were not sharpening their musical skills, the members fought flames at establishments that subscribed to the company's services. Atlantic City consolidated all its volunteer fire companies into one public department in 1904. (ACFPL.)

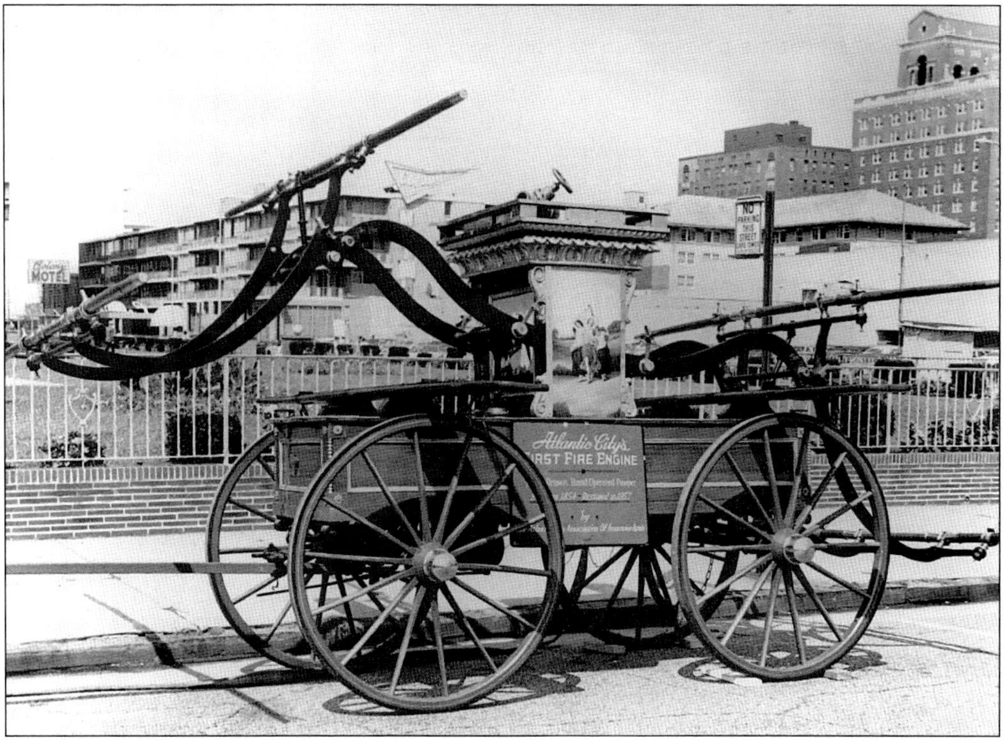

Atlantic City acquired its first fire engine in 1857. The horse-drawn, hand-operated pumper, seen above in 1965, was restored by the Atlantic City Association of Insurance Agents in 1957 for promotional use in city parades. By 1910, the city boasted a steam pumper, below, but still relied on horses to pull the apparatus to this fire, which was across the street from the Hotel de Ville, a leading establishment of its day. (ACFPL.)

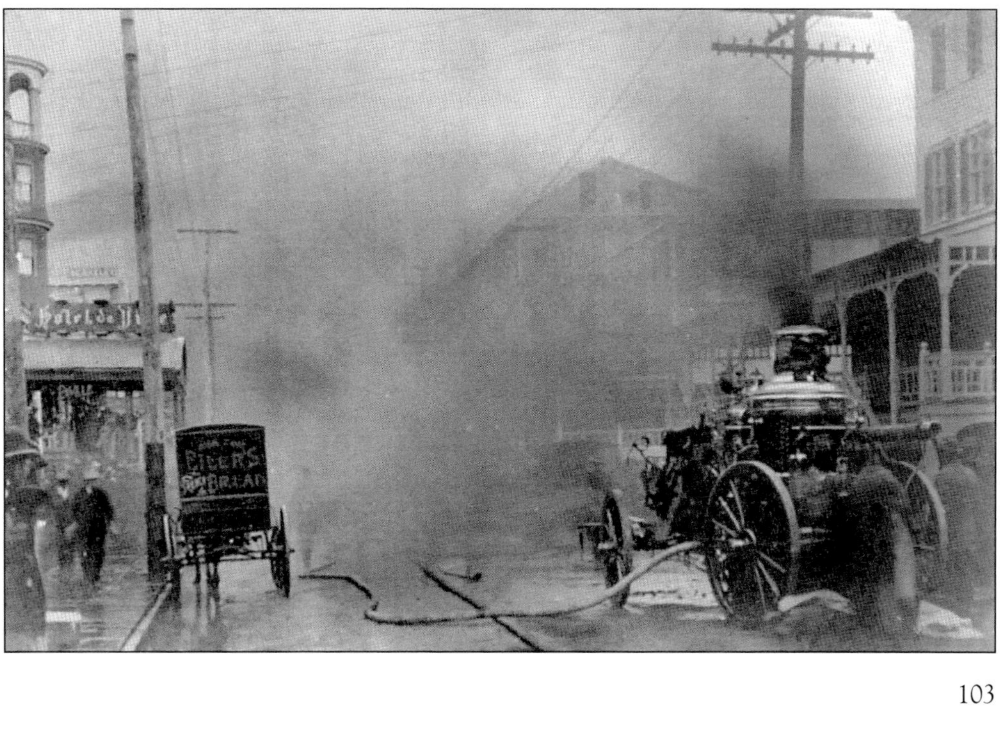

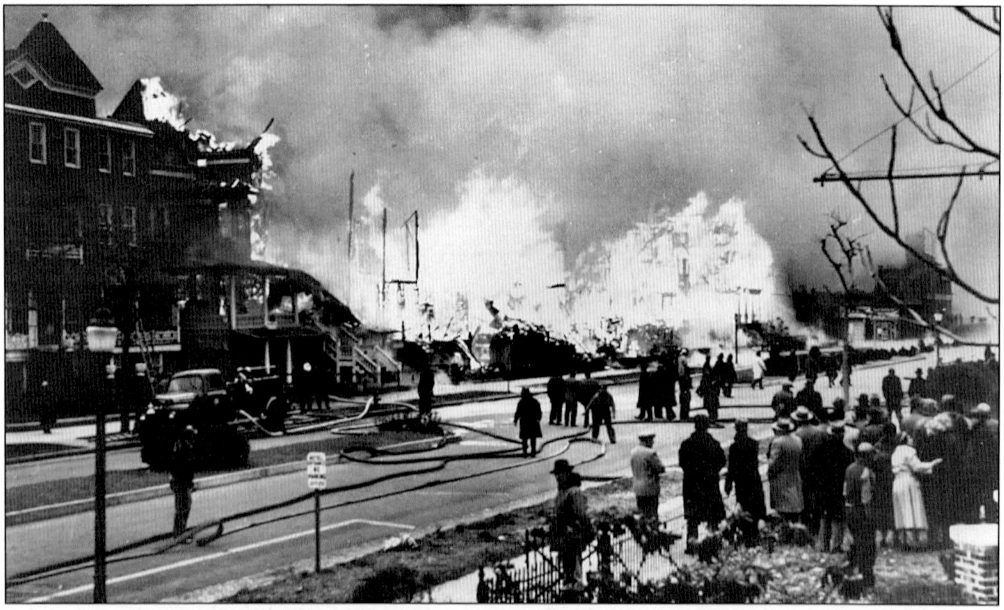

During the Congress Hotel fire of January 7, 1952, more than 40 pieces of modern equipment could not save the blocks bounded by the Boardwalk, St. Charles Place, States Avenue, and New Jersey Avenue. Some 400 firefighters from 17 municipalities battled freezing temperatures to stop its spread, shown above. Winds gusting more than 40 miles per hour lofted flaming debris across streets and spread the fire to smaller buildings, below. (ACFPL.)

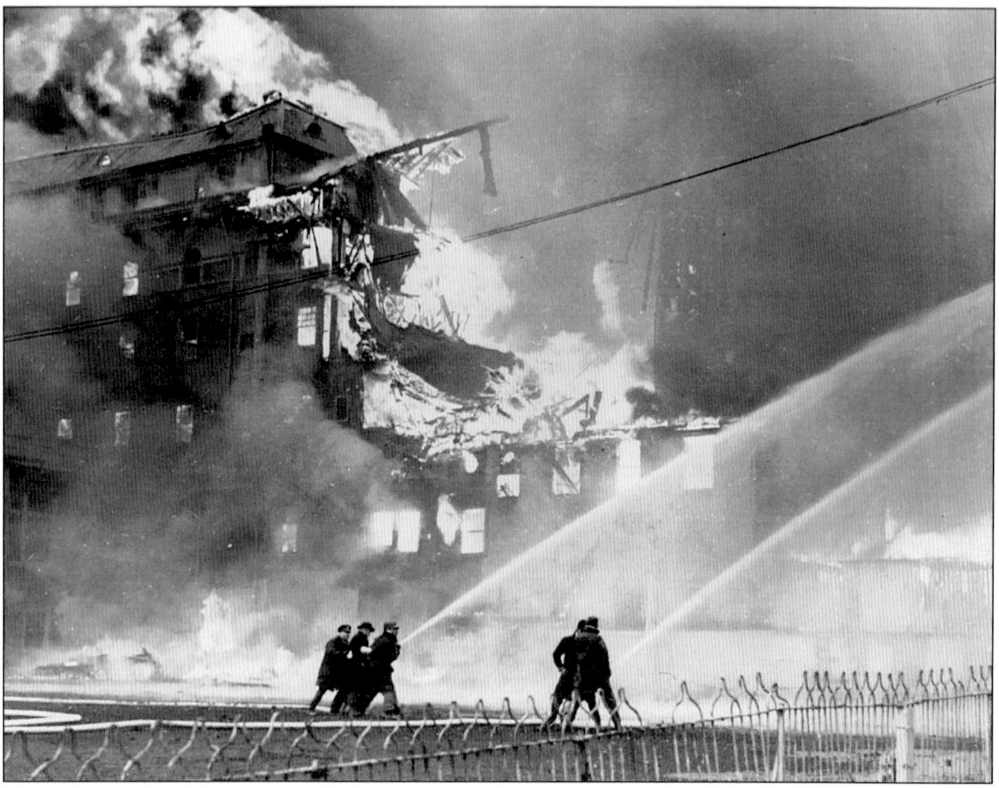

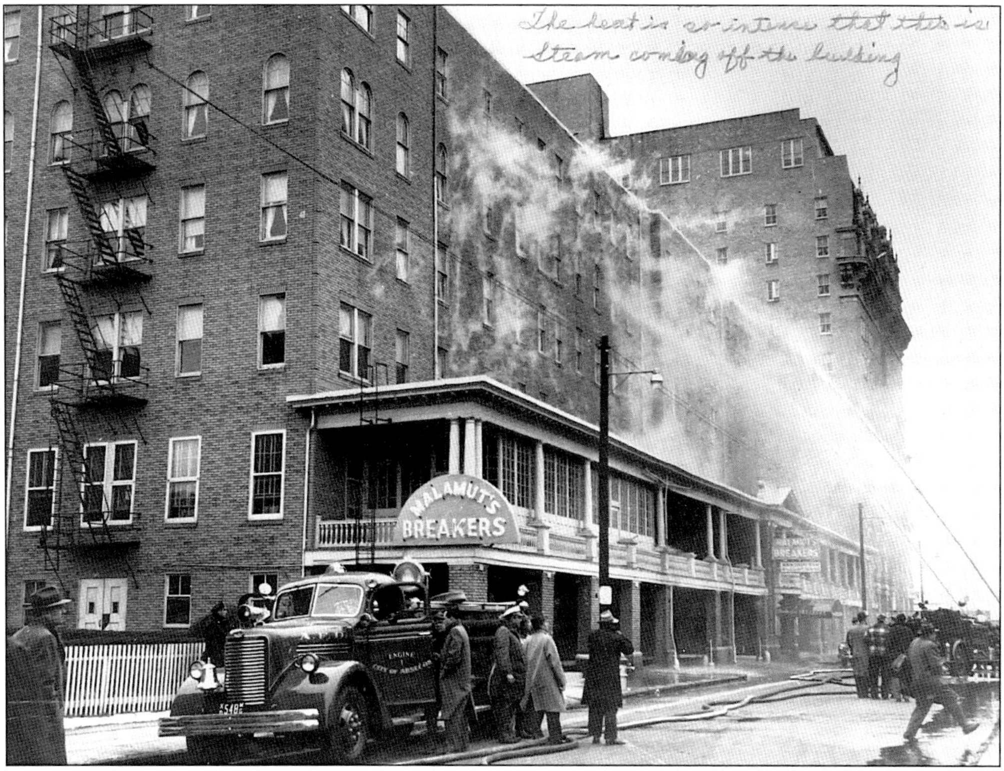

The intense heat set other buildings afire. Firefighters saved the Breakers Hotel, above, by cooling it with their hoses; the hot bricks turned the water into steam. No one died in the fire, as businesses were closed for the season. However, the fire consumed four hotels, the Globe Theater, three stores, a fire truck, and 10 guesthouses, seen below. Twelve other buildings also suffered damage. (ACFPL.)

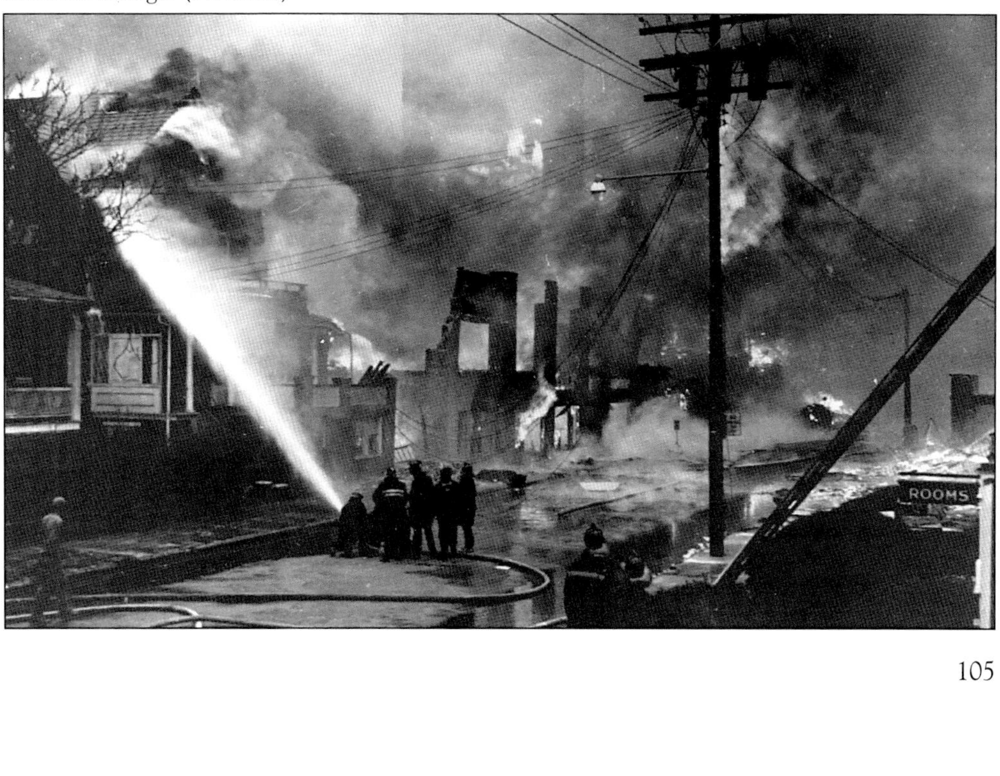

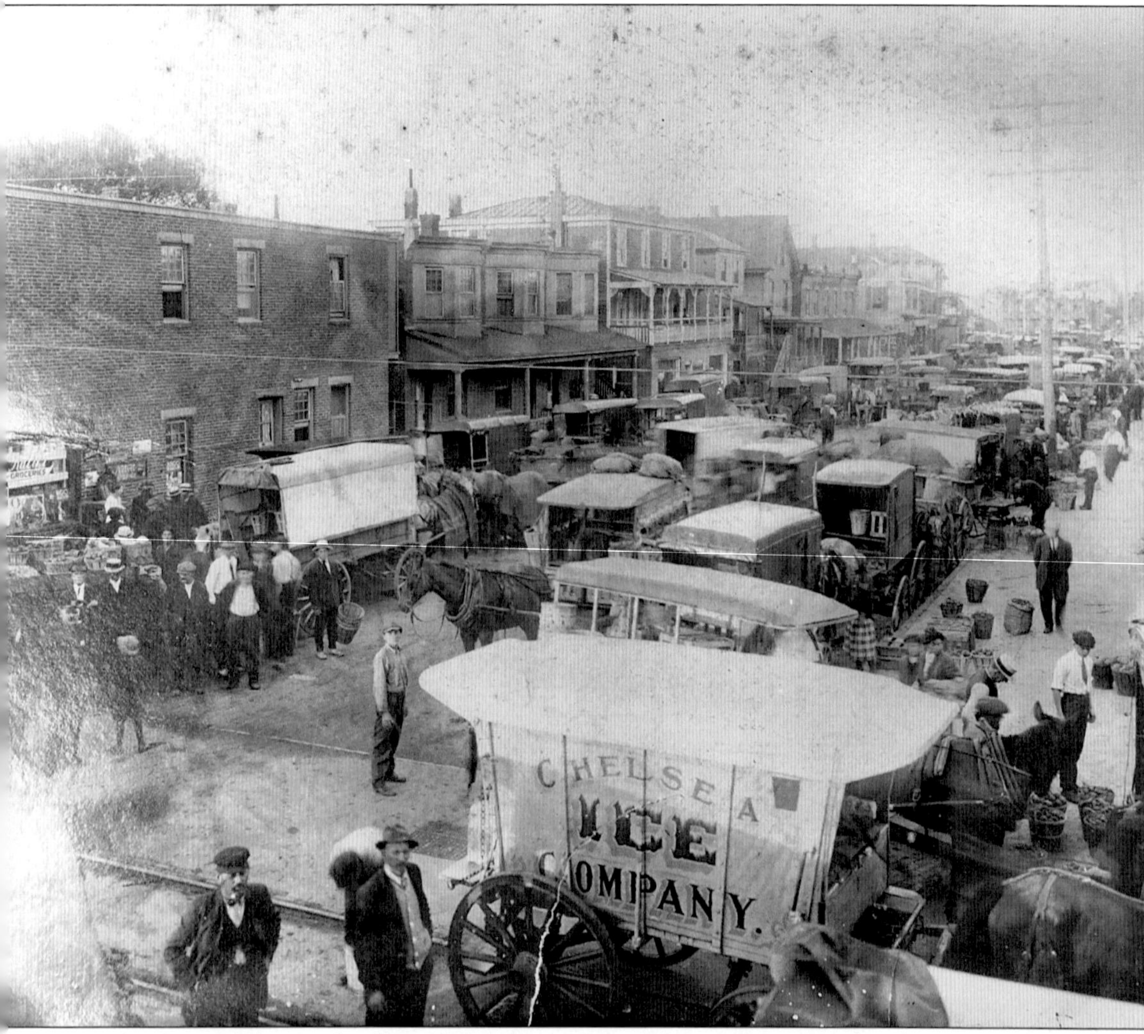

The farms of the Garden State fed Atlantic City and its visitors. For decades, all meat, milk, grain, and produce crossed the bay via the railroad. These goods were carted for sale to the open-air market, seen above in 1876. Atlantic City imported everything from the mainland. Even drinking water was brought in until city engineers discovered the Pinelands aquifer 1,500 feet beneath the sand. (ACFPL.)

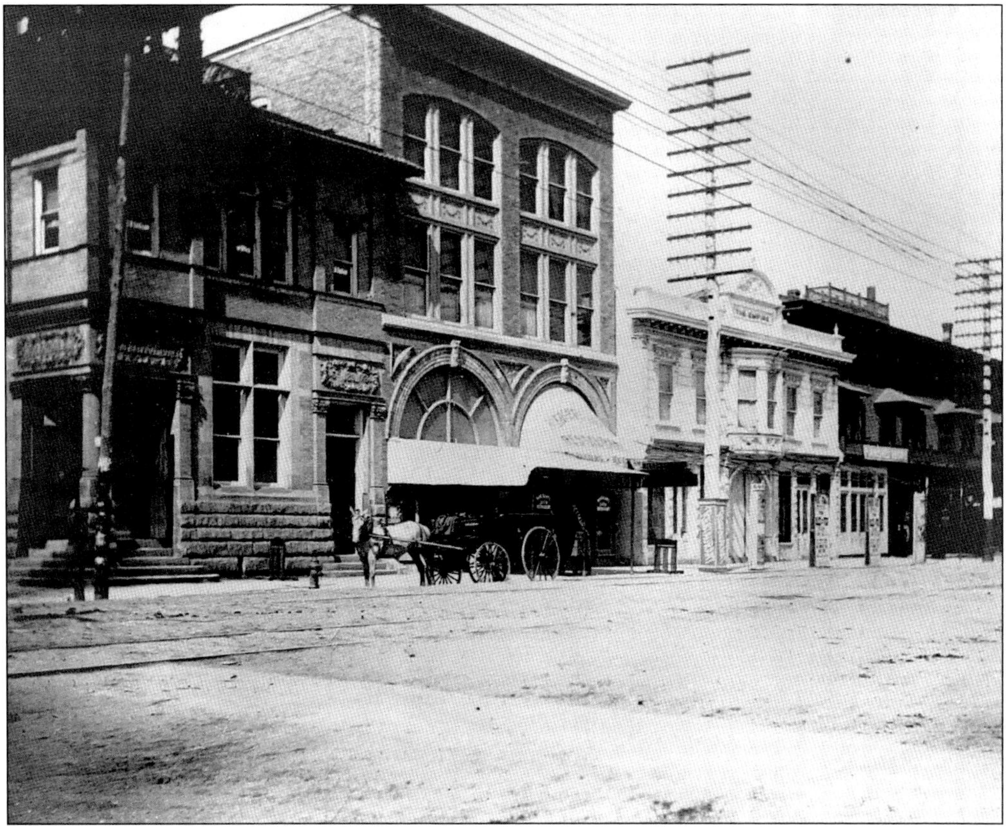

The city's streets were made of sand well into the 20th century, even after electrical and telephone lines had made inroads by 1900, above. Horses and carriages, like this one outside a restaurant near the intersection of New Jersey and Atlantic Avenues, kept the pace of Atlantic City manageable for decades. (ACFPL.)

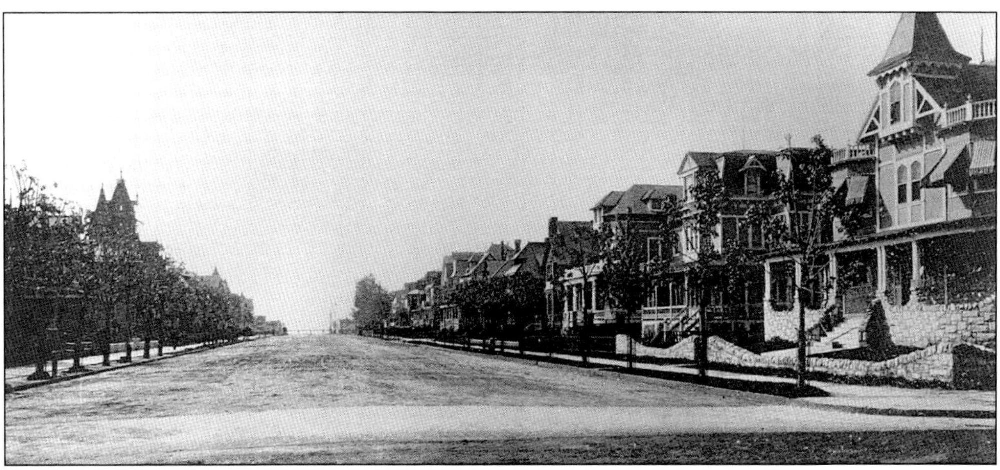

Atlantic City gloried in its grand Victorian cottages and tree-lined boulevards. As late as 1920, States Avenue, above, stretched past columned porches to the ocean, with the Boardwalk barely visible in the distance. However, development in the 20th century converted the cottages into rooming houses. The streets were narrowed and the trees removed. (ACFPL.)

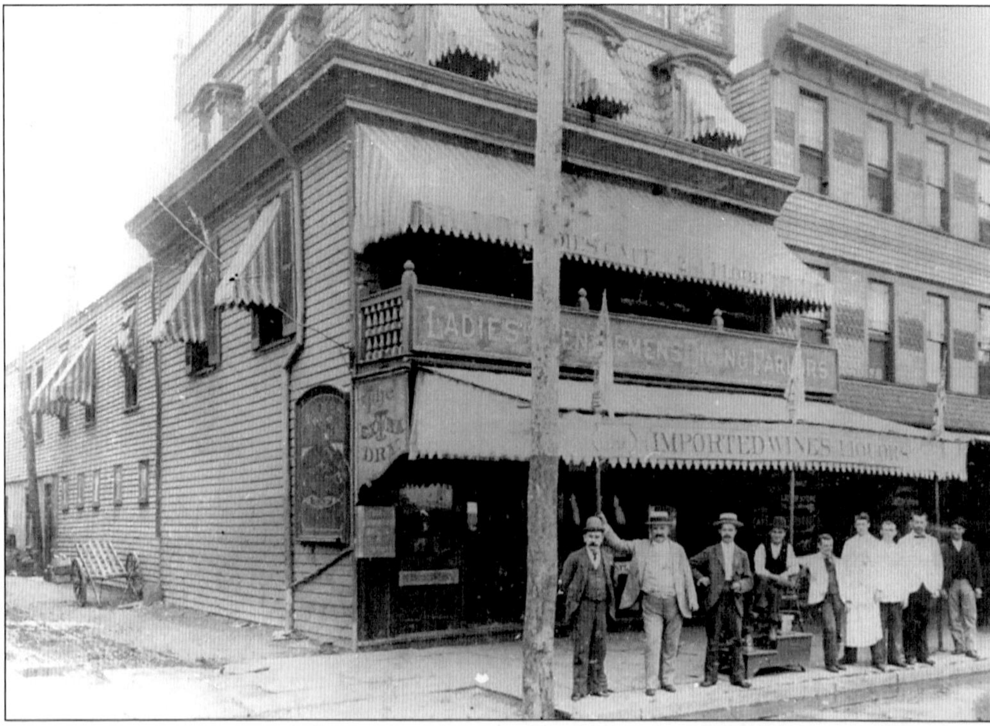

Restaurants were a major Atlantic City business. In 1900, the Extra Dry restaurant, above, advertised its imported wines, liquors, and dining parlors for men and women. Such parlors were an important consideration in a time when a woman risked her reputation if she walked the streets unescorted or dined alone. (ACFPL.)

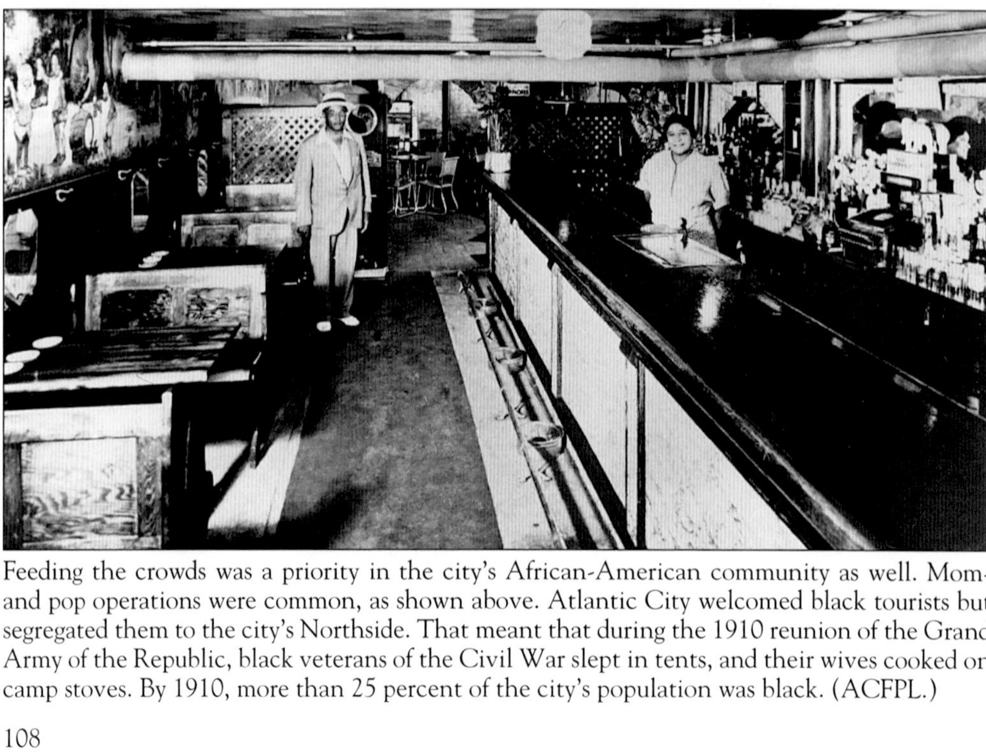

Feeding the crowds was a priority in the city's African-American community as well. Mom-and pop operations were common, as shown above. Atlantic City welcomed black tourists but segregated them to the city's Northside. That meant that during the 1910 reunion of the Grand Army of the Republic, black veterans of the Civil War slept in tents, and their wives cooked on camp stoves. By 1910, more than 25 percent of the city's population was black. (ACFPL.)

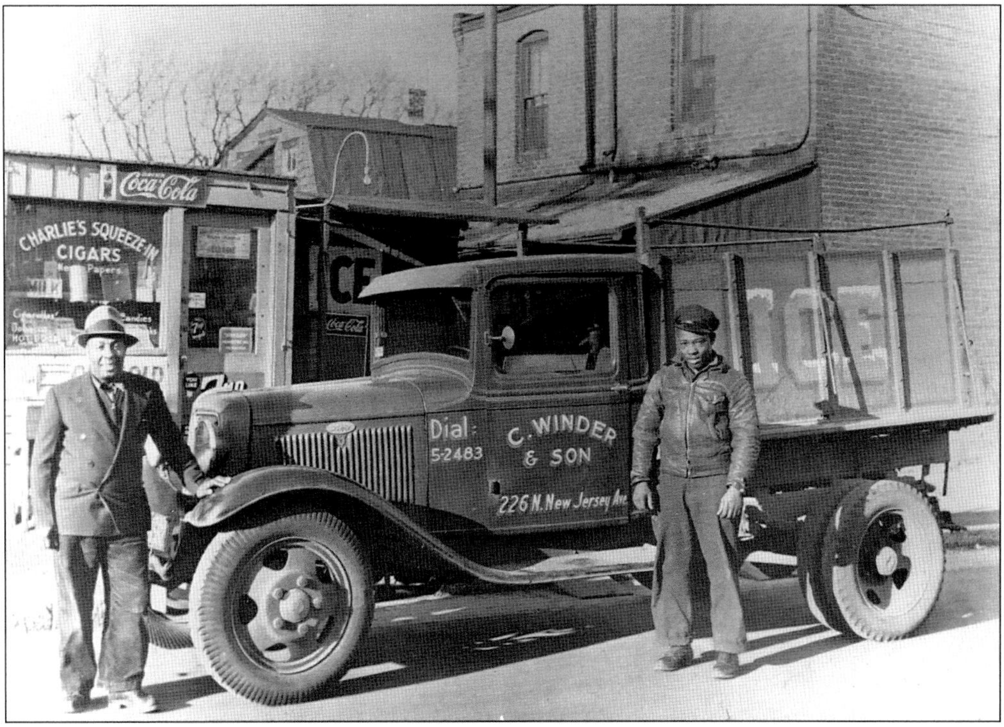

The ice business was lucrative in Atlantic City, where the political leaders had declared that was a "wide-open town" well before Prohibition. C. Winder & Son had a well-known Northside delivery service. However, by the time this photograph was taken in the 1930s, the concession had been sold to a Mr. Perry, above left. (ACFPL.)

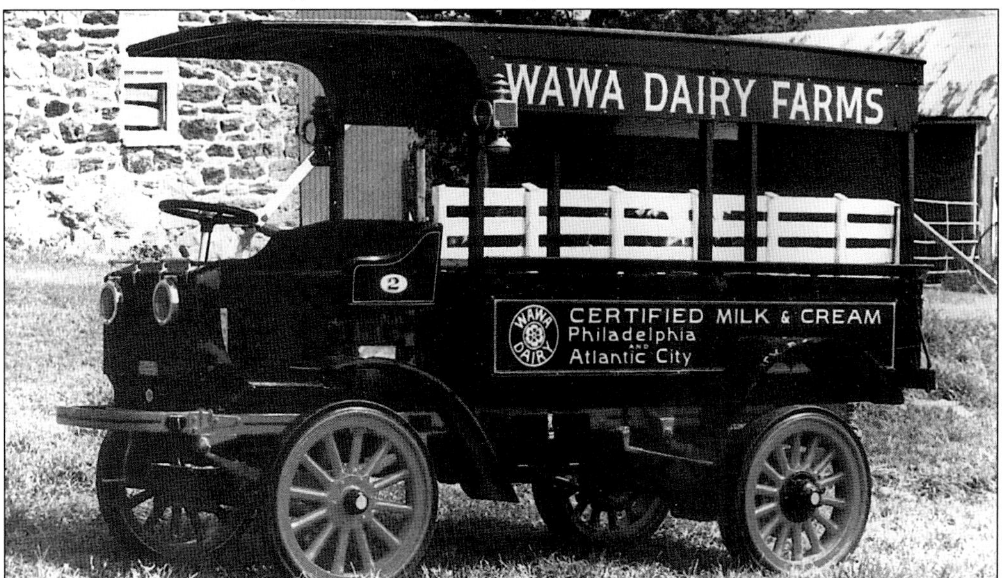

Daily milk delivery followed Philadelphians from home to Atlantic City. Milk wagons and later trucks, above in 1923, of the Wawa Dairy Farms were local institutions that supermarkets and convenience stores displaced in the 1950s. (ACFPL.)

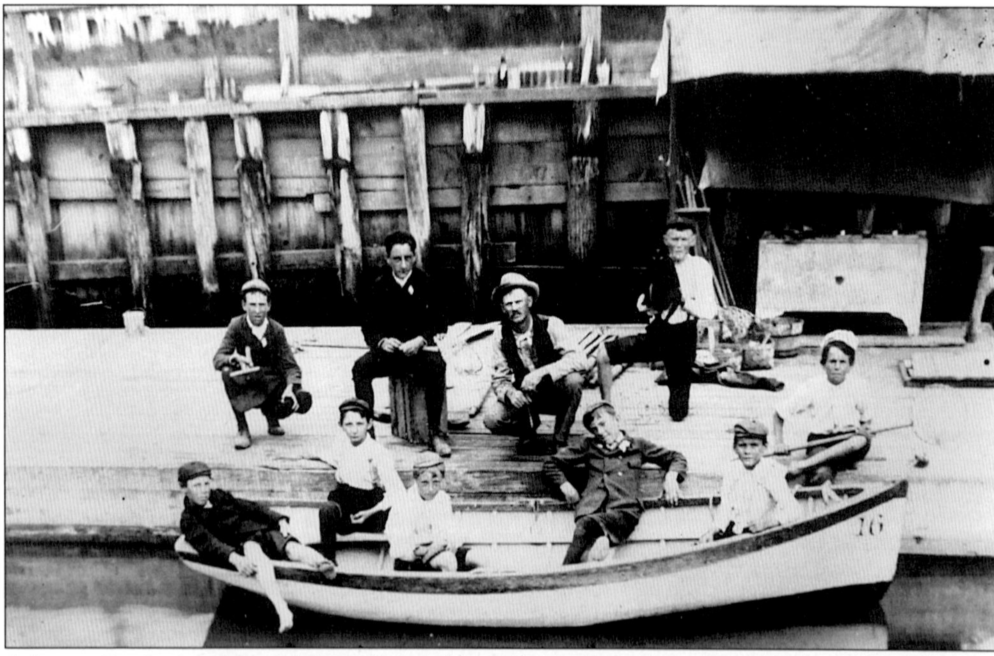

Atlantic City's commercial fishing fleet fed the palates of eastern cities and supplied fare to local establishments. The fleet was headquartered in the marinas of the Northside and Inlet sections, among them the Fenton and Leeds docks, seen above in 1890. Another dock at Gardner's Basin now houses the New Jersey State Marina. (ACFPL.)

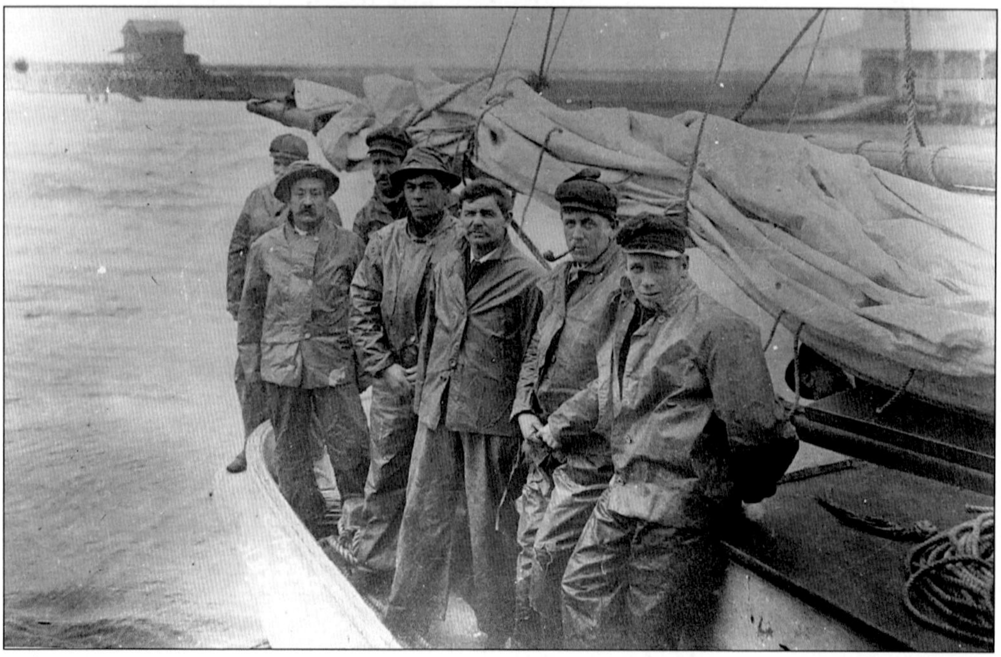

Fishing was and remains one of the most dangerous of occupations. To bring in their catch in 1906, the fishermen of the *Alberta*, above, prepared for the worst that the sea and sky could deliver in a time before weather forecasting. Little is left of the commercial fleet now, but Atlantic City retains a sizable sport-fishing fleet. (ACFPL.)

The best of the fleet's haul made it to the tables of the city's restaurants. The Knife and Fork, still in business today, was one of Atlantic City's famous eateries. Another, now gone, was Captain Starn's on the inlet. In 1955, the captain himself, center right, posed with waitresses in the restaurant's "dry-docked" boat for a promotional photograph. (ACFPL.)

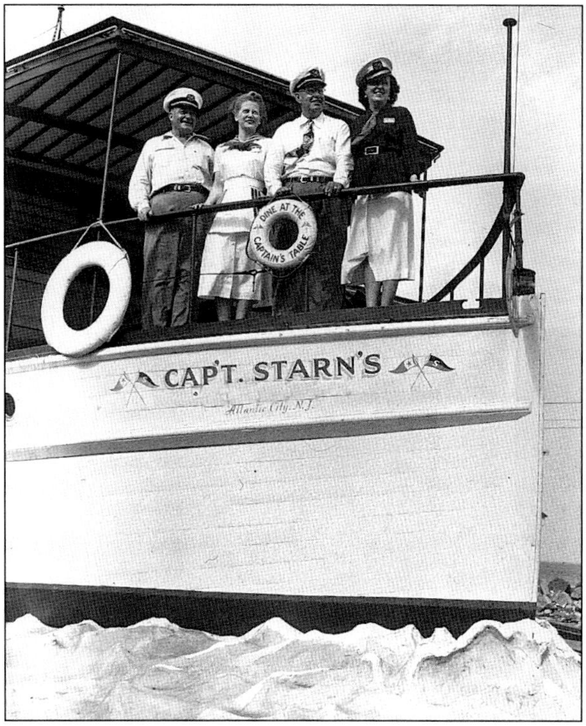

Captain Starn's major competitor was Hackney's, which had evolved from a pushcart in 1912 into a 3,000-seat restaurant before a fire destroyed it in 1963. Owner Harry Hackney, second from right below, promoted the restaurant with red plastic lobsters, a float in the Miss America Parade topped with an oversized lobster, and celebrity endorsements. A young Jerry Lewis fingers a lobster in 1955, below. (ACFPL.)

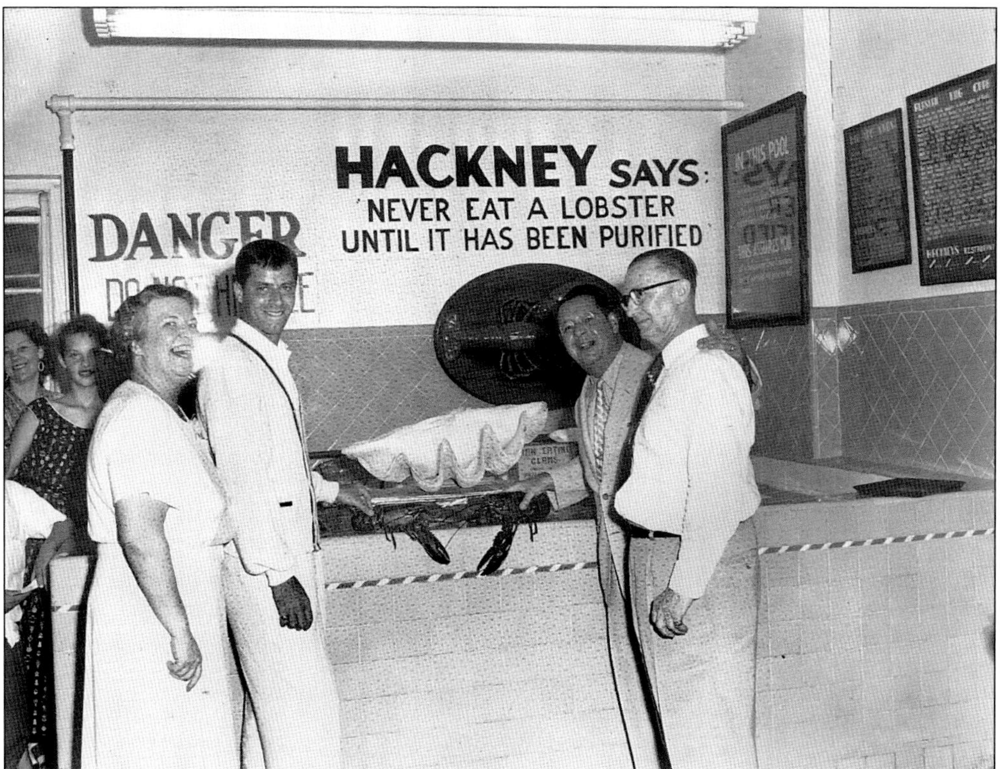

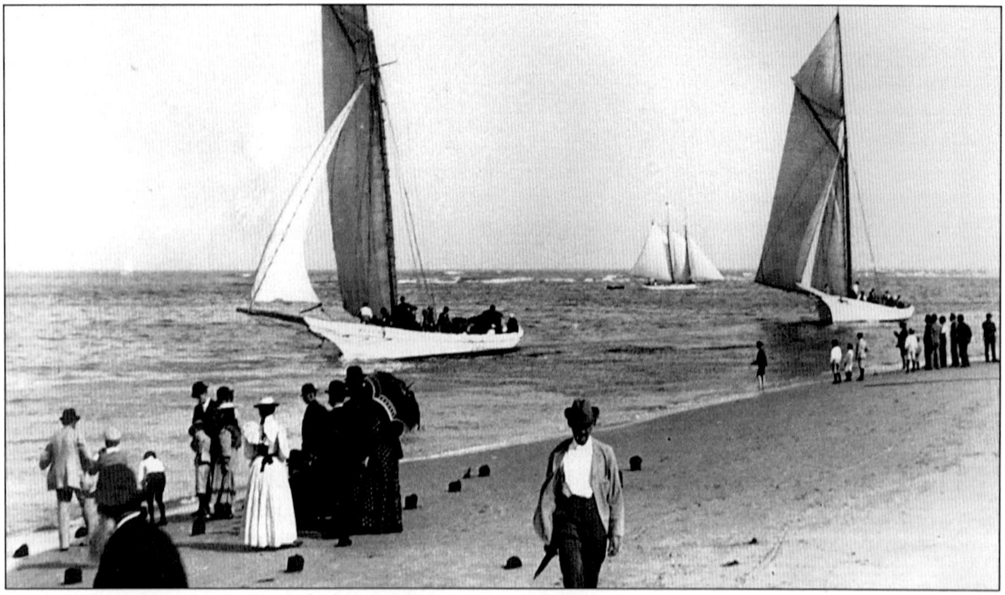

If residents were not fishing or serving fish, they still found employment on the sea by offering yachting excursions for tourists. In 1900, skippers picked up their fares directly from the beach, above, and deposited them there again after a run through the waves. (ACFPL.)

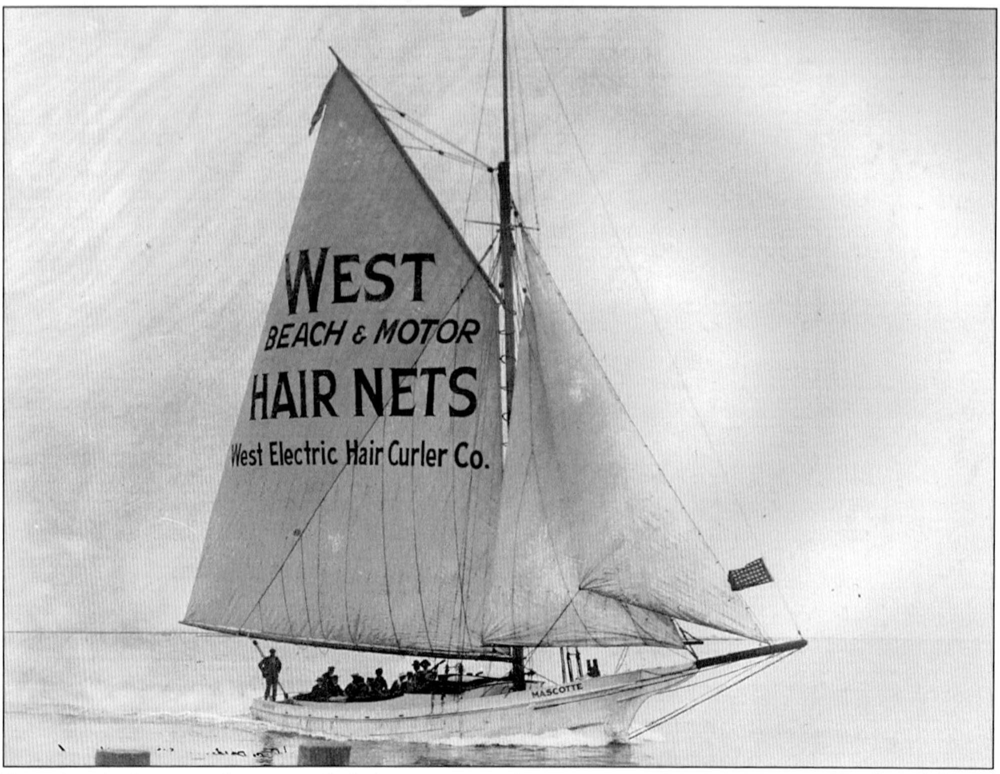

Decades before airplanes trailed banners pitching suntan lotion across the beachfront, enterprising sailors leased their sail space for advertising and plied the waters off Atlantic City's beach. In 1935, the *Mascotte*, seen above, managed two very different sponsors. (ACFPL.)

An annual highlight for both residents and tourists, the Morris Guards Marlin Fishing Tournament drew sportsmen and women to Atlantic City to hook the big one. Winners like the 1965 couple at right could count on a good catch until over-fishing thinned the stock by the 1970s. The waters off Atlantic City remain fertile grounds for smaller game species. (ACFPL.)

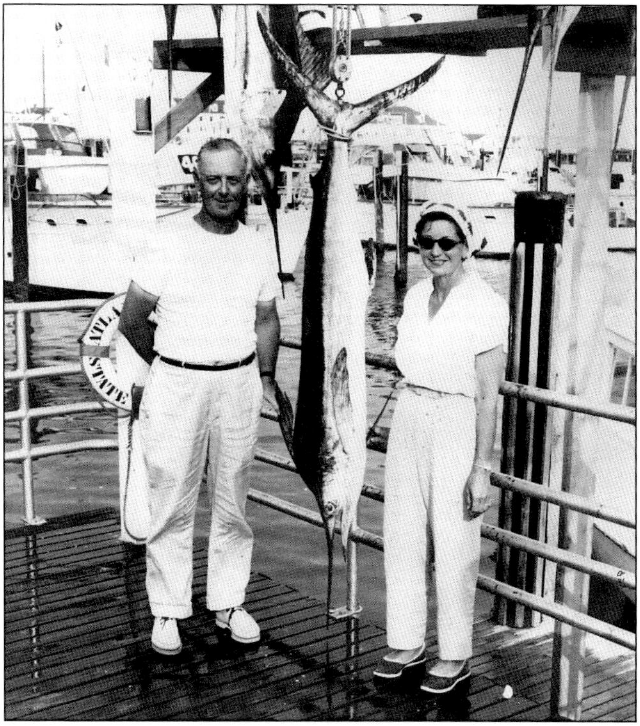

Atlantic City's citizens also found recreation away from the sea. The New Jersey Pine Barrens nearby and the wilds of Pennsylvania offered another experience of the great outdoors. Residents of the city's Northside, below, proudly show off their eight-point buck. (ACFPL.)

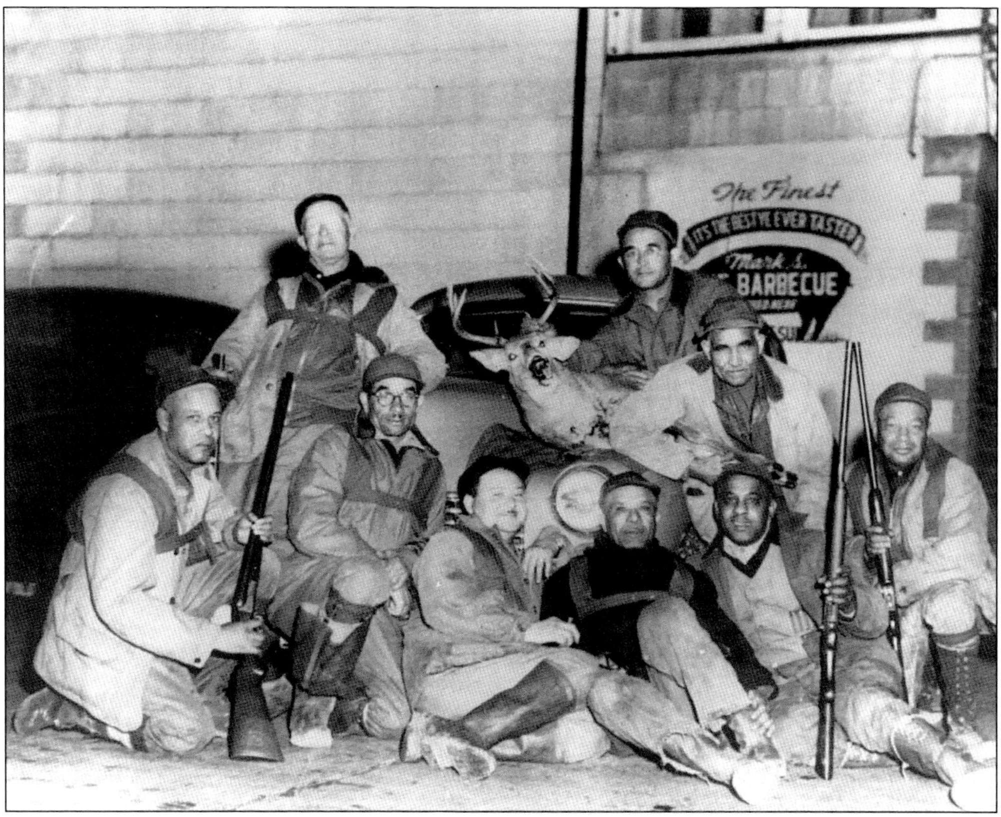

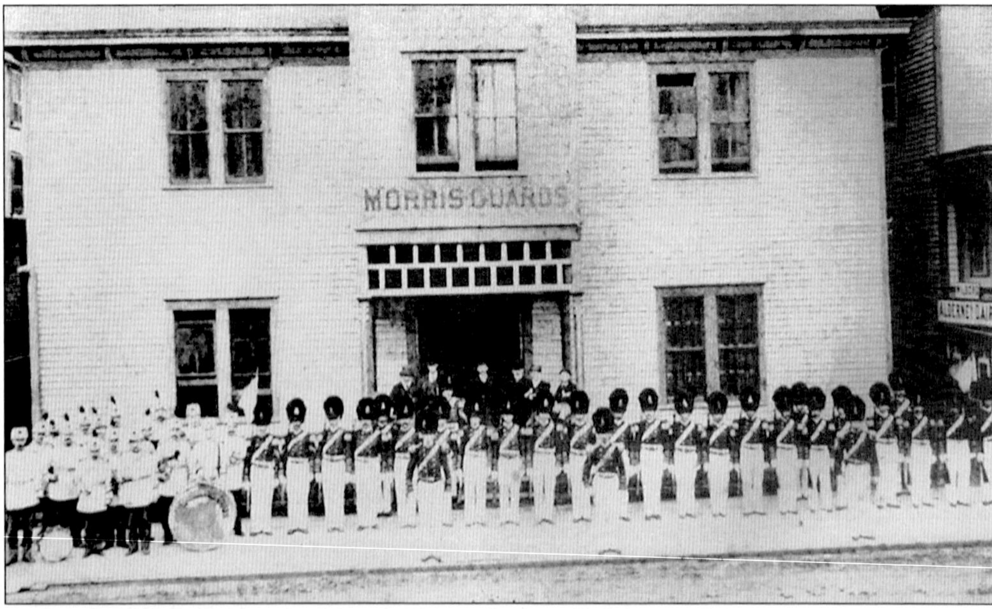

Organized in 1887 and named for Civil War hero Colonel Daniel Morris, the Morris Guards were originally an independent military company. They sent a entire unit to the Spanish-American War and volunteered for WW I and WWII, but by then members served only as individuals. The Morris Guards' drum and bugle corps, above, was one of its service programs in the 1890s. (ACFPL.)

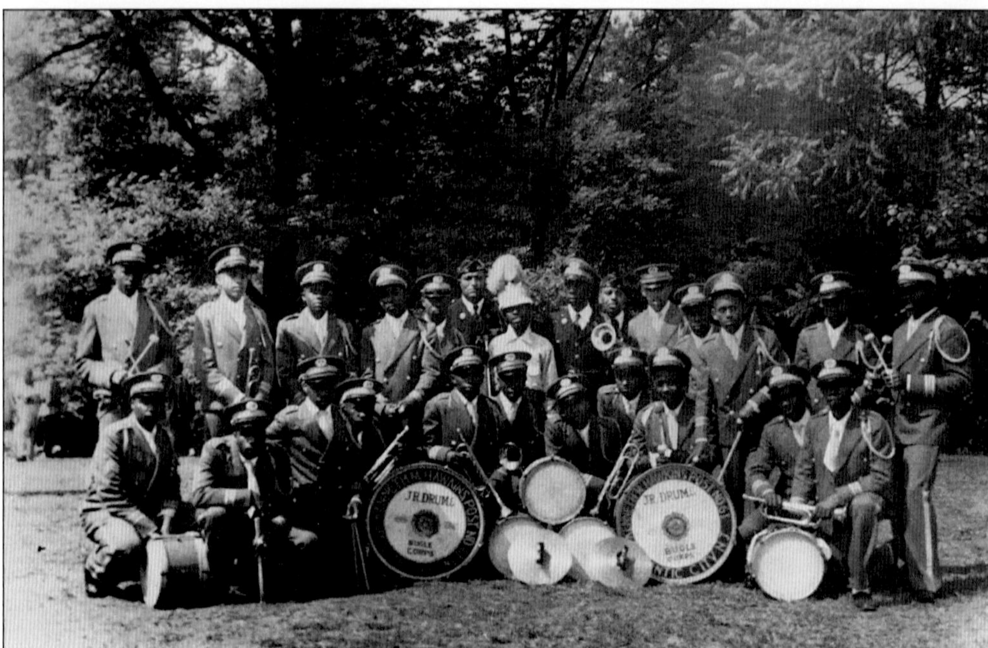

Excluded from participating in the Morris Guards, Atlantic City's African-American community formed the Kenneth Hawkins American Legion Post with its own drum and bugle corps, seen above. Like drum corps programs today, the post's program sought to provide a wholesome outlet for the community's youth. (ACFPL.)

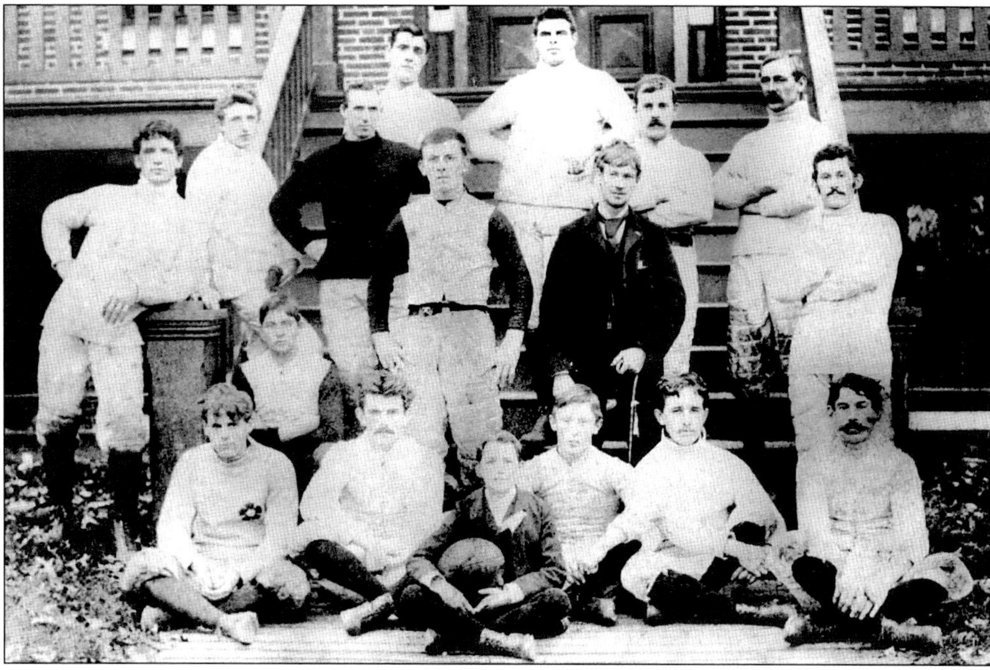

Youth sports programs were prominent in Atlantic City life. The Morris Guards sponsored football teams, as seen above in 1893, and basketball teams. Atlantic City High School still boasts competitive teams, including a strong swimming program. (ACFPL.)

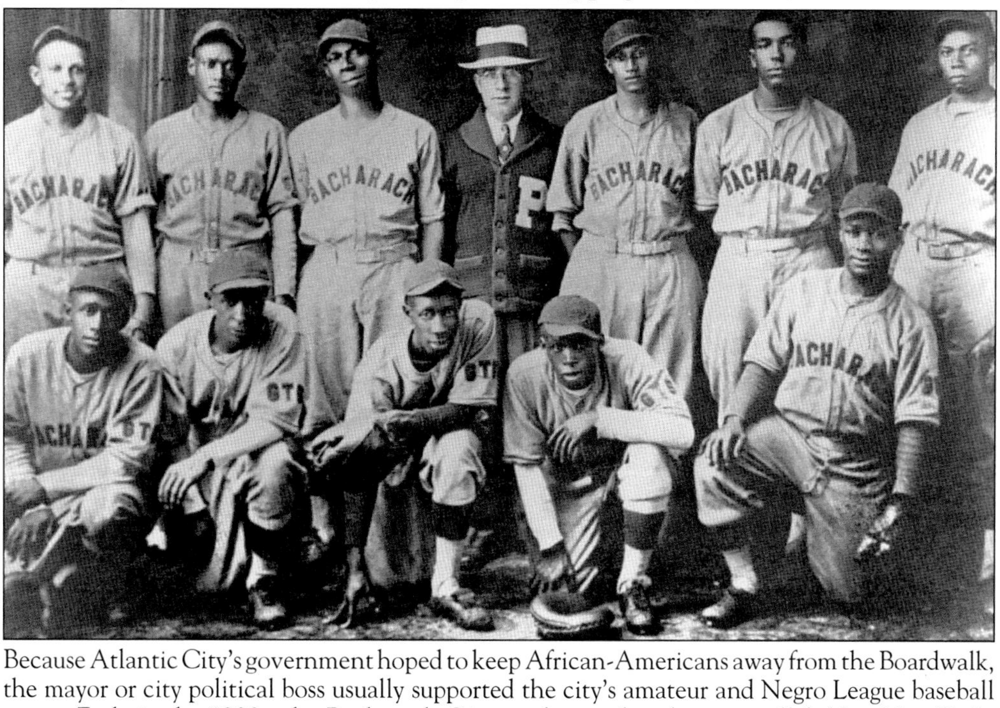

Because Atlantic City's government hoped to keep African-Americans away from the Boardwalk, the mayor or city political boss usually supported the city's amateur and Negro League baseball teams. Early in the 1900s, the Bacharach Giants, above, played on a small field at New York, Adriatic, and Kentucky Avenues. They enjoyed their best years with future Hall-of-Famer John Henry "Pop" Lloyd at shortstop. (ACFPL.)

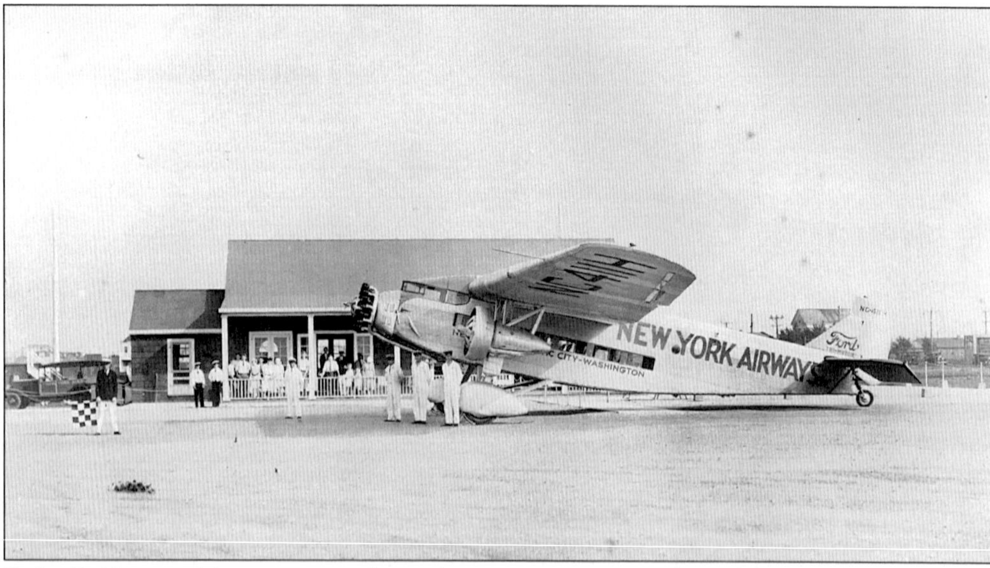

Bader Field, named for a mayor, welcomed pioneering aviators, their planes, and the occasional dirigible. The *America*, for one, took off from Bader Field in an attempt to become the first airship to cross the Atlantic Ocean. It crashed at sea, although its crew was rescued. Regular passenger flights began in the 1930s when New York Airways, above, and other airlines opened daily service. (ACFPL.)

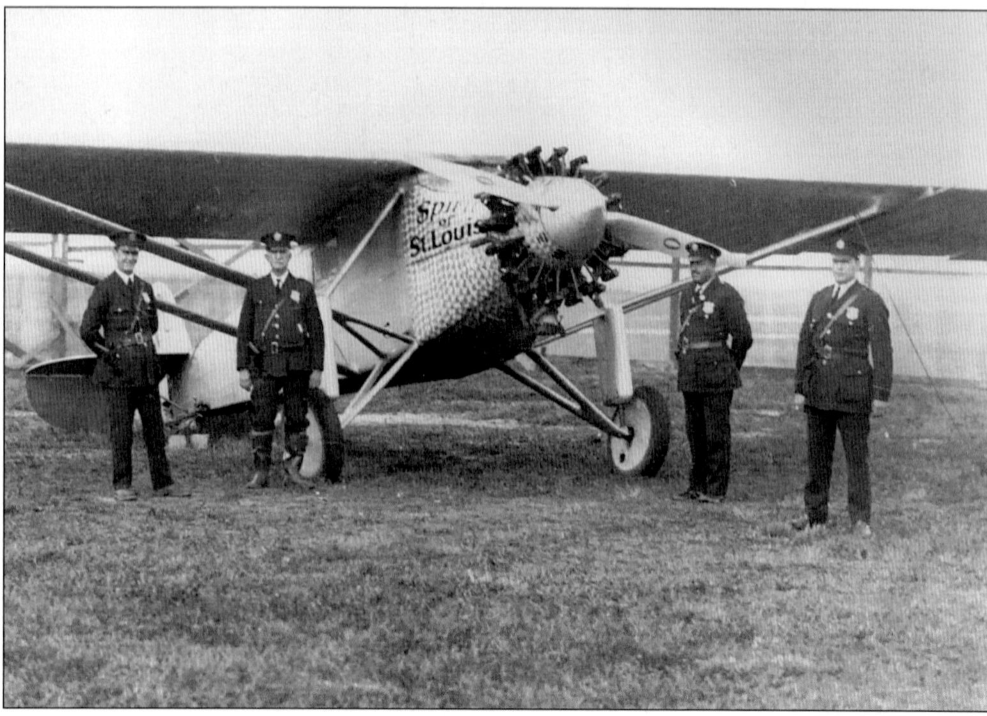

After his historic flight in 1927, Charles Lindbergh stopped at Bader Field, where police guarded his *Spirit of St. Louis*, above. The first airfield in the nation to call itself an airport, Bader Field served Atlantic City until its runways proved too short for modern jets to negotiate. The Air Force facility in Pomona now handles the city's air traffic. (ACFPL.)

America's cycling craze in the late 19th century also captured Atlantic City's imagination. Businessman Albert Wootton, at right with his staff, tried to capitalize on it by branching out from his usual line of business as a ship's chandler. (ACFPL.)

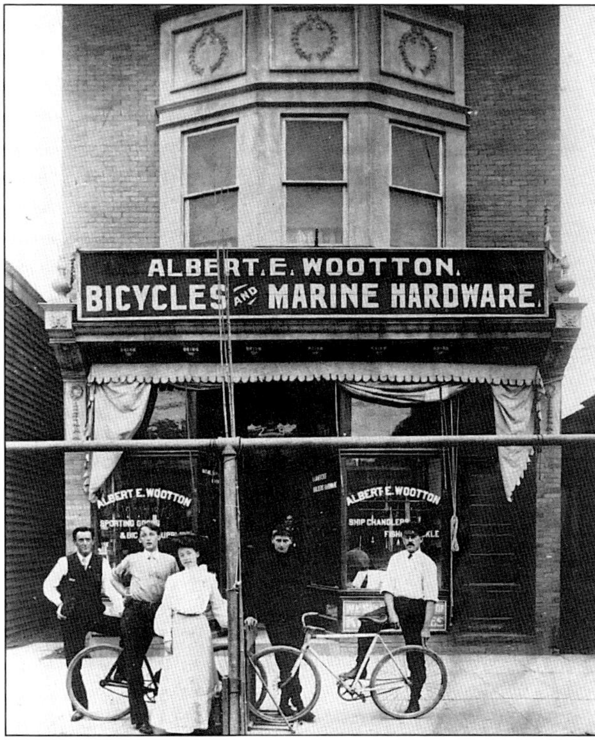

One of Wootton's bicycles may have made it to the velodrome, below, for racing. This photograph was once half of a card, the two images of which offered a semblance of a three-dimensional image when viewed through a stereopticon. (ACFPL.)

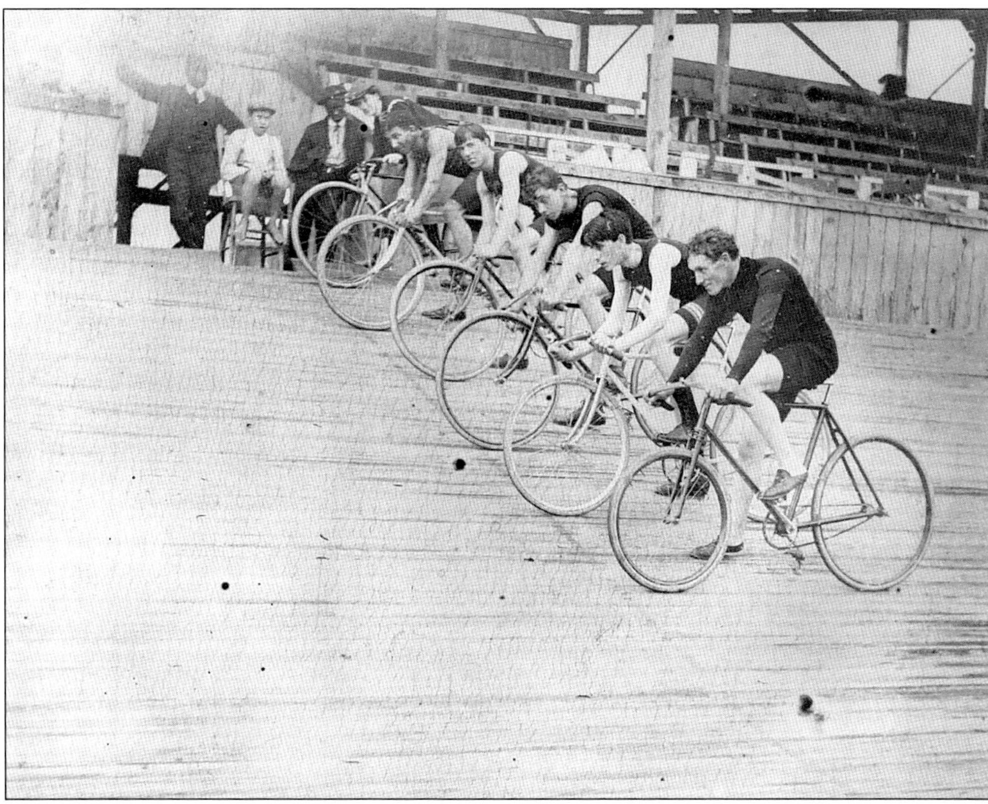

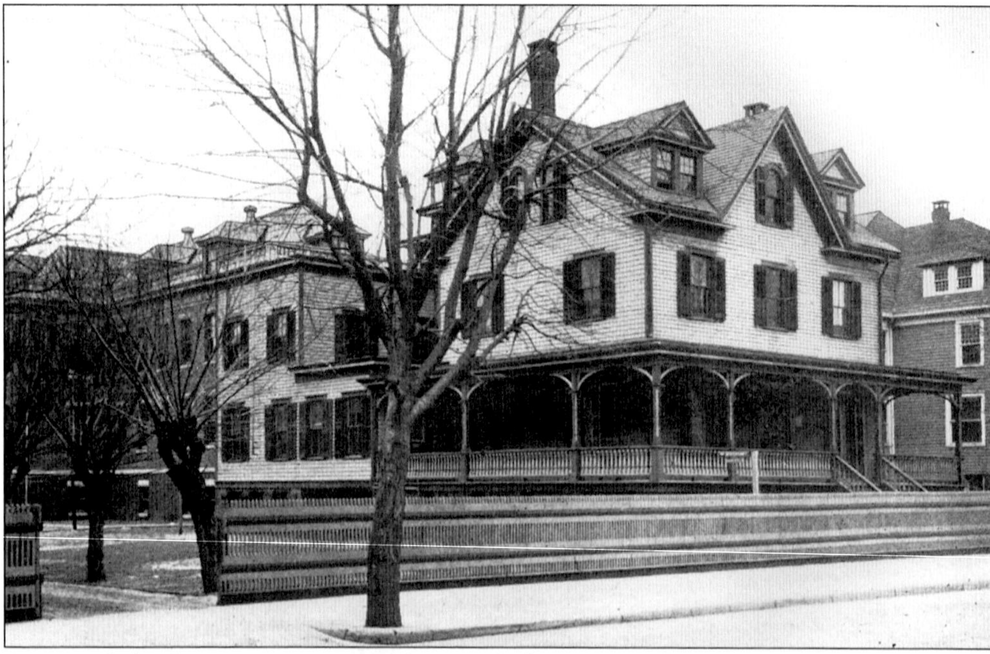

Civic pride bred civic institutions. Along with departments for fire, police, streets, and the beach patrol, Atlantic City saw the need for a hospital and converted a residence in 1898, above, to provide one. The wooden structure featured a main building, above right, and the Boice Annex, above left. For the ill, infirm, or injured, traveling to the hospital meant a rough ride in its horse-drawn ambulance, below. (ACFPL.)

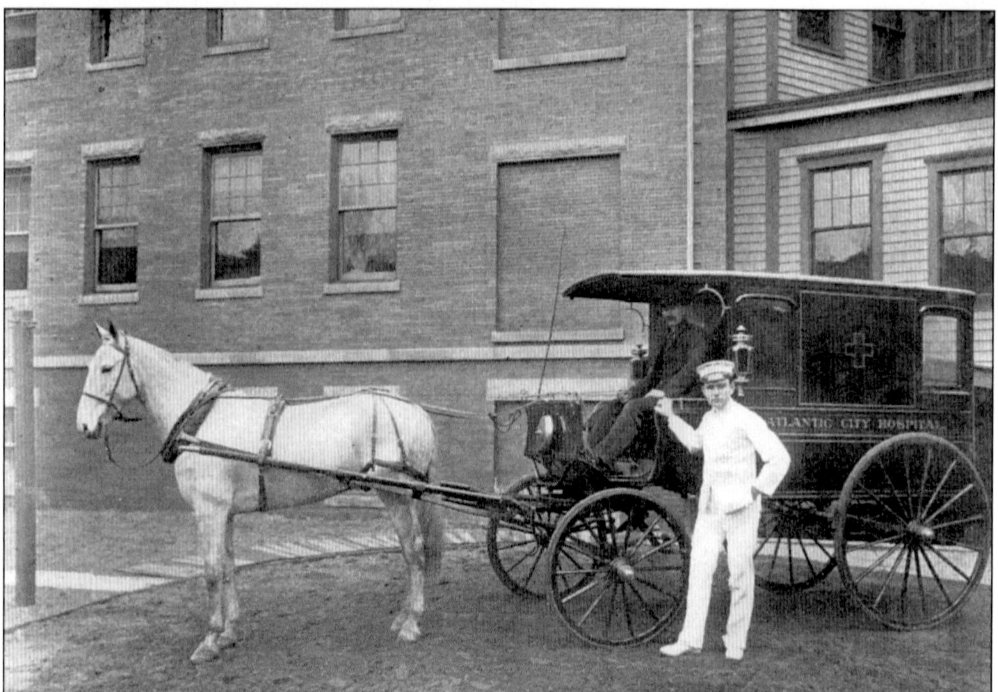

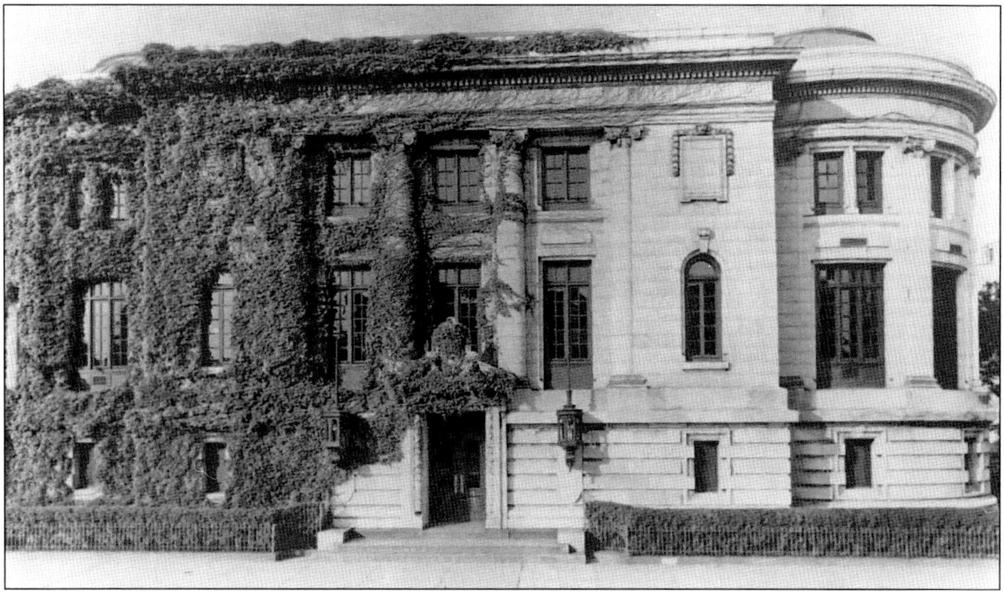

The old Atlantic City Library at Pacific and Illinois Avenues, above, had chiseled over its main door "Open to All." Built in 1908 and now in disrepair, that building was replaced in 1995 by a far larger main branch at Atlantic and Tennessee Avenues in the city government complex. From the beginning, the library built a reputation as an institution where all residents could share civic duties, as on the advisory committee meeting, below, in the 1940s or 1950s. (ACFPL, ACFPL.)

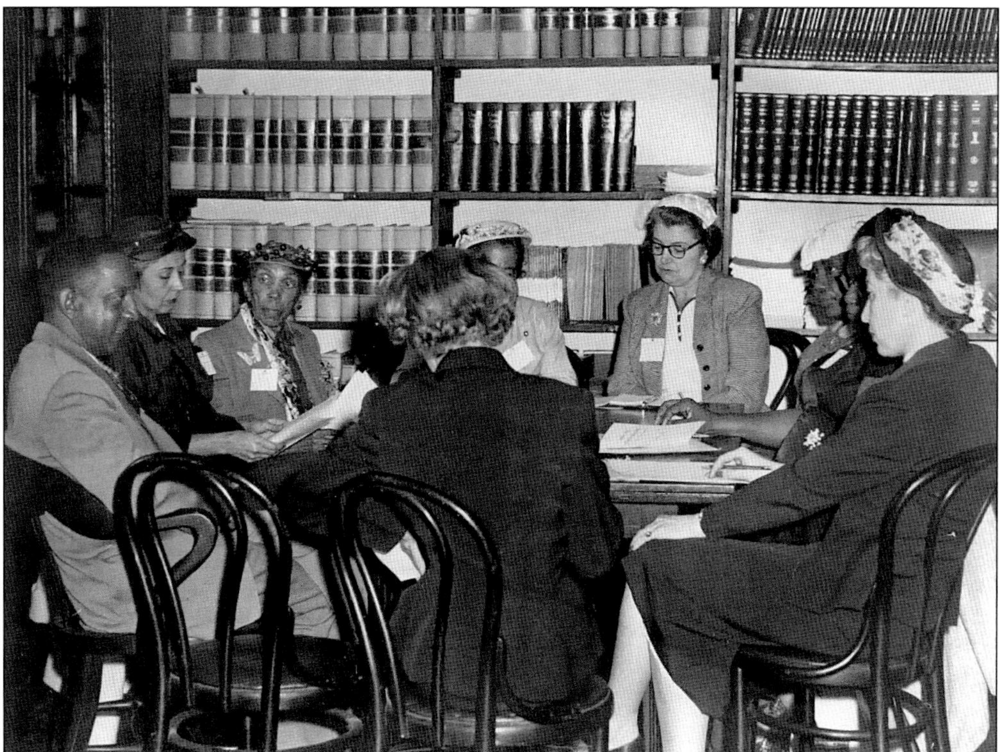

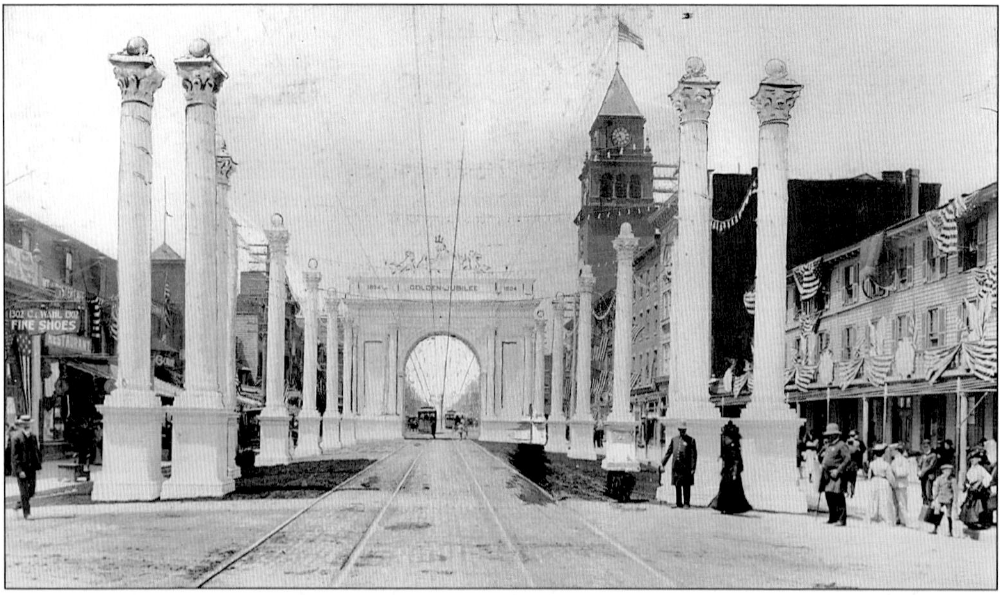

Atlantic City spared no expense in 1904 to celebrate the 50th anniversary of its founding. The city decked out Atlantic Avenue with a colonnade and triumphant arch, above, straddling the trolley tracks near the intersection with South Carolina. Then the city staged a parade. Every major civic, religious, and community group entered floats, below. In its love of parades, Atlantic City revealed a big-city genius for promotion and a small-town love of spectacle. (ACFPL.)

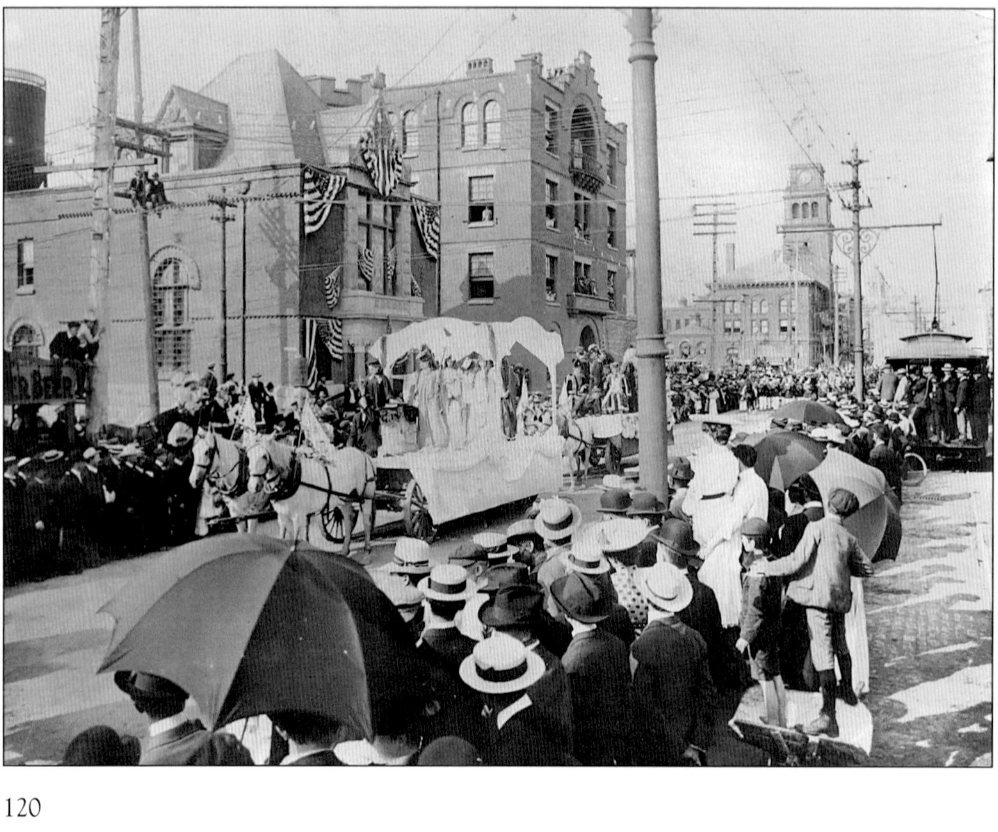

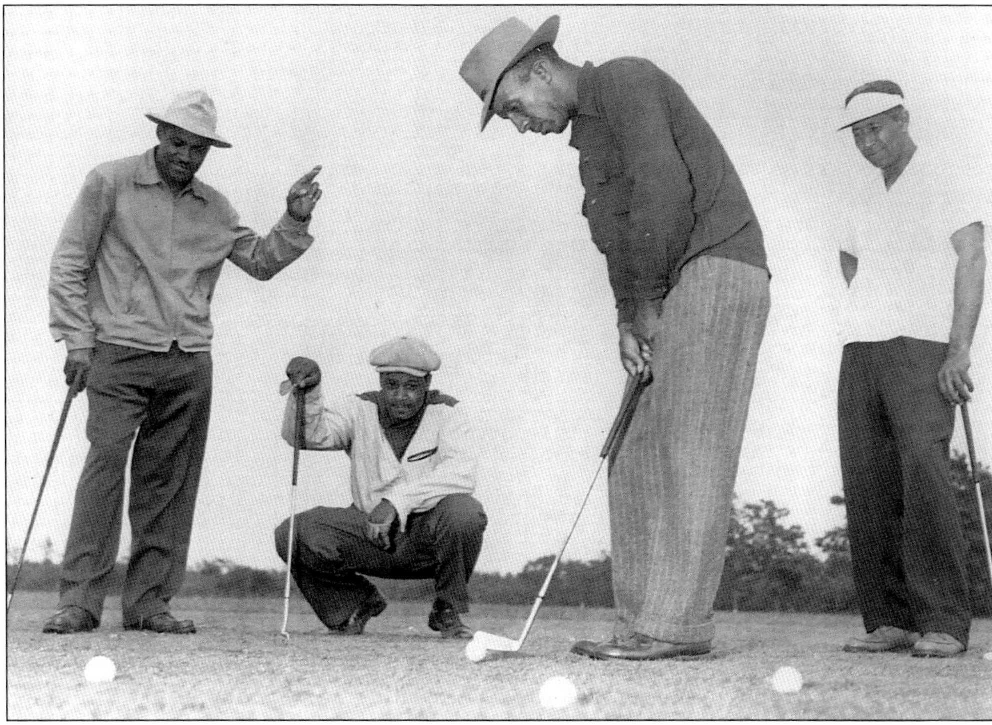

Country clubs were rarely open to African-Americans, except for Apex Country Club in Egg Harbor, above. Local businesswoman Sarah Spencer Washington—who built a fortune on beauty salons, beauty publications, and the Apex Hair and News Company—bought a farm and vineyard in 1934 and converted it into a golf club for the city's black residents. Other Atlantic City diversions included outings on Absecon Bay and the ocean, such as this one aboard Captain Gale's good ship *Princeton*, below. (ACFPL.)

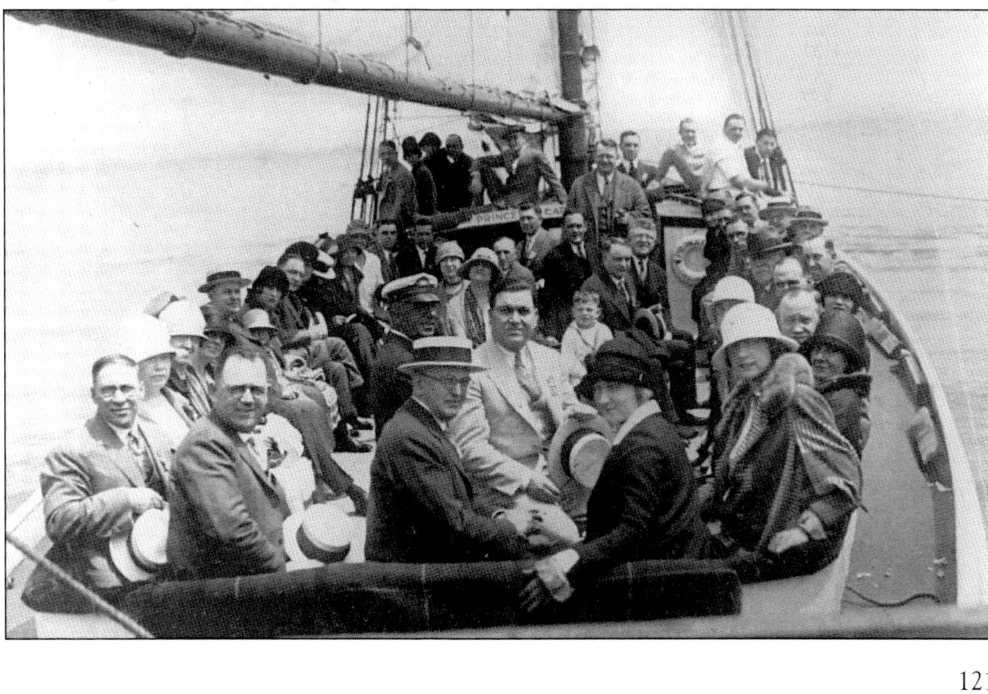

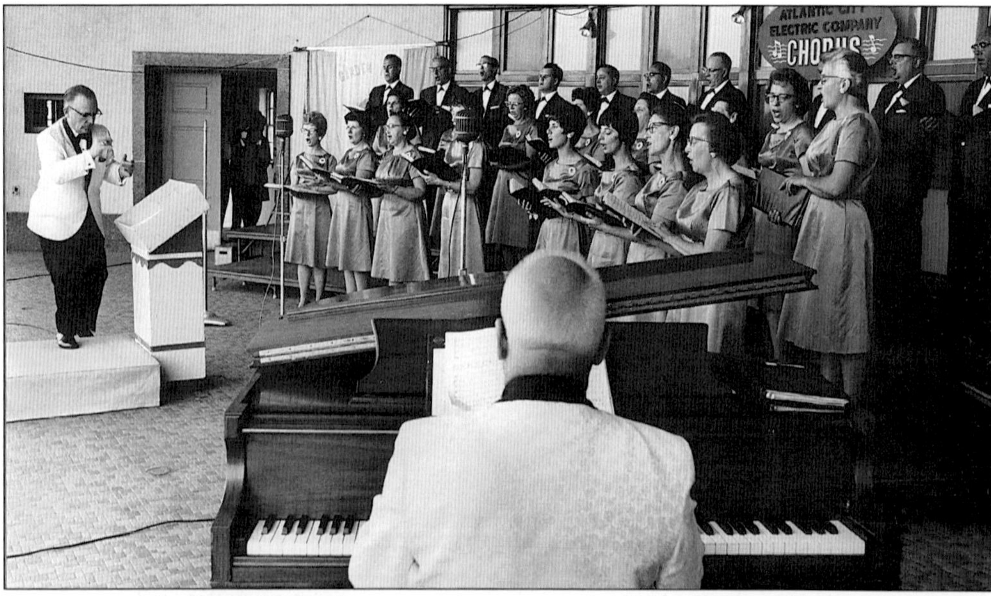

For years, employees of the local power utility sang in the Atlantic City Electric Chorus. The group performed at public functions and for tourists, as above, through the 1950s and 1960s at the company's promotional stand on the Boardwalk. To this day, retirees recall Atlantic City Electric as a corporation with a family-like feeling. The utility is now part of Conectiv. (Conectiv.)

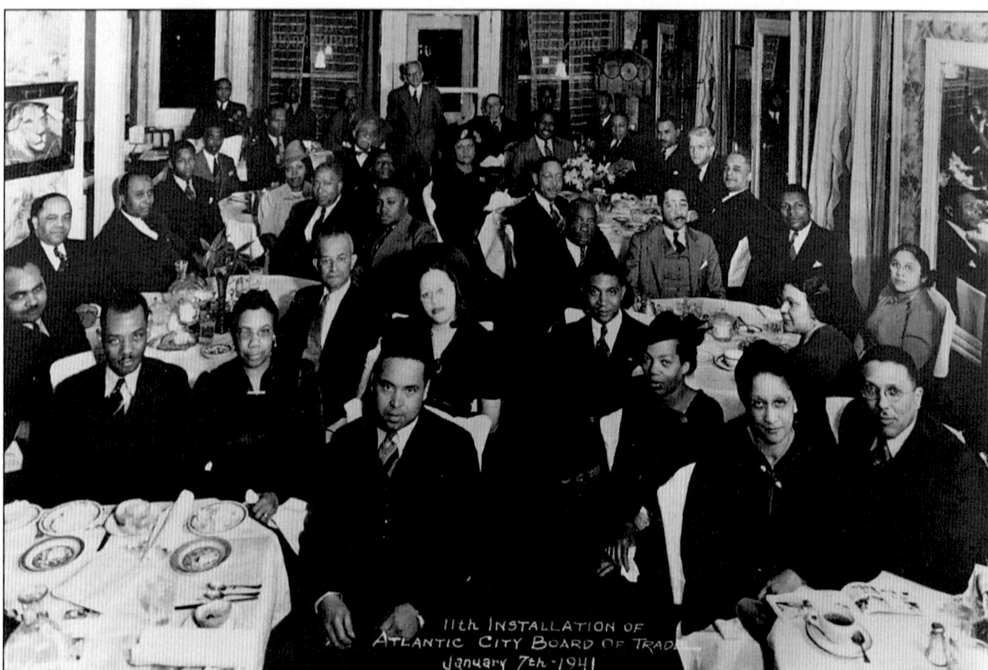

Excluded from the chamber of commerce, black business people formed the Atlantic City Board of Trade in 1930. At events such as its gathering in 1941, above, the board dealt with economic challenges and mustered its political influence to deal with city government. (ACFPL.)

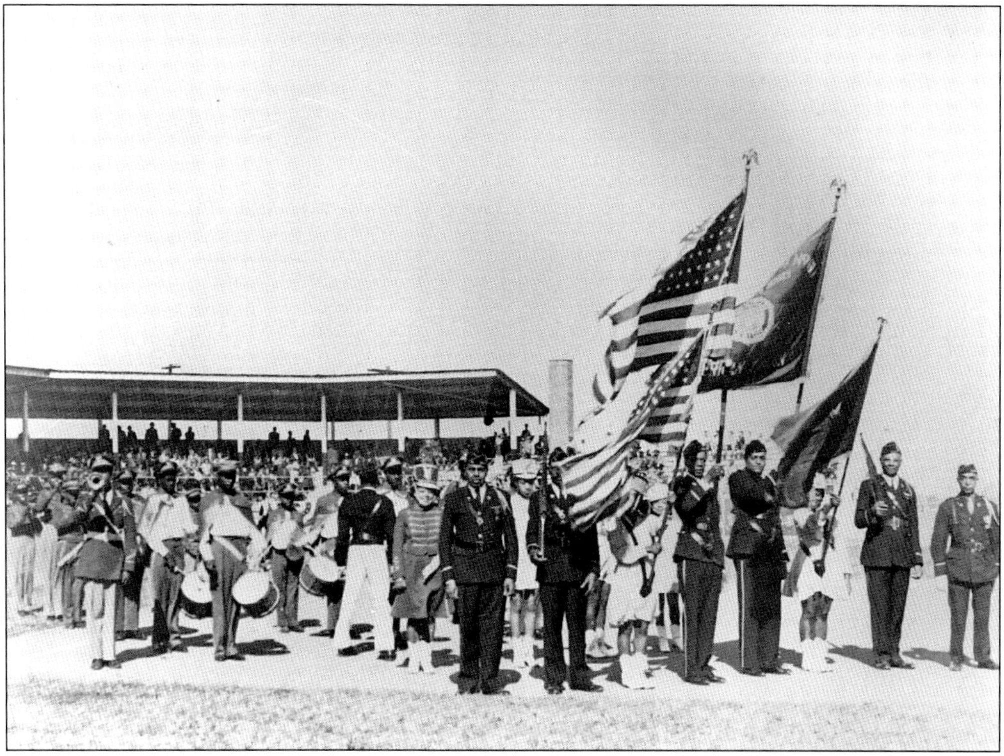

John Henry "Pop" Lloyd (1884–1964) was such a presence in Atlantic City that the city dedicated a baseball stadium to him in 1949, above, at Huron Avenue and Martin Luther King Boulevard. Lloyd, right, played for the Bacharachs and coached the city's Johnson Stars in the Negro League. After baseball, he worked as a janitor in the city's school system until his death in 1964. He was inducted into the Baseball Hall of Fame in 1977. (ACFPL.)

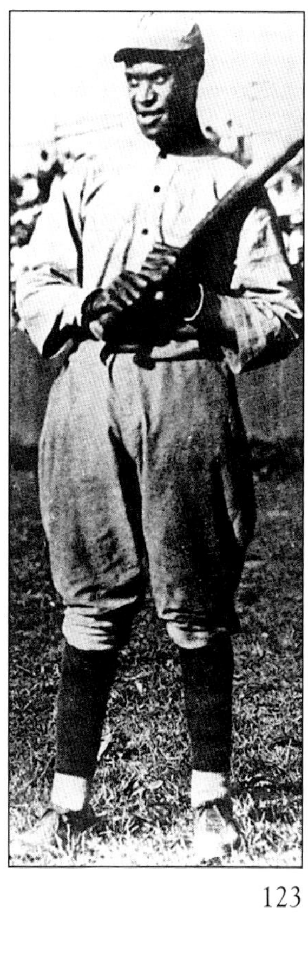

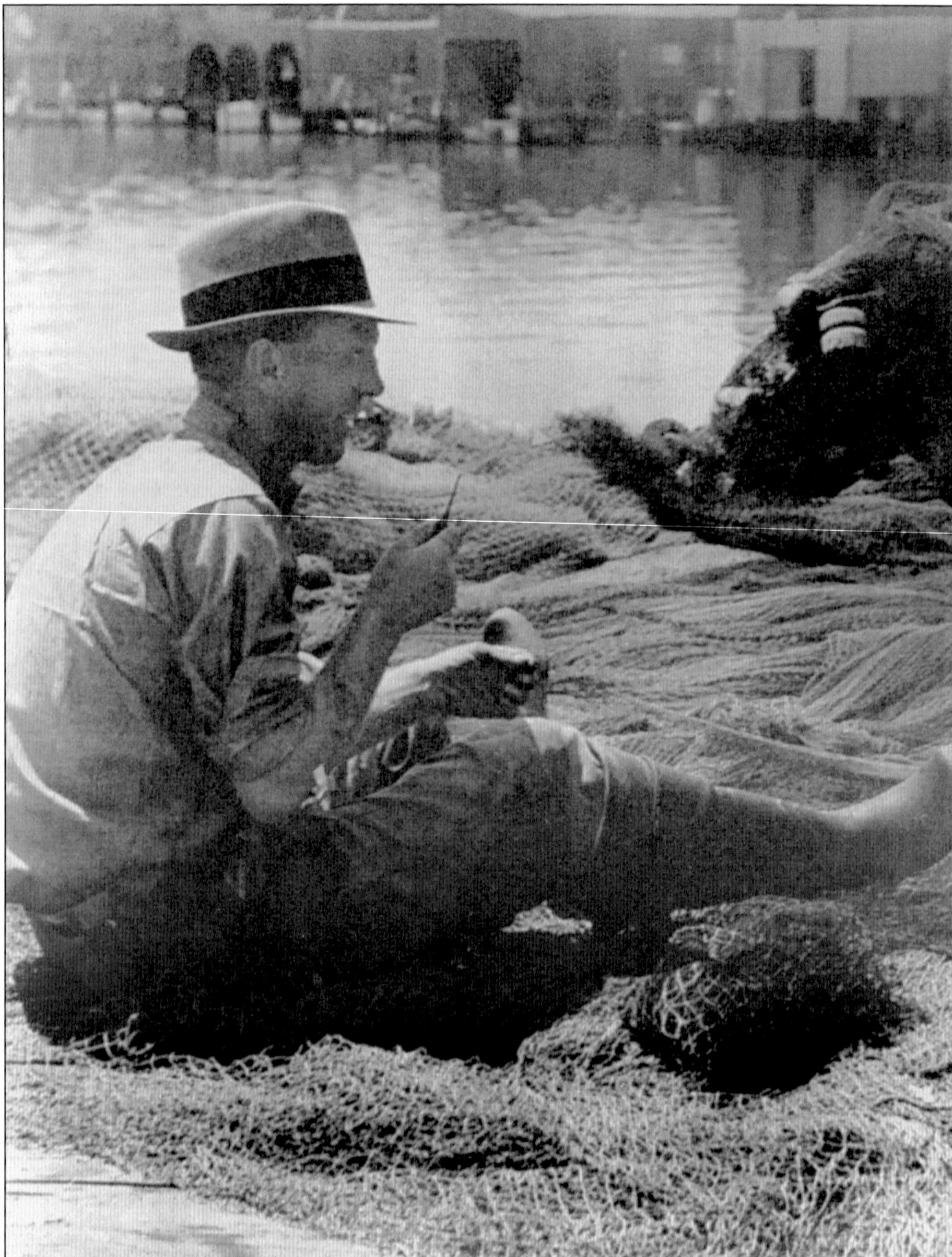

Until its decline in the late 1950s and the 1960s, Atlantic City remained two towns: a working town and a resort promoting fantasies. Fishermen still mended their nets as showgirls pulled on fishnets in the city's nightclubs. Citizens continued to work and entrepreneurs to dream until competition from resorts such as Miami Beach and changing tastes in tourism sapped the city's vitality. (ACFPL.)

Nine

STILL DREAMING

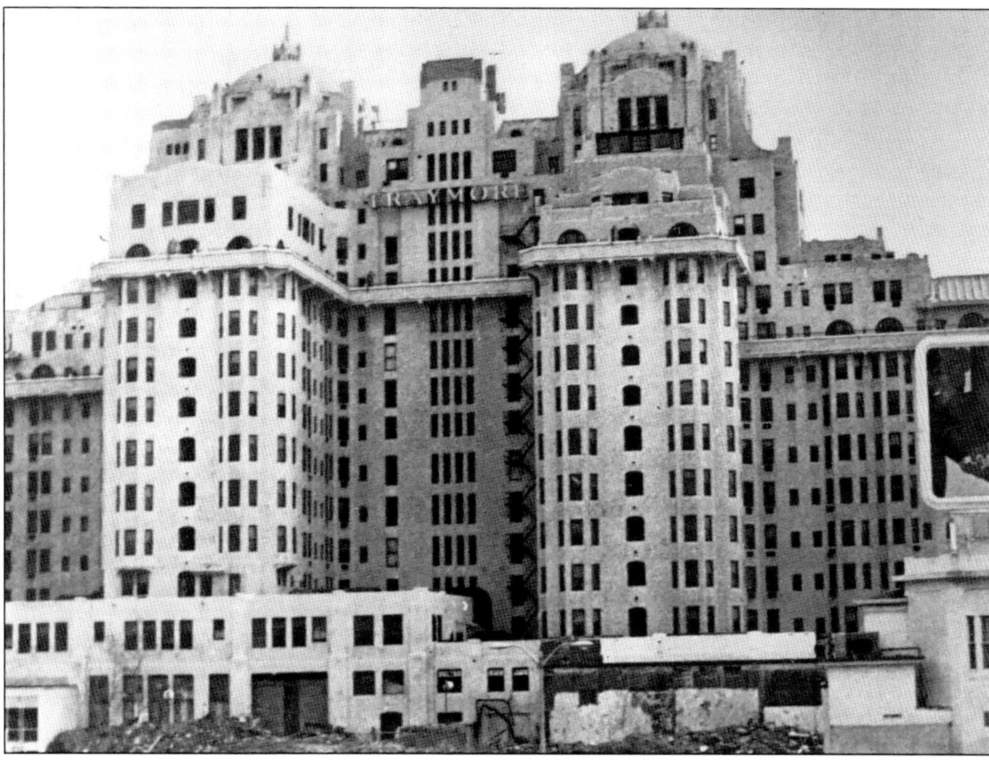

Dreams have always been Atlantic City's long suit. However, as both city residents and tourists awaited the results of the statewide approval of gambling casinos in 1976, dreams verged on nightmares. The city would change dramatically; to students of architecture and tradition this meant some (if not most) of the imposing Boardwalk structures would disappear. Many wondered what possibly might replace the past. Boardwalk denizens watched the Hotel Traymore as it was prepared for demolition, sighing over the imminent demise of the fine old hotel. (ACFPL.)

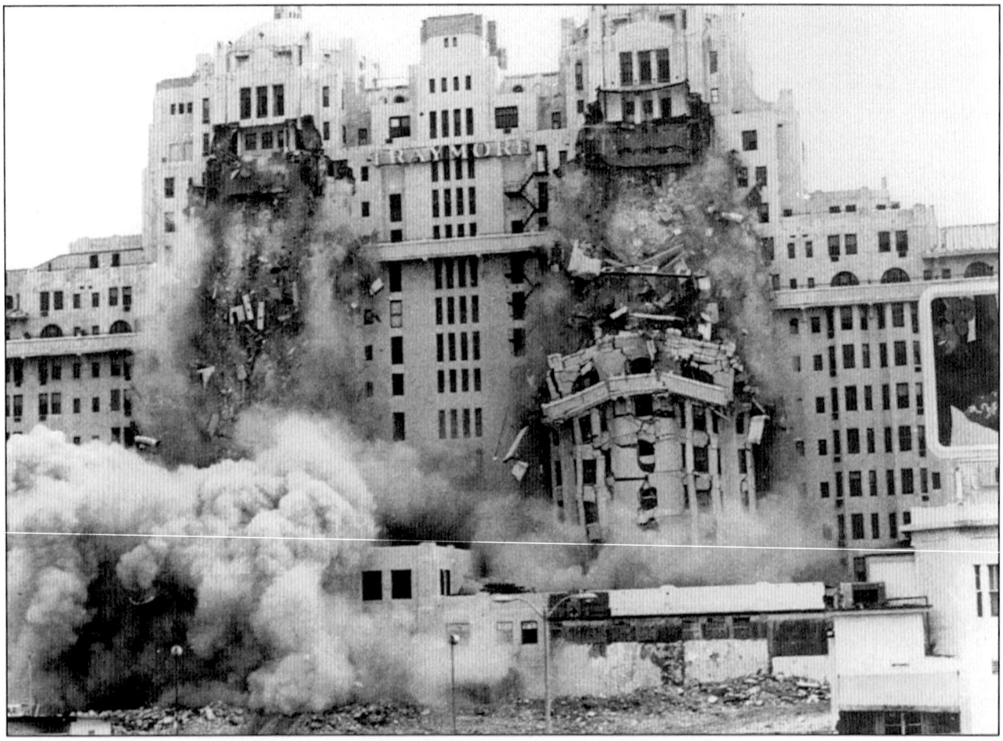

The final blows to the Traymore were swift and awesome. Artfully placed dynamite, above, sliced away the facades of the familiar twin towers. Then, huge caches of explosives leveled in seconds what had taken three-quarters of a century to build, below. The Traymore had vanished and so had much of the city's past. Would there be dreams enough to replace nostalgia? (ACFPL.)

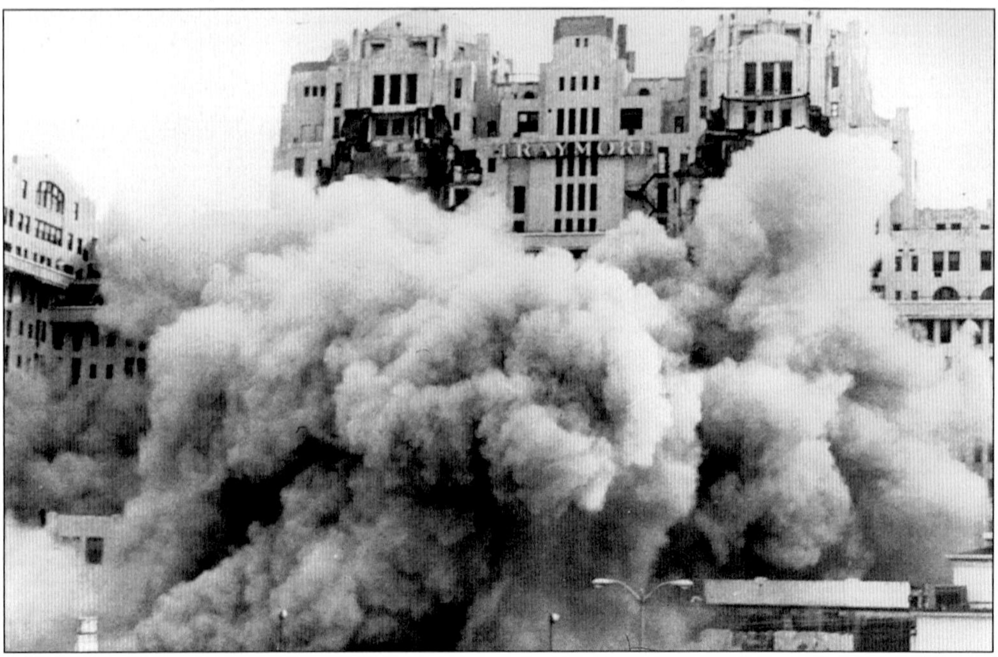

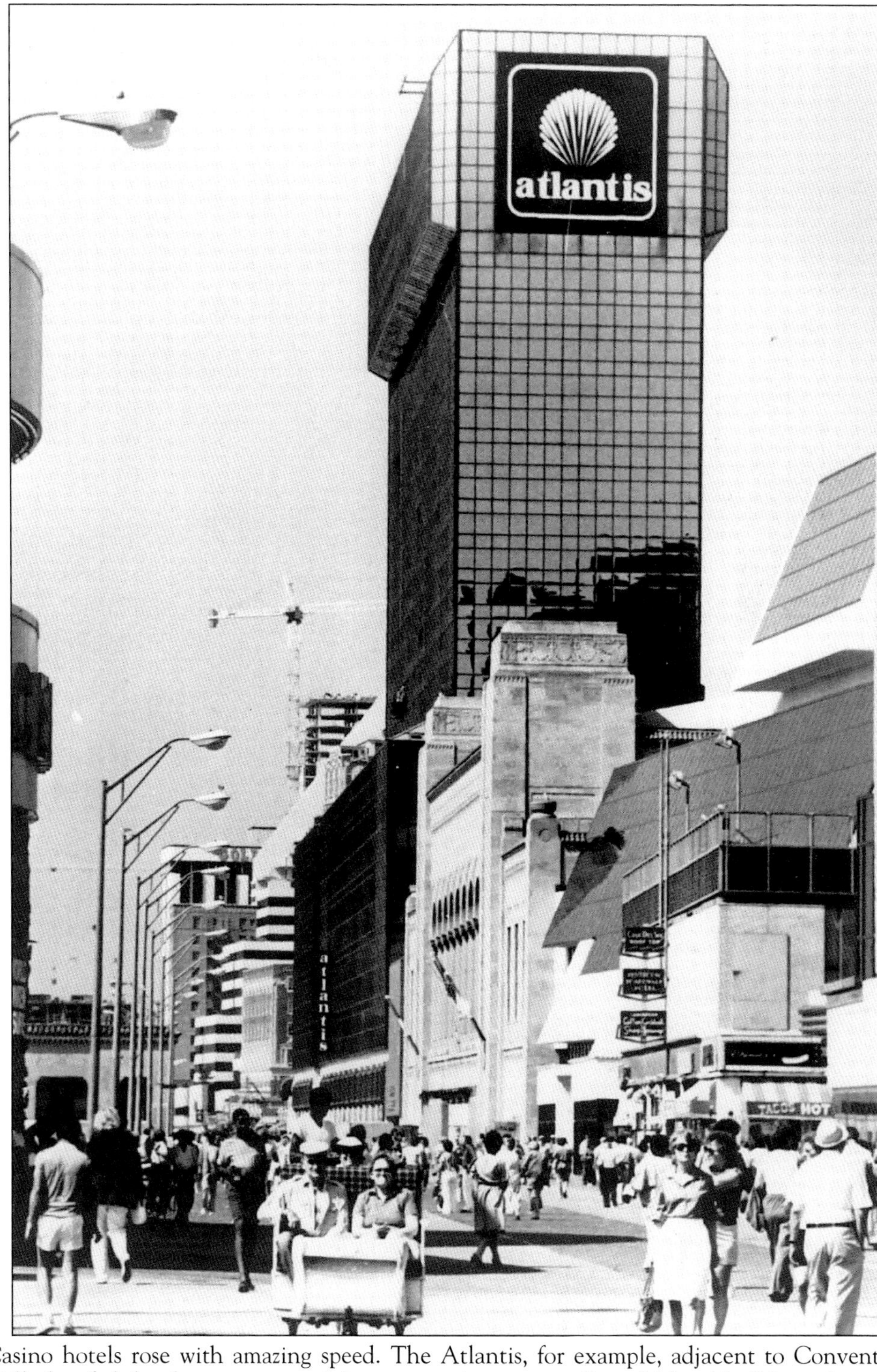

Casino hotels rose with amazing speed. The Atlantis, for example, adjacent to Convention Hall, dwarfed that huge structure. Most new casinos were tall, multi-level buildings, featuring stark architectural patterns. Tourists still strolled the Boardwalk or rode in traditional old roller chairs. (ACFPL.)

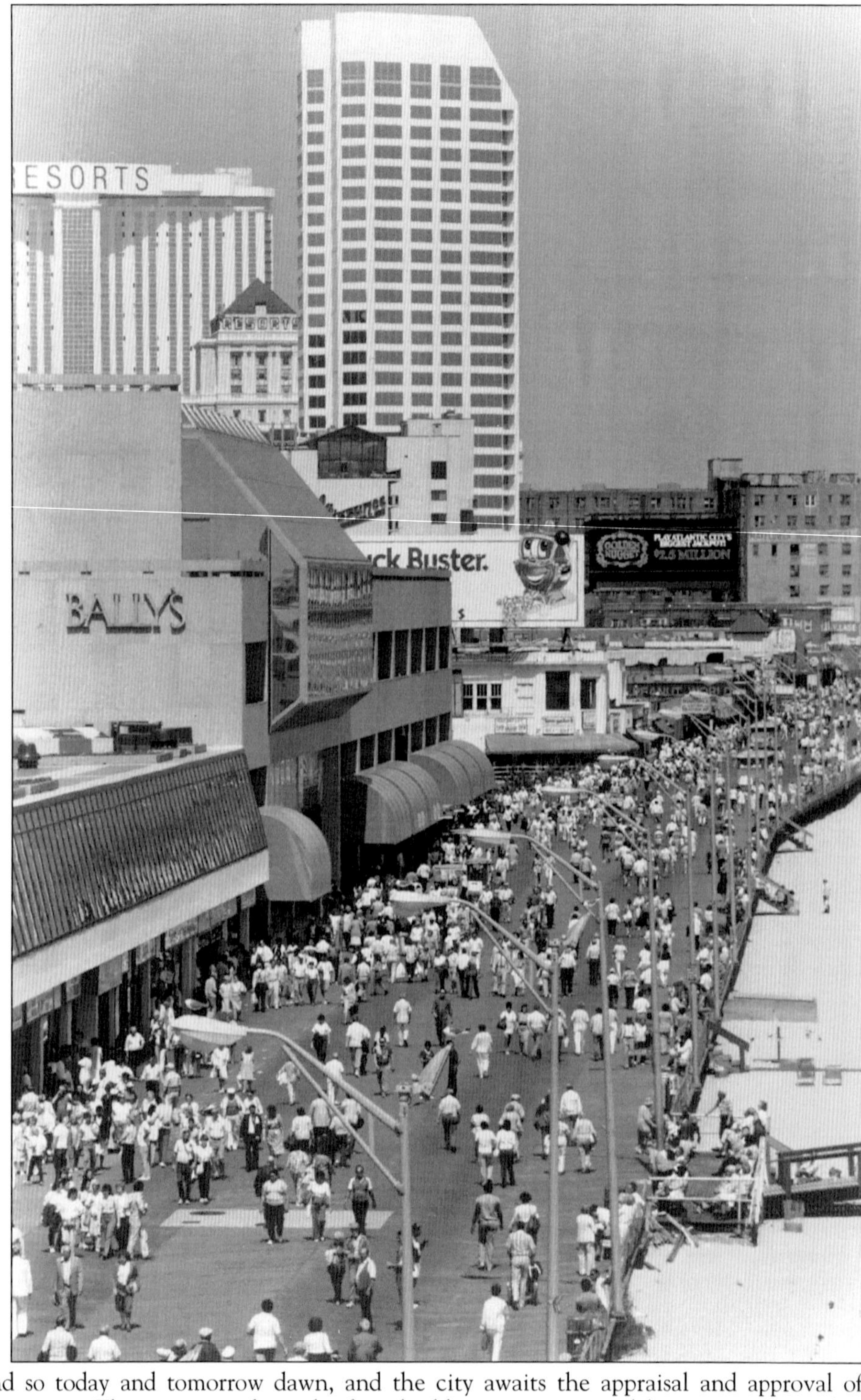

And so today and tomorrow dawn, and the city awaits the appraisal and approval of new generations. The city is transformed as far as buildings are concerned, but on any sunny afternoon in summertime, crowds of tourists stroll the unique Boardwalk. There is ample room to dream. (ACFPL.)